New Directions for Special Collections

D1073269

New Directions for Special Collections

An Anthology of Practice

LYNNE M. THOMAS AND
BETH M. WHITTAKER, EDITORS

 LIBRARIES
UNLIMITED™

An Imprint of ABC-CLIO, LLC
Santa Barbara, California • Denver, Colorado

Copyright © 2017 by Lynne M. Thomas and Beth M. Whittaker

All rights reserved. No part of this publication may be reproduced, stored in a
retrieval system, or transmitted, in any form or by any means, electronic,
mechanical, photocopying, recording, or otherwise, except for the inclusion of brief
quotations in a review, without prior permission in writing from the publisher.

Library of Congress Cataloging-in-Publication Data

Names: Thomas, Lynne M., editor. | Whittaker, Beth M., 1970- editor.
Title: New directions for special collections : an anthology of practice / Lynne M.
    Thomas and Beth M. Whittaker, editors.
Description: Santa Barbara, California : Libraries Unlimited, an imprint of
    ABC-CLIO, LLC, [2017] | Includes bibliographical references and index.
Identifiers: LCCN 2016024837 (print) | LCCN 2016045513 (ebook) | ISBN
    9781440842900 (hardcopy : acid-free paper) | ISBN 9781440842917 (ebook)
Subjects: LCSH: Libraries—United States—Special collections. | Special
    libraries—United States—Administration. | Archives—United States—
    Administration. | Special librarians—Employment—United States.
    | Archivists—Employment—United States.
Classification: LCC Z688.A3 U645 2017 (print) | LCC Z688.A3 (ebook)
    | DDC 025.17—dc23
LC record available at https://lccn.loc.gov/2016024837

ISBN: 978–1–4408–4290–0
EISBN: 978–1–4408–4291–7

21 20 19 18 17   2 3 4 5

This book is also available as an eBook.

Libraries Unlimited
An Imprint of ABC-CLIO, LLC

ABC-CLIO, LLC
130 Cremona Drive, P.O. Box 1911
Santa Barbara, California 93116-1911
www.abc-clio.com

This book is printed on acid-free paper ∞

Manufactured in the United States of America

For Michael and Caitlin, as always.
—Lynne M. Thomas

For Sarah and James, who waited patiently, and
for David, who stood beside me all the way.
—Beth M. Whittaker

Contents

Introduction

Lynne M. Thomas and Beth M. Whittaker

We were gratified by the responses to our earlier book *Special Collections 2.0: New Technologies for Rare Books, Manuscripts, and Archival Collections*. It was, of course, out of date even before it was in print, as we acknowledged in the afterword:

> We believe that the unique characteristics of special collections libraries, archives, and museums, and the unique skills of the professionals who work in these settings lead to exciting possibilities to use new technologies in transformative ways ... We also hope to contribute to an ongoing discussion about the changing nature of cultural heritage institutions, their priorities, and the ways in which they operate. (xi)

Of course the environments in which we work continue to change, and the need for robust discussion about the possibilities to use new technologies in transformative ways shows no sign of abating. Rather than try to rewrite the book to provide an update that would also be immediately obsolete, we decided to try another approach; we would actively seek other perspectives and other voices to capture their thoughts about the "changing nature" of our work. An open call brought in an embarrassment of exciting proposals; many made it to this book.

One of our first dilemmas was what to call ourselves and the work that we do. "Special collections librarians and archivists" is a mouthful, but in our experience, this is the best way to discuss our various roles and perspectives. Sometimes, the same person is both. Often we work side by side. Many times, special collections librarians and archivists may have more in common with each other than we do with colleagues in other parts of our large organizations. Other times, we are frustrated by the lack of common vocabulary, and insist on important differences between books, manuscripts, photographs, and other kinds of collection material. We regret the disconnect between our organizations and our cultures, and hoped to help bridge this by intentionally seeking both perspectives in this book.

Our title, "New Directions for Special Collections," has at least two meanings. Some authors addressed duties that might be new to a particular individual—being more involved in fund-raising and working with donors, for example, or trying to incorporate student assistants into processing workflows. Other contributors took on work that is new to us as a field, such as rethinking reference or managing archival appraisal of digital records. We challenged our contributors to always ask, "What is the lesson? What can others learn from this so that when the software or budget or staffing changes (as it always will), we will have the knowledge to make good decisions?" Finally, we felt it important to include a different kind of writing as well. We asked several authors with outstanding experience in their fields to talk very frankly and personally about the state of their work today and how they see it developing in the future.

Because of these multiple interpretations of "new directions," this book is intentionally told in a variety of voices and with different aspects of the broad "special collections and archives" audience in mind. We believe there is something in this book for everyone, from the student considering a career path to the seasoned professional hoping to make the most of the tail end of his or her career. In short, this book demonstrates how numerous professionals have addressed and integrated "the new normal" into their day-to-day work in special collections and archives, in all its profound impact and meaning. We believe the authors bring a valuable perspective and will contribute to the ongoing discussions in our professions.

Of course, we could not include everything. We know the breadth of chapter topics, from K–12 outreach to documenting social protest movements and from instruction to metadata to preservation, is leaving out something, likely something very important. We cannot cover it all, but we hope that we provide a robust snapshot of life in 21st-century special collections.

Chapter 1
The Rare Book Librarian's Day, Revisited

Melanie Griffin

In 1986, Daniel Traister wrote an article, titled "The Rare Book Librarian's Day," that sought to dispel myths about the figure of the rare books librarian.[1] Traister wrote against the idea that rare books librarians spend their days conducting and assisting with Research (with an intentionally capitalized "r"), frequently employing the specialized historical and bibliographic skills acquired through years of study. While Traister's study was and still is a useful thought piece, detailing as it does the distance between perception and reality, it also unquestioningly highlights at least two other divides between the perception of the profession of rare books librarianship and reality for most practitioners. Traister, then curator of Special Collections at the University of Pennsylvania, writes with a view from the Ivy League as well as from an administrator's office.

While Traister's perspective is from 1986, my first encounter with this view of the profession was in library school in 2008 while I was studying to become a special collections librarian. Despite the terminology change from "rare books" to "special collections," Traister's experience as an Ivy League administrator was presented to me as what I should expect in a future career in special collections, especially if one wanted to be considered "successful." One should expect, for example, to work with donors like the one Traister references, who have materials that we want to accession into our collections and a chauffeur to help load those materials into our cars.[2] This individual experience was used to normalize a privileged, experienced view of the profession, a view that my classmates and I realized was statistically impossible for most, or perhaps any, of us to obtain. This point of view was further privileged as we discussed the Rare Books and Manuscripts Section's "Competencies for Special Collections Professionals."[3] The competencies are dauntingly comprehensive and describe experience and expertise that we hope to find in the profession, rather than what we might more typically expect to find on any given day in any given shop, particularly a small and underfunded shop.

When I began my first professional position as a special collections librarian, I discovered that my suspicion in graduate school was right on target: the professional literature's definition and depiction of "special collections librarians" may skew toward large, well-funded institutions,[4] but the reality of my situation required a different approach. While my university has a Carnegie classification of "Research University" with very high research activity, the library is not a member institution of the Association of Research Libraries (ARL), and the university is very focused on student success, not necessarily research. The great recession of 2008 is still an economic reality here. Funds are tight, expectations are high, and staffing levels have continuously plummeted over the past five years.

Following Traister's structure and outlining a typical day as a nonmanagerial special collections librarian at a teaching-oriented Research One institution without ARL member status highlights important similarities and differences in our perspectives. On any given day, I arrive in the morning, check e-mail and phone messages, and discover that the staff member and two of the students scheduled to work at our reference desk have called in sick. As our reading room coordinator recently changed positions and this person has not been replaced due to budget cuts, I spend the next 30 minutes scrambling to find substitutes. There aren't many, and the department's curators (there are two of us) change meeting times and decide how to fill the gaps while still making our other scheduled obligations. With one crisis averted, I return to voice mail and e-mail. The morning's opening tasks are completed between messages: I turn on computers and the patron-accessible overhead scanner in the reading room, discover that a light has burned out in the reading room, and call maintenance to replace it. I watch for the student who did not call in sick to let him know of the change in the desk schedule. I spend the next two hours of the day on the public services desk, helping art history students working on a required class assignment as well as volunteers from the local genealogical society working to digitize records of genealogical interest. I call the scanner's tech support company to schedule maintenance, as the publicly accessible scanner is malfunctioning once more.

After the student assistant arrives and takes over the public services desk, it is time to go next door to teach a class session on the history of book production for a history of the English language seminar. Fortunately, I had pulled some 30 objects illustrating 5,000 years of manuscript and printing tradition for the class the day before rather than waiting until the usually quiet two hours first thing in the morning. Returning from teaching the class session, I discover that our director of development will be dropping by in a few minutes with surprise potential donors who would like to see objects from special collections; all we know about the donors is that they are interested in art.

After the development visit, my lunch break allows time to take out the department's trash and collect our mail. Then the student working at the reference desk needs help with queries he was unable to answer independently and with cataloging questions that arose in his morning's technical services work. When our department's cataloger retired, supervision of all in-department cataloging and coordination of all original cataloging that needs to be outsourced fell to me. In the afternoon, I am called back to the reference desk to say "thank you but no thank you," explaining to a would-be donor who would like to donate historic newspapers to my university that they would be duplicative and are in poor condition. I then finish moving 50 or so boxes of recently donated children's literature from temporary storage to our processing area. After moving the boxes and separating dime novels from what looks suspiciously like molded rat poop, I run upstairs to the digital collections department, where I advise on creating a crosswalk for metadata from one content management system to another. My transfer from digital collections to special collections meant that a replacement metadata librarian was not hired; most of my previous job functions remain my responsibility. That meeting runs late and I leave it for another meeting on the library's Web site redesign. My day ends as it began: answering e-mail. I leave campus at the end of my office "work" day, only to go home, turn on my laptop, and begin working again. My position is classified as nontenure earning faculty; research and service are requirements for continued appointment. Most days have no time for research or service. I spend many of my evenings researching and writing articles and contributing to the Rare Books and Manuscripts Section of the Association of College & Research Libraries as the senior web editor.

Toward a More Holistic Understanding of Special Collections Librarianship

There are similarities and differences between Traister's day and my own. Traister classifies his primary job function as "talking to people."[5] On days like the one I just described, I would classify mine as "making sure the wheels don't fall off." On less frenetic days, perhaps "connecting people with really cool stuff" would be more appropriate. Spending time working with donors of various calibers and working with the public, talking to people, and taking care of the administrative tasks that library school never really taught us constitute a major component of our similar days.

Traister describes a well-resourced institution with significant collections across a variety of disciplines and eras; my institution has two main collecting strengths and teaching collections across a variety of others. When Traister has friends of the library visit, he pulls "a Shakespeare First Folio; Audubon's *Birds of America*; a copy of Martyn's *English Entomologist* ... a letter from Thomas Jefferson on the occasion of Benjamin Franklin's death; a manuscript poem on women by Elizabeth Barrett Browning; and other more or less similar stuff";[6] materials of this caliber are nowhere to be found in my department. Most visitors would not look at the collections Traister discusses in his essay and, as a potential donor notably did one day while touring our science fiction collection, ask why they are housed in a special collections department.[7] Traister's donor has a chauffeur to help load the car; our donor boxed up molded animal droppings and mailed them along with the materials. Traister describes the staff he has working behind the scenes to connect researchers, students, and the community to those resources; I am one of those behind-the-scenes people *and* taking on much of Traister's role. Traister alludes to spaces, including exhibition and lecture spaces, in his department that would make librarians in less well-endowed institutions like mine green with envy. My office measures 6 feet by 9 feet when it is empty of all furniture, and our teaching space doubles as the only lecture space on campus that is free for students and faculty to reserve. The department's air-conditioning system was installed new when the building was constructed in the 1970s, resulting in a constant battle to keep temperature and humidity under control in central Florida.

My day as described, however, is simply another data point on the "special collections professional" continuum, just as Traister's is. How can

Table 1.1   Institutions and Positions of Interviewees

Institution Type	Position Held
Historical society	Special collections and manuscripts librarian
Liberal arts college	Music librarian
Private university	Paraprofessional staff member
State university (ARL library)	Cataloging librarian
State university (ARL library, stand-alone special collections library)	Curator
State university (ARL library)	Head of special collections and archives

we move beyond individual profiles such as these and find commonalities that cut across the field while also acknowledging the significant differences that are to be found in various positions, functions, and types of institutions where we work? What does it really mean to be a special collections librarian?

To begin to answer these questions, it is helpful to present a series of comparative portraits of special collections librarians from a diverse array of institutions and job functions, ranging from a lone arranger at a historical society to an administrator at an ARL special collections department (see Table 1.1). The goal of these six portraits is to move beyond the individual experience and toward a more holistic understanding of special collections librarianship, drawn from the unique experiences of special collections librarians in a variety of environments, to explore the differences and commonalities found in the array of work experiences suggested by the term "special collections librarianship."

Before presenting these comparative portraits and analyzing them in the composite, it is important to note particular elements of them individually. The librarian portraits featured here, selected on the basis of job function and library type, illustrate the diversity of perspectives within the field. Another important consideration is the use of pseudonyms in these portraits. In addition to employing pseudonyms, I have attempted to avoid describing the institutions where the interviewees work in ways that make either the interviewee or the institution immediately recognizable. The field of special collections librarianship is, however, an extremely small one; many of the librarians profiled below will be identifiable to many readers. Despite this fact, none of the interviewees expressed concern over being recognized, and many indicated that they had given similar interviews for different purposes under their real names. I employed pseudonyms to focus more on the individual's experiences and less on the individual's institutional affiliation and particularities found at specific libraries. All too often, institutional names become shorthand for the type of experiences, environments, and work that are expected to occur at that particular (type of) library. Pseudonyms helped avoid this shorthand. It is also important to note, however, that these portraits reflect individuals and that the profiles below are real, lived experiences. To underscore and highlight the experiential nature of these portraits, I have retained and presented some personal data and used pseudonymous names rather than relying upon job classification as an identifier.

These portraits build upon the framework begun by Traister's "day in the life"; they point to common themes across the profession while also illuminating differences to what has generally been perceived as the rule.

The questions I asked interviewees (see Appendix 1.1) were inspired by Traister's reflections on his day as a rare books librarian, and the answers offered highlight a multiplicity of experiences and add depth to an understanding of what it means to be a rare books or special collections librarian. I take Traister's position as a starting point not to undercut it, but rather to orient the pluralities of experience highlighted here. What is it that we do? What makes a special collections librarian a special collections librarian? Is it our job function, the materials we work with, or a combination of the two? The answer uncovered in these six interviews is a resounding "it depends"—on the position held and the type of institution in which a particular librarian works.

For Kelly,[8] the special collections and manuscripts librarian at a state-affiliated historical society, a typical day looks very different now, at the end of three years at the historical society, than it did when she first began.[9] Kelly is part of the collections department, but she is the only librarian on staff. Her colleagues, also members of the collections department, are museum curators responsible for three-dimensional objects. As the only "paper" person on staff, Kelly has slowly become responsible for a wide range of collections: institutional archives, state history materials, rare maps, the personal library of the historic home's original owner, early printed books from the region, and travel literature. Her collections are scattered across 20 buildings, only one of which was designed to hold library and museum materials. The other buildings on the site were originally houses, and they come with the structural challenges associated with using historic construction in ways that it was never intended to be used.

While Kelly began as the society's archivist, responsible solely for documenting the site's history through its institutional archives, due to budget cuts she eventually assumed responsibility as registrar and manuscripts curator. Most recently, her days have included fielding phone calls from researchers at neighboring universities, usually faculty members or graduate students working on theses and dissertations or genealogists who are planning research trips; helping other staff members at the society who want to use the collections in their work; attending meetings for exhibit design and programming; talking with donors; processing collections; marshaling volunteers, ranging from high school students to museum studies graduate students to retirees, and finding appropriate projects for them; and physically moving manuscript collections from their old homes in one of the 20 buildings on site to a newly renovated collections storage facility that recently opened. Her office, meanwhile, is across campus from this storage facility. While she has been able to move most of the manuscript and institutional archives materials to this secure storage facility, many of the rare book collections Kelly is responsible for are on permanent display in the other buildings on site. When asked about atypical days that she enjoys and finds professionally fulfilling, Kelly describes finding time to process more collections. The flip side, though, are the days that do not bring professional joy: days spent with taking care of administrative tasks due to loss of staff, interviewing candidates to replace those lost staff members, and a seemingly endless stream of administrative meetings and calls from prospective donors who found a "rare" book in the attic and who, after watching *Pawn Stars*, became convinced of the book's value. A large portion of her job, Kelly notes, can be summed up as "keeping track of stuff,"[10] both physically and intellectually.

Paige, the music librarian at a small liberal arts college, has days that are somewhat similar to Kelly's despite the very different setting.[11] Paige is the only professional librarian in the music library on campus, which includes both circulating music collections and music-related special collections. As a solo librarian, Paige spends a large chunk of each day on administrative tasks, despite the fact that she is not technically an administrator. Each morning, for example, Paige troubleshoots staffing problems at the branch, checks in with student workers, and puts out building-related fires that arose overnight, which may range from placing plastic sheets over shelves to protect materials from a leak to tracking down maintenance to fix a malfunctioning toilet.

Space limitations have required Paige to be creative in making sure that collections are secure and researchers have space to work with materials. Paige's office, for example, is where rare items in the music library live; her office is considered a location code in the library's catalog. In addition to administrative duties and the normal office-related tasks common across seemingly all librarian positions, Paige devotes the rest of her day to work on long-term projects, including planning and implementing large-scale digitization projects, doing the leg work to purchase and process new acquisitions, dealing with donors, attending meetings, fulfilling responsibilities to faculty governance on campus, and preparing for and leading instruction sessions, all of which are related to musicology, music history, or performance. Paige notes that the format she most frequently acquires for her special collections is the music manuscript facsimile; the price point is feasible for her institution, and the materials stand up to repeated usage in the classroom. Like Kelly, Paige has job responsibilities that she dislikes (dealing with unsolicited gifts) as well as responsibilities that she enjoys and would like to be able to spend more time on (purchasing materials for use in the classroom and then working with students to show them how to use those materials). Paige describes her primary job function as providing subject expertise.

Catherine, meanwhile, is a paraprofessional staff member in the Special Collections and Archives departments at a private university, a position she holds while pursuing a PhD in book history.[12] Catherine's day-to-day work is essential for the department to continue serving patrons: she oversees the reading room, managing the registration process, the paging of materials, and security in public services areas. She also works six hours per week as a special collections cataloger, manages acquisitions for a subset of the department, supervises all of the student assistants and interns in the department, and is responsible for updating the department's Web site. The department's collecting strengths include church history and religious books, such as Bibles, prayer books, and hymnals. In addition to these research collections, the department also has strong teaching collections in the history of the book and author-specific American literature. Given this scope, Catherine works with researchers in church and religious history visiting from around the world, but she works more frequently with undergraduate and graduate students learning about the history of book production.

In addition to regularly assigned duties, Catherine was active in the library's recent project to renovate the department's reading room, so unlike Kelly and Paige, Catherine does not spend major portions of her day working around less-than-ideal space constraints. Catherine's office is in direct sight lines of the reading room, and a curved mirror allows her to keep an eye on student assistants who are processing collections. As is to be expected in a public services oriented position, Catherine's professional frustrations and joys both come from her interactions with patrons: there are, of course, problem patrons who expect either research or photoduplication services that are not offered by the department, but there are also opportunities to help new, frequently undergraduate, researchers learn the skills necessary for them to complete their projects. For Catherine, a jargon-free way of describing her work is "helping researchers find and get what they need."[13]

Christopher is a cataloging librarian in a special collections library at an ARL institution.[14] There are currently four different special collections libraries on campus, all devoted to either different formats or different subjects. Christopher works at the special collections library charged with documenting the history and culture of the state. While he is formally assigned to catalog published materials, over the years his job has evolved to include cataloging manuscripts and oral history materials as well as creating metadata for digital projects. In addition to local descriptive work, Christopher also spends a portion of each day supervising the two project catalogers who report to him and contributing to national cooperative cataloging projects, including the Cooperative Online Serials Program (CONSER) and the Name Authority Cooperative Program (NACO). Working to create name authority records is Christopher's favorite part of his job; it requires research into the personal names and corporate bodies he is describing, and it requires technical expertise. Christopher is also currently serving as co-principal investigator on a national digitization grant, where he works on all aspects of grant and project management except for budget reporting; his daily work may include making presentations on grant activities, holding workshops, resolving questions about cataloging or metadata, editing quarterly reports, reviewing supplemental grant applications, attending advisory board meetings, or making sure that deliverables were produced on schedule. It is through this grant-funded project that Christopher engages in work with events, planning and implementing public programming and statewide workshops related to the digitization project. In addition to his cataloging and grant work, Christopher is also responsible for regular shifts on the library's public services desk, fluctuating from two hours per week to two hours per day, depending on current staffing levels. He does not, however, routinely interact with library donors or attend or plan regular library events. When asked to describe his primary job function, Christopher replied, "describing sources of information."[15]

Space is increasingly problematic for Christopher and his colleagues, which number 8 faculty librarians and approximately 10 full-time staff members within the special collections library. While the primary rare books and special collections department is located in a new building adjacent to the university's main library, Christopher's department is typically housed in one of the university's early 19th-century buildings. Recent years, however, have seen required renovations to address mold, lead, and other public safety concerns. With almost constant construction in a historic building not originally intended to house archives and books, Christopher has spent quite a lot of time shuffling between offices. For a while, his "office" was a table behind the reference desk with no walls separating him from public spaces. He has also worked in temporary office "nooks" off of stacks space and in shared office space. Currently, the entire building is closed for major renovations, so Christopher is working out of the campus's main library. While there are decided perks, including an actual office with both doors and walls, he is also working in a different building than his public service colleagues and the materials he is responsible for cataloging.

Erin is a subject specialist curator at a large, stand-alone special collections library affiliated with a state university with ARL membership status.[16] While all of the librarians I interviewed hold master's degrees in both librarianship and an academic discipline, Erin is the only interviewee who currently holds a doctorate as well. Like Catherine's space, Erin's reading room has also recently been renovated and maximizes the workflows staff have put in place to ensure the safety of collections. A reception desk and cloakroom with lockers are located outside of the reading room, and the reading room includes many individual desks, all with power outlets, rather than large tables. Erin's office, however, is a floor away from the reading room, in an area that is not accessible to patrons but is conveniently located to the stacks.

When asked to describe her typical day, Erin notes that the connector between her days is not a specific activity itself but the range of activity. On any given day, Erin will spend time on collection development, which might include corresponding with a donor or a bookseller or reading catalogs; working with the cataloging department, which reports through and is housed in the main library, not special collections, to set priorities for accessioning new materials; helping student workers create descriptions for finding aids; and taking care of teaching responsibilities, including preparing for class visits, which might be for a nearby high school studying medieval manuscript culture or a graduate seminar studying a particular literary author, talking with faculty about upcoming courses, or teaching a semester-long course in book history that is offered through the English department. Erin describes her primary job function as making connections between people, resources, and materials. Making these connections also provides Erin the part of her job that she enjoys the most; when I asked her about days she loved, Erin talked about facilitating "transformative" moments in the classroom or with individual patrons in the reading room, where her instruction leads the student or researcher to a magical "a ha" moment.[17]

Although not everyday occurrences, Erin is also very active in public facing, formal programming with her library and university. Her special collections library mounts three exhibitions a year, all of which include a public programming component, and other events on campus frequently use materials loaned from special collections to augment their own public programming. Erin helps with all of these events, with tasks ranging from conceiving of, researching, and mounting a full exhibition; mentoring a student from the museum studies program who is working to mount a small-scale exhibition in the library; attending exhibition-related events; and traveling with and supervising materials that have been loaned to other events on campus.

Michelle is the head of Special Collections and Archives at a state university with one of the smaller ARL member libraries.[18] Michelle is one of 50 FTE at the library, and 5 full-time professional staff report to Michelle through either Special Collections or the Archives, which are separate administrative entities and are housed in different buildings. As an administrator, Michelle describes a day that, in many ways, sounds much like the day Traister reports: she spends a lot of time talking with people. Michelle begins her day with voice messages and e-mail, and then she attends both formal and informal meetings with the staff she supervises, with the library's management team, with current and prospective patrons, with library development to generate support for the collections, and with library staff in other departments to increase awareness of collections and resources. Michelle also oversees the entirety of the department's exhibition program, and she, more so than any of the other librarians I interviewed, is also the public face of Special Collections and Archives for donor relations work. Working in conjunction with the library's development office, Michelle attends both formal and informal meetings with existing donors, gives tours to existing and prospective donors, works to establish relationships with new or potential donors, evaluates offers, and prepares proposals for collections that the university would like to receive via donation.

Michelle was unique among the special collections professionals I interviewed in that she was recruited for the position she currently holds; while she was not actively seeking to move into special collections management, when the opportunity presented itself, she decided to jump. It is not a decision she regrets. Michelle speaks of an active, engaged staff who are knowledgeable of the collections her departments oversee, and also of well-developed and managed collections, ranging from a very robust and historically sound university archives to rare book and manuscript collections in history of science and technology, history of performing arts, travel and exploration literature, and fine press printing. While the learning curve has been steep, particularly with regard to formal human resources procedures, such as delivering performance evaluations, there have also been opportunities to gain the new knowledge needed, including university-sponsored manager's training.

What Do We Talk about When We Talk about Special Collections Librarianship?

In the original "The Rare Book Librarian's Day," Traister writes against a particular typology of the rare book librarian, against the idea that rare book librarians are research librarians who "read and write about our incunabula, our renaissance bookbindings, Shakespeare's First Folio, Elzevier imprints, Jonathan Swift's publications, nineteenth-century American publishing or book illustration, the first editions of William Carlos Williams; we caress each lovely book."[19] As a result, Traister highlights the prosaic nature of much special collections work, and there are certainly echoes of the quotidian in the ethnographic portraits presented here. Space, or lack thereof, is a perennial problem for many special collections librarians, as illustrated here by Paige's office serving as a location code in the catalog and Christopher's continuous hunt for an office. Many of us, like Kelly, make do with space that was never intended to house collections. We also spend quite a lot of time on general workplace management: changing toner in copiers, making sure student assistants show up for work, training and supervising volunteers, calling maintenance, and generally ensuring that the department continues to function.

Writing against a particular typology, one that privileges the view from special collections departments that collect Elzevier imprints, Jonathan Swift, and early Shakespeareana at the exclusion of other experiences, creates limits. The social grammar of special collections librarianship is much broader than a focus on the exceedingly and immediately obviously rare would suggest. The collections that we house and make available to researchers are very different based on the location and mission of the department; the special collections I surveyed in this chapter range from the "traditional" rare book collection to personal papers, state history, performing arts, religious studies, popular culture, literature, and science and technology. It is important to note this breadth, in terms of both content and scarcity. Special collections librarian Melissa Hubbard recently alluded to this point on Twitter, noting that "The special collections as 'crown jewels' metaphor always irks me. It reduces us to expensive and sparkly . . . I just want to stand up and shout, 'a lot of our stuff is homely and under-valued, but it will still*blow your mind*!' "[20] Special collections are not just homes to the exceedingly rare and the lavishly shiny. Some collections include materials such as these, but many more offer depth and breadth to the researcher and to the student and require both the librarian and the user to look beyond the binding or imprint and to focus on the content.

Similarly, our collections are used by very different populations: genealogists, undergraduates, PhD candidates, visiting faculty members from other institutions, and even high school students. While all of the special collections librarians interviewed mentioned seeing users from each of these demographics, different collections serve different purposes, and this is reflected in the user base that frequents each department's reading room. Christopher and Kelly, for example, see many genealogists with seasonal fluctuation in visiting graduate students and faculty, while Catherine and Paige work frequently with undergraduate students and less frequently with graduate students and faculty members who have very specific research interests that mirror their collection's strengths. Erin, meanwhile, works with a patron base that looks the most like the one Traister described, consisting largely of graduate students and faculty, but she also speaks of working with visiting classes of high school students. The differences here are important in that they serve to illustrate the important range of activity that occurs in our collections and that special collections librarians support.

The first substantive question asked of all interviewees was simple: how did you become a special collections librarian? Everyone interviewed spoke of an initial love of materials, of objects, and of books, but they also spoke of a growing desire, typically gained through internships and early career experience, to help people and to make connections between different resources, and between researchers and materials. While it is true that many of our tasks are administrative and that no one spends his or her day exclusively as a research librarian in the model against which Traister wrote, all of the librarians interviewed did note that having a working knowledge of both the collections under their care and the research methods involved in using those collections was important. Paige, for example, works exclusively with music materials, music students, and music researchers; without functional research literacy in the field, she would be unable to serve her patrons. Erin also noted that days with extra time for getting to know the collections she curates are days well spent, because she always finds materials that will help her promote the collections, assist patrons with reference queries, or better able to perform collection development activities more strategically.

Traister concludes his "day in the life" portrait by noting, "training for special collections librarians needs a clearer definition of 'research librarianship.' The expectations of those who enter the field will be constantly disappointed by reality if its daily necessities are not more realistically emphasized."[21] These portraits support Traister's argument and add nuance to it. Special collections librarians do not spend their days lovingly caressing Elzevier imprints, and, more importantly, many of us do not even have Elzevier imprints in our collections. While we will spend more time than we may care to itemize calling maintenance or moving our office yet again, it is also important to recognize the specialized knowledge behind the public services we provide. We may spend 90 percent of our days filing things, as Traister points out, but we know what those things are when we file them. We can help other people access them after they have been filed, and we know how they can be used when they are retrieved. Most importantly, perhaps, we know not to write off that homely little book on the bottom shelf.

Appendix 1.1: Interview Protocol

1. What is your official job title? What is your official classification (e.g., faculty, administrative, staff)?

2. How did you become a special collections librarian?

3. What is your educational background?

4. So, what do you do? Describe a "typical" day.

5. Describe an atypical day that you absolutely detest.

6. Describe an atypical day that you love and wish you had more of.

7. Describe the institution where you work. How many librarians are there in your organization? In your special collections department?

8. Describe your work space (office, processing area, stacks, security, etc.).

9. Describe your patrons. Who are they and what do they do with your collections?

10. Describe the types of materials your institution collects and that you work with on a daily basis.

11. Describe your work, if any, with donors.

12. Describe your work with partner libraries, including loan of materials.

13. Describe your library's facilities and your role in making sure that the facilities work correctly.

14. Describe your work with events.

15. Describe what you do when you have "friends" of the library pop in for a visit.

16. Describe your work with students (interns, volunteers, employees).

17. How would you describe your primary job function?

Notes

1. Daniel Traister, "The Rare Book Librarian's Day," *Rare Books & Manuscripts Librarianship* 1, no. 2 (1986): 93–105.

2. Ibid., 96.

3. Rare Books and Manuscripts Section's Task Force on Core Competencies for Special Collections Librarians, "Guidelines: Competencies for Special Collections Professionals," ACRL, 2008, accessed January 15, 2015, http://www.ala.org/acrl/standards/comp4specollect.

4. This tendency of promulgating a view "from the top" persists; see, for example, John H. Overholt, "Five Theses on the Future of Special Collections," *RBM* 14, no. 1 (2013): 15–20. The future here is seen from and defined by experience at Harvard's Houghton Library.

5. Traister, "The Rare Book Librarian's Day," 100.

6. Ibid., 98.

7. While there is, of course, an answer to this question, it is not always readily apparent to potential donors, even after we discuss the importance of preservation.

8. All names are pseudonyms, but the gender of the interviewee has been preserved in the pseudonym chosen.

9. Personal interview, March 26, 2015.

10. Ibid.

11. Personal interview, March 25, 2015.

12. Personal interview, April 15, 2015.

13. Ibid.

14. Personal interview, April 20, 2015.

15. Ibid.

16. Personal interview, April 21, 2015.

17. Ibid.

18. Personal interview, April 22, 2015.

19. Traister, "The Rare Book Librarian's Day," 95.

20. Melissa Hubbard, Twitter post, May 18, 2015, https://twitter.com/melissa_hubbard (asterisks in original).

21. Traister, "The Rare Book Librarian's Day," 105.

Chapter 2
Reading Room and Reference (Re)Vision: The Transformation of Reader Services

Mattie Taormina and Marilyn Rackley

In 2009, Stephen Davison asked in his article, "If We Build It, Will They Come?" We answer with a resounding "Yes!" Even with fragmentary metadata, missing context, selected (but not entire) digital collections online, wobbly user interfaces, and scantily described finding aids and catalog records, patrons still come.[1] Reference and reading room staff continue to create patron-centered services when and where their users need them.[2] When Davison wrote his article six years ago, he noted that the digitization of materials for user access and web-based exhibits attracted a wider variety of users than ever before, and this is especially, but not exclusively, true for academic libraries.[3] He perceptively noted that the profession was "participating in a transformation that has only just begun."[4]

In the last 10 years, through grants, institutional commitments, the Hidden Collections Initiative, more product, less process (MPLP)–inspired workflows, and advances in storage and technology, cultural heritage repositories nationwide have undertaken digitization programs.[5] This amplified access to materials has attracted different types of users, changed research methods, and adjusted reference services to continue offering the best patron experience possible. The transformation for special collections and archives reference is in full swing.

Today's special collections and archives reference librarians still need to hone and develop traditional archival and rare book bibliographical skills. They also need to know how best to attract new users; meet and understand users' changing needs, behaviors, and expectations; integrate special collections materials into academic courses; maintain a strong web and social media presence; and create and expand outreach programs.[6] Patrons' use of technology over the last 10 years has transformed reference departments and reading room interactions, and new materials, such as born-digital holdings, are creating new reader services.[7] Accordingly, these changes must guide hiring decisions and reading room practices; flexible, tech-savvy, transliterate librarians best serve the scholars and research methods of the present and future.[8]

A Different Kind of Reference Staff

At its core, special collections reference is still about providing quality service that best meets the needs of users whether they be remote or on-site.[9] To continue to be effective and relevant to users in the ever-changing reading room of the 21st century, more than skills need to be addressed: we need a new mind-set. We need to hire staff possessing an eagerness and curiosity for learning both general and specialized archival software(s), and teaching others (present authors included) how they work.

Reference will always require strong, demonstrated skills in communication, teamwork, and creative problem solving. These skills can also lend themselves to a deep and quick embrace of technology. Both recent and long-term reference and reading room staff need to have an openness and ability to embrace technological changes. We cannot afford to have someone fearful, resistant, and set against learning new technologies working with the public. We are beyond the time when administrators can put someone "exceptionally nice" in reference services solely based on their stellar interpersonal soft skills and solid knowledge of finding aids, MARC records, and other traditional tools to work at the desk.[10] This indeed would have been a very good hire in the past, but today's public service reference staff must possess both a passion for helping people and an openness toward technology. We know that just one disagreeable interaction with an unfriendly staff member is enough to scare away the timid student or repel an important donor.[11] The time has come when both "traditional" and "tech" qualities must be weighted equally in hiring decisions.[12]

Not much in the professional literature emphasizes this needed attitude toward technology by special collections and archival reference staff in such plain, strong terms. The core competencies of the Association for College & Research Libraries help future professionals plan their career paths, and help administrators write or review position descriptions to make sound hiring decisions. The 2008 competencies gently suggested that special collections public service professionals should "also develop skills and knowledge to respond to trends in higher education as well as to rapidly changing technologies and the resulting shifts in user expectations."[13]

Purposefully tying technology to reference and reading room staff truthfully reflects what is happening in our reading rooms. The classic archival reference interview is increasingly focused on explaining software, web interfaces, and other technological tools. Today's reference practitioners must have knowledge of current technology so that the person behind the desk, answering the phone and e-mail, and monitoring the chat and Twitter accounts can readily accept and eagerly adapt to—or intelligently challenge—changing future technologies. The new 2016 competencies reflect a better understanding of the need for reference staff to possess a deeper technological prowess.

Research Is Changing

As our rare materials become more accessible online, the academic special collections and archival reading room crowd has expanded. Alongside the perennial genealogist and historian now sits the film studies, art, and science students, joined by the lawyer, museum curator, and general, nonacademic user. With the advent of Common Core State Standards, more K–12 students are coming in as well.[14]

Early efforts to digitize large amounts of visually appealing material have brought in an assortment of TV/media producers and documentarians. This group's service needs require more flexibility from reading room staff, sometimes challenging established service models. Their remote reference requests generally begin with: "Since you hold the papers of (person), can you look through the photos and pick the best image of (person) surrounded by students, teaching a class?" They often have reduced timelines too: "We want to show (image A) in our 3 p.m. broadcast."

When these users personally visit the archives, their quest for visually appealing materials that only they can identify ("I'll know it when I see it") motivates them to ask to "see the whole collection" or "spread out everything on the table so I can get a feel for what's there" or "browse your stacks and look through all the boxes." Often, these users are unfamiliar with off-site storage practices, preservation of original order of materials, and other care and handling measures that tend to be standard reading room observances.

Changing academic research needs also directly impact reference and reading room services. Patrons bring their own expectations of technology into the reading room, and their research methodology has dramatically changed in the last nine years. Stanford was one of the first special collections to allow patrons to use their digital cameras in the reading room for duplication purposes in 2006. Almost 10 years later, many patrons no longer spend their limited research time going through boxes, taking meticulous notes, and carefully selecting materials for photocopying. Now on-site scholars choose to take hundreds of pictures—sometimes without reading the materials—and assess and organize them upon returning home. This new research pattern challenges traditional duplication limits; requests to duplicate entire collections in this manner are frequent.[15]

Digital cameras are not the only gadgets patrons want to bring into the reading room to do their research. They want to bring in headphones, iPads, and mini handheld and flatbed scanners. Some patrons want the repository to provide them with an ever-increasing array of tech: tripod camera stands, single-lens reflex and document cameras, smartboards, and a variety of scanners, all with the expectation that whoever is behind the desk will be able to provide training and technical assistance with these tools whenever needed.

Lastly, as academic research has become more interdisciplinary, professors and students have new ways they wish to engage with materials. Professors want to hold office hours with students in the reading room to discuss the student's paper with the item in hand. Student groups frequently want to work with a document or book collectively, hunched over the item, actively talking and discussing its information. They want to make their own movies or create original art from library materials. Like the documentarians, these visually intensive uses require "the team" to be able to pull lots of sources, spread them out, move them around, and openly discuss how the materials can best support the scope of their project.

Our Spaces Need to Change

All of these described uses can often conflict with the physical designs of many current special collections and archival reading rooms. Many reference and reading room professionals have to work around their reading room's design to adequately give patrons service. These rooms were created around the needs of a traditional researcher who is frequently becoming outnumbered: a scholar working in silence with rare books or archival materials in solo pursuit. With this persona in mind, reading rooms were designated as quiet spaces since it is hard to concentrate on raw data over the din of conversation. Seats face forward, not only for security reasons but also because lone researchers rarely need to talk to anyone while they are here. This model is breaking down under the weight of the modern interdisciplinary undergraduate and graduate learning experience.

In 2003, Traister noted that, "once readers arrive and have what they need in hand, they need a reading room situation that functions for them": a comfortable, quiet, reading room with large tables, plenty of outlets, and free WiFi.[16] Twelve years later, patrons not only require these basic amenities, but also need flexible seating, adjustable tables for accessibility, a way to listen to audio visual materials, group-talk space, and—with more large, formats coming in—wide tables with no obstructions (like a lamp) in the middle. As special collections and archives reference librarians attempt to accommodate these new users, they still have patrons that need their room to be silent. It is essential that we rethink our standard reading room policies and procedures and spaces with these users and use patterns in mind and factor in more flexibility where possible.

Reference Services Have Evolved

"Digitization is a start, but providing innovative digital services on top of the digital collections is essential to meet the needs of an expanding audience for special collections materials."[17] Overholt notes that "Special Collections will increasingly serve an audience that does not, and in many cases need not, cross its threshold."[18] For many reference and reading room practitioners, this statement has been true for several years, really taking hold when library catalogs, archival finding aids, and primary resources were made electronically discoverable and e-mail was introduced.[19] Today's reader services departments provide more virtual reference than ever before, changing the types of reference services they offer, and the way they communicate with their patrons.[20]

Some reference and reading room staff have chosen to communicate with remote patrons by "flipping" their reading rooms. Like the concept of the flipped classroom, reader services staff have created videos detailing care and handling and reading room policies so that patrons can watch the videos before they arrive to do research, reducing the time patrons spend on repository-required administrative tasks.[21] These new communication paths with patrons mean that reference transactions can be more focused and detailed rather than librarians and users spending valuable time seeking information that really should be self-service.[22] They also require reference staff to learn new technology skills like web design and video creation and editing, to name a few.

Paradoxically, some users may not want to talk to reference and reading room staff at all. Self-reliant, they believe that they can find all the information they require—or "good enough" information—by simply typing search terms into an internet browser and suitable sources will appear. "[U]sers seeking information have many alternative avenues to pursue; the excellence of our collections and user services are often secondary to patrons, who seek convenience and ease of use first."[23] Young scholars lack an understanding of how archival descriptive tools such as finding aids and other metadata are created and why these tools provide different search results than a search engine.

The profession is also beginning to question if traditionally collected statistics still accurately capture the varied and complex reference transactions that occur now that usage may be by remote, anonymous users.[24] As administrators crave more efficient and intensive use statistics, how much longer can academic special collections and archive departments continue without software for managing user services such as Aeon and AXAEM? We must move toward developing open-source statistical software that will reclaim reference staff time spent manually capturing these vital numbers.

Transparency

Reference staff are quite familiar with incorporating information and archival literacy into their reference transactions; technological changes in our materials and a prominent online presence require us to be ever-transliterate so that we can successfully teach this literacy skill to our patrons. Our digital processes make it even more essential that we practice critical librarianship with our patrons so that we are transparent about the ways we participate in power and privilege over the information we acquire, represent, and process.[25]

For example, when a collection is digitally sampled and only the "important" parts of a collection (usually selected by a curator) are scanned and posted online, the question of what is made digital and how it is presented becomes very important.[26] Jackie Dooley cautioned us in 2009 that users did not want us to mediate and filter their online digital content discovery, that we needed to adopt "wholesale" rather than "retail" or specialized scanning of collections, and that we need to "stop doing scholars' interpretive work."[27] Davidson issued a similar warning, as administrative, donor, or curatorial decisions on scanning only what is deemed "most important" in a collection and giving that portion priority (or privilege) is power directly affecting scholarship.[28] MPLP-processing decisions and other metadata creation affect scholarship as well: items with more complete information become more discoverable and subsequently those sources are favored over others.[29]

We need to be transparent on why some sources get better metadata which ensures their use while other sources languish and are not easily discoverable. The OCLC report "Taking Our Pulse" found that "insufficiently discoverable metadata" is a significant challenge in meeting user needs.[30] Reference librarians are now fielding questions from several different systems of metadata: the catalog record, the finding aid, and now digital collections online. Not all the metadata corresponds, especially when supplemental metadata exists only in one place.[31]

How important is our power over metadata? The Digital Public Library of America recently issued a research paper detailing how large-scale digital collections can best meet classroom needs. Teachers make decisions about the usefulness of an item based on any contextual information they can find about a digital object. "Participants [K–12 students and teachers] shared frustrating experiences with digital cultural heritage content that appears useful but loses their attention with inadequate context or overly extensive metadata."[32]

We need to be more transparent about our workflows. Why do some collections get processed over others? Reader services often fields these questions and struggles with how to explain them. Not processing or scanning collections is an exercise in power too. No one outside of an archive or special collections knows what happens when we acquire a collection: not our users and, in some cases, not our administrators. The collection comes in and that is all they know until a finding aid is created—sometimes many years later. Users often have no knowledge of how long conservation treatments take, what processing or reformatting actually means and the steps involved, or the money that is necessary to create digital collections and the copyright/donor dance that is required. Processing were a good first step in trying to make these processes more clear, but there is a need to do more.

We need to own the part we play in exercising power and privilege over materials, and the easiest way to do that is to be transparent in our reference exchanges, in our finding aids, and with our digital metadata. Consistent inclusion of a processing note in the finding aid and in the digital record that describes the level of processing and scanning that was applied to the collection and why helps reference staff and patrons alike know what power we exercised over the description they are viewing.[33]

Embracing the Born-Digital

B. J. Daigle declared in 2012 that "[b]orn digital materials mark a new world order for archives."[34] Special collections departments now acquire archives and manuscript collections that include both paper-based and born-digital components (hybrid collections) and, in some cases, all digital components.[35] Our materials' formats are so varied, and so sophisticated, that in addition to our comprehension of traditional books, papers, textiles, and photographs, we must also possess a working knowledge of hard drives, flash drives, mobile devices, floppies, audio/video formats, web pages, and various social media platforms to facilitate both preservation and access for our patrons.

Special collections and archives are making efforts to understand this new world order. Within the past two years, the Society of American Archivists' (SAA) Reference, Access and Outreach section has created a taskforce gathering, analyzing, and making available information to practitioners looking for solutions for addressing access to born-digital materials.[36]

Existing articles and case studies describing efforts at processing born-digital materials regularly mention the need to ensure access to these materials and not just their preservation. For example, when the Wilson Special Collections Library staff at the University of North Carolina at Chapel Hill began planning how to deal with electronic records, they noted the need to work with reference and instruction staff in determining how to best present the digital objects.[37] However, reference and outreach issues, independent of the provision of access, are not often specifically addressed in the professional literature.

Facilitating access to born-digital materials not only accelerates the transformation in reference services that has already begun but also introduces new issues and challenges. Understanding and helping researchers use these materials either in the reading room or remotely may require a level of technical understanding beyond that required to help users navigate paper-based records. Much of the literature that describes acquiring, pre-serving, processing, and providing access to born-digital materials includes detailed evaluations and descriptions of sophisticated software tools needed to handle these types of materials in the collecting repository and to provide access without damage to the integrity and authenticity of the originals.[38] The literature also debates whether to provide access to collection materials via emulation or migration.[39]

While the role of reader services is not to process or preserve these materials, if we are to provide meaningful assistance to users accessing them, we need to understand how these tools have been used in our institu-tions to preserve and, in some cases, manipulate them. Decisions made by special collections staff have both practical and theoretical impacts on user research. When working with paper-based records, researchers may expect reference staff to help them understand not only the context of the creation of the materials but also the context of their accession into the collection and the work staff have performed to make them accessible. "This sort of information [regarding processing] would go a long way toward docu-menting the archival context of the records. And, if made available to the public, this information would enable users to make their own decisions about the possible meaning or order(s) of a particular collection," and thus judge the impact of the archivist's decisions on their research endeavors.[40] Archival description also serves as a guarantor of the authenticity of the records. "Archivists explain the records—and the additions or changes to them over time—to demonstrate to all interested persons that we have pro-tected their authenticity."[41]

When working with born-digital materials, researchers may have an even greater need to understand the archival context of the materials when they may be removed from the technological context of their creation and when the original files may not be accessible. Just as we need to be transpar-ent about the ways in which we exercise power and privilege in making deci-sions about paper materials, we need to be transparent about the decisions and processes that have affected preservation and access to electronic records. Researchers may want and need to know about the staff decisions that lead to the particular ways in which the staff decided to make those materials accessible.

What do researchers then need to understand about digital forensics, checksums, disk images, migration, and so on in order to effectively conduct their research? Some researchers will not have the technology background to understand these processes and will need assistance from knowledgeable reference staff. When the Manuscript, Archives, and Rare Book Library at Emory University received author Salman Rushdie's computers, the unit formed a team to process and make the contents accessible. The team settled on a multistrategy approach that included providing researchers access to an emulated version of the author's desktop to allow them to experience Rushdie's computer as he himself would have done. Emory's emulation was designed to be so accurate that users would even see the same error messages Rushdie might have seen when using his computer. However, this emulated environment proved to be disorienting for some researchers, who may not have been familiar with the operating systems and software applications Rushdie used on his earlier computers.[42] Emory's research services needs to be able to help researchers understand what they are experiencing through the emulation, obsolete operating systems, and outdated software applica-tions, including what emulation is and why the choice to emulate this par-ticular environment was made within the repository.

Archivists are recognizing that long-standing approaches to providing access in the reading room or even online may no longer be viable with born-digital materials. The nature of born-digital materials lends itself to the use of different research approaches. While certain researchers may continue to pore over a small set of documents, other researchers will need to use different methods to deal with the sheer quantities of materials being created, preserved, and made available.

When the Library of Virginia released the e-mail records of former Virginia governor Tim Kaine, it noted that

> our system is geared towards delivering more traditional digital content, such as digitized maps, manuscripts, and photographs. Though the emails are full-text searchable, the results set for a given keyword search can easily number in the thousands given the sheer volume of total records in the collection. We thus tried a number of approaches to help users navigate the collection.[43]

Reference staff will need to help researchers understand and take advantage of these new options, as basic as full-text searches or as sophisticated as text-mining and data visualization, while also facilitating more traditional styles of research with born-digital materials. Researchers may also come prepared with their own research and data analysis tools and expect the repository to provide the data in a format compatible with their tools.[44]

Reference staff encounter a different set of expectations in an age when most born-digital materials can, at least from a technical perspective, be made accessible online almost as soon as they are accessioned. If "Can't I just see the whole collection?" seems like a reasonable request to users of large paper collections, it would certainly seem like a reasonable request when the whole collection is made up of few enough files or data to fit on a single laptop, flash drive, or hard drive. Digital remote access to archives, special collections, and other reference and library media is the current state of the industry; this is what patrons are demanding from their libraries. Special collections professionals, however, recognize that donor agreements and copyright law may prevent the repository from making these materials available outside of the controlled environment of the reading room.

Reading room staff often also play the role of security guard in the reading room to ensure the security and safety of materials. Collection materials in these new formats require that reader services revisit their care and handling and security measures. We need to craft access policies and procedures that ensure the security and long-term viability of the materials while still promoting access. Electronic materials may be made accessible via a variety of hardware options, including external hard drives, flash drives, laptops, and websites. Should users be allowed to access an original flash drive via a computer like they would an audio cassette or CD-ROM, or should the drive be "reformatted" as is the practice for tape-based materials like VHS tapes?

Even when born-digital materials are made available to researchers on larger physical media, like collection laptops, the security role of the repository staff may need to change. It is unlikely the researcher would try to leave the reading room with an entire laptop, but it is possible that researchers may try to copy, delete, or otherwise alter collection files. Reference staff will need to understand the technical measures put in place to maintain the security and authenticity of the materials while being knowledgeable about possible ways to circumvent those measures.

Regardless of whether collection materials are used in the reading room or remotely online, repository staff must implement policies and procedures for services that go beyond the provision of access. It has also traditionally been the purview of reader services to provide reproductions of materials to researchers, in the form of photocopies, prints, low-resolution scans, high-resolutions scans, and audio-visual reproductions. The provision of reproduction services takes into account donor restrictions on use of materials, copyright laws, and the cost of staff time in making the actual reproductions.

While all of these considerations require us to exercise our judgment in providing reproductions, most repositories have created general guidelines when dealing with requests for duplication of physical materials in their collections. Reference staff will need to determine which, if any, of those considerations apply when researchers request copies of materials that exist primarily in digital formats. Do the same institution-specific limitations on number of pages or percentage of collection materials apply when the number of pages is no longer a valid way to determine materials extent? What costs should apply when providing reproductions involve only a transfer of files and not labor-intensive scanning or other reformatting?

Born-digital materials will be preserved, accessed, and used in ways that we cannot even imagine yet. While many special collections professionals are making thoughtful attempts to incorporate access to electronic materials by integrating them descriptively with related paper materials or by including folders of electronic documents in a finding aid next to folders of paper documents, others are dreaming up new ways to describe electronic materials by presenting the sentiments expressed in a particular collection in easy-to-analyze visualizations.[45] The landscape of skills and knowledge needed to provide reference services for born-digital materials will change rapidly and require even more technical skills and training than it does today. Policies and procedures will be needed for accessing these materials in both the reading room and the virtual reading room that will keep pace with these rapid changes. Facilitating access to every type of resource, regardless of its format, will continue to keep reference staff relevant and invaluable to both patrons and administration.

Lean In for Reference Services

While it is satisfying to see so many conference sessions and articles on outreach, teaching, social media, and exhibits (many functions considered public services), the profession as a whole has not been as focused on reference as it might be. Fundamentally, reference is the core of public services, and in many small repositories and historical societies, it is the only function when instruction and exhibit spaces are not possibilities. It might be time for a call to action or a lean-in specifically for reference services.[46] Like the criticisms lobbied against Sandberg's book, one can only lean in toward the table and be part of the change and leadership, if one first has been invited to where the table actually is. Many times, it seems that reference and reading room staff are not invited to that table.

Administrators may assume librarians and archivists learn reference skills through their degree-granting educational programs, but it is often not the case. MLIS degree programs usually offer a general library reference class in their programs, but nothing specifically focused on the special collections environment.[47] General reference courses do not adequately prepare a reference practitioner to work in and provide effective service to patrons who use special collections and archival reading rooms. According to Bastian and Yakel, "little emphasis has been placed on reference knowledge in formal archival education"; only 6 out of 62 archival educational programs in 2006 offered a course specially devoted to reference work.[48]

It is also rare for educational opportunities focused on reference to be offered at professional societies' conferences. In the early 1990s, SAA did not offer its reference-related workshop "because not enough archivists or their supervisors were willing to pay to learn about this topic."[49] A survey of the past 12 years of workshops offered by the SAA and the Rare Books and Manuscripts Section (RBMS) of the American Library Association found that SAA last offered a reference workshop in 2006, and RBMS has yet to offer one.

Professionals usually backfill their education or keep abreast of new developments in the field by reading the scholarly literature. Depending upon one's access to different journals and how much time one can devote to this type of exploration, this approach may not prove helpful to reference staff. A survey of the last 10 years of articles in the *Journal of Archival Organization*, *RBM*, and the *American Archivist* shows the profession exploring issues pertaining to technology and processing, cataloging, and different formats, and how the digital metamorphosis has impacted outreach, social media, faculty, and classes. Few explored the impact all these digital efforts have had on the core, day-to-day function of reference. That is not to say that members of RBMS and SAA have not written specifically on reference in their local, regional, and state publications in the last 10 years; it just means that these three prominent national publications have not covered the topic in any depth.

Why are reference and reading room issues left out? Maybe we have contributed to this omission: perhaps we have not advertised to our colleagues what we can bring to the table, or maybe we are too busy working the desk and e-mailing patrons to make time for planning meetings, exploring new technologies, proposing panels, and writing essays. Making reference a side note in a panel or an article on related topics makes it incredibly difficult for professionals in reference services to focus on changes specifically happening to that area, to know what is expected of them, and devalues this core part of their profession.

Besides reference not being mentioned prominently in degree programs, professional conferences, and the scholarly literature, one wonders if dedicated reference and reading room staff are present at digital project planning meetings. At large institutions, when teams are assembled for new scanning projects, website design, catalog augmentation, and digital collection creation, is there a reference staff member on the team? When a collection comes in and processing or conservation treatment decisions are being arranged, is a reference staff member at the table? Involving reference staff from a project's beginning is vital, as Mary Jo Pugh aptly states:

> Reference specialists can identify the research needs of major user constituencies, such as staff of the parent institution, genealogists, scholars, students, or press, and develop strategies to meet them. Reference staff can advocate user needs in institutional planning.[50]

Pugh also describes access considerations of archival materials: "The use of archives is often seen as a linear model at the end of other functions similar to a caboose at the end of a train."[51] If the library or archive is truly committed to creating user-centered products (and the products being an online catalog, digital collections website, etc.), then the obvious decision is to start and end conversations about those products with the people who represent those users: reference staff. As obvious as this is, this inclusion is not consistently happening.

"The Report of My Death Was an Exaggeration"

In the early 2000s, several scholarly articles predicted the demise of reference, based on a belief that because of tools like Google Books and keyword-searchable online finding aids and catalogs records, reference queries would decline as more and more content went online. Reference mediation would be a thing of the past. This belief—coming mostly from people not in close contact with the day-to-day operations of the reading room or even with a background in special collections—has proven false but its early assertion devalued the position of reference in the profession.[52]

More access to information actually has increased the need for reference assistance. Two art museum archivists, Snyder and Botten, recently wrote:

> The huge growth in our digital collections has led to a similar expansion among the number and variety of our online visitors. Though we had always considered ourselves a specialized repository with a core audience of experienced academic researchers, our online collections attracted a greater number of undergraduate students, casual researchers, art enthusiasts, and genealogists, many of whom submit reference questions through our online form.[53]

As much as the profession has tried to create helpful websites and databases full of information useful to the user in order to mitigate how much archivist-mediation the patron might need, this digital push has not caused an abatement in reference queries. Reference now commonly consists of very focused and complex questions, or overwhelmed users needing help navigating through the wealth of information online.[54] The focused users are able to locate the basic information they need, and now have very specific and detailed reference questions such as, "I need the full title page transcription and collation of this book, and need to know about the paper (including watermarks), any ornamentation, and lastly, if the binding is contemporary to publication. Oh, and can I get leaf measurements (height and width)?" or "You have an artist book there and I want to know exactly how the gatherings were sewn into the binding, how many gatherings there are total, how many sheets are in each gathering, and the measurements of the images that are on the pages" or even this query: "Neither the Google Book scan nor your catalog record tell me about your copy's provenance or if it has a half title page."

The overwhelmed user creates an uptick in basic reference questions (like hours, location, e-mail address, and how to request copies) because some department websites are buried under many layers of the parent institution's website. Or, the website is discoverable but overpacked with so much information (or maybe not packed enough in some cases) that it is not useful.[55] A 2010 survey of University of Illinois at Chicago special collections' users by Valerie Harris and Ann Weller found that 99.2 percent of the respondents considered it important to have ready access to a librarian or archivist in order to conduct their research.[56] The survey found that researchers valued reference service over other traditional services such as photocopying, digital imaging, and access to wireless Internet.[57] Clearly these high numbers imply that whatever digital efforts the profession has made, they may not be as helpful to patrons as previously thought.

If it's all online, why do users keep coming? As materials go online, it does not make users stay away; it seems to have the opposite effect. Many reference staff report increases in reading room use, reference, and classes over the last 10 years.[58] For example, at the 2015 RBMS conference, Sarah Sherman mentioned in her presentation that the Getty Institute's requests for classes have dramatically gone up due to their growing online presence.[59] Reference staff routinely field a growing amount of requests for high-resolution images from patrons wishing to publish materials found online and queries for related content in the physical collection that may not have been added to the online collection.[60]

John Overholt wrote, "We can't know what uses will be made of our collections once we put them in the world's hands . . . we will be constantly surprised by the uses made of our collections in ways we could have never imagined and on scales we could never have accomplished on our own."[61] We cannot know the exact skills that will be needed in the future nor foresee all the different ways we will need to provide access for our future materials' formats. Instead, we can focus on hiring reference staff with the right attitude toward technology, while still remembering that creating a patron-centered library requires librarians with people skills, technological competence, the ability to empathize with patrons, and flexibility to adapt to change—all important personality characteristics.[62]

Reader services needs people with a willingness to build both their technical and people skills. Reference departments need to cultivate new skills and approaches to users' ever-changing research needs. The future of reference is forward thinking, is welcoming, and keeps pace with ever-changing patrons and their research methods no matter what form materials take.

Notes

1. Stephen Davison, "If We Build It, Will They Come? Strategies for Teaching and Research with Digital Special Collections," *RBM: A Journal of Rare Books, Manuscripts and Cultural Heritage* 10, no. 1 (March 20, 2009): 37–50.

2. To see the most current thoughts on creating a user-driven public services culture, please consult "User-driven Culture in Special Collections: A Manifesto," http://www.user-driven.org/, which was also presented as a panel at the 56th Annual RBMS Conference, Oakland, 2015. Robin M. Katz, Leah Richardson, Sarah M. Horowitz, and Elizabeth Call, "#UserDriven | Creating a User-Driven Culture in Special Collections," accessed July 13, 2015, http://www.user-driven.org/.

3. The authors acknowledge that the views expressed in this chapter have been informed by their experiences working in what many would consider privileged academic research libraries. Where the reader works might have varying levels of personnel or different departmental structures, but the types of questions and challenges highlighted in this chapter are familiar to most repositories, regardless of the size or funding, as they deal with reference questions from a variety of researchers with differing needs.

4. Davison, "If We Build It," 37.

5. See Barbara M. Jones, "Hidden Collections, Scholarly Barriers: Creating Access to Unprocessed Special Collections Materials in North America's Research Libraries, a White Paper for the Association of Research Libraries Task Force on Special Collections," June 6, 2003, http://old.arl.org/bm~doc/hiddencollswhitepaperjun6.pdf. http://connection.ebscohost.com/c/articles/95005739/from-reference-desk-inbox.

6. This is an adapted list from an original list of concerns respondents had toward digitization, but it relates perfectly to public services generally. Found in Jackie Dooley and Katherine Luce, "Taking Our Pulse: The OCLC Research Survey of Special Collections and Archives," 69, accessed July 12, 2015, http://www.oclc.org/content/dam/research/publications/library/2010/2010-11.pdf.

7. For an outstanding assortment of essays on the different facets of modern public services, see Kate Theimer, ed., *Reference and Access: Innovative Practices for Archives and Special Collections* (Lanham, MD: Rowman & Littlefield, 2014).

8. "Transliteracy is the ability to read, write and interact across a range of platforms, tools and media from signing and orality through handwriting, print, TV, radio, film to digital networks." It is the ability to use information from a multitude of information sources to satisfy an information need. Found in Anamika Megwalu, "Encouraging Transliteracy through Reference Instructions," *The Reference Librarian* 56, no. 2 (April 3, 2015): 157–160.

9. For a fascinating take on how MLIS graduate programs are not teaching basic bibliographic skills at the expense of newer, technological ones and the impact this has had on reference, please see Daniel Traister, "Public Services and Outreach in Rare Book, Manuscript, and Special Collections Libraries," *Library Trends* 52, no. 1 (Summer 2003): 87–108.

10. Having exceptionally nice reference staff is still of paramount importance and a welcome change from when Daniel Traister observed in 2003, "Anyone who works in this field must be aware that readers have long regarded staff as major constituents of the formidability and repulsiveness of many rare book collections large and small"; Traister, "Public Services and Outreach," 88.

11. See Todd Gilman's piece, "A Gentle Reminder," in the Chronicle of Higher Education. Both the original story and the reader comments explore the tension that comes from trying to protect collections while making them accessible. Accessed July 11, 2015, http://chronicle.com/article/A-Gentle-Reminder-to/65235/.

12. We will not be discussing generational differences in ratio to technological skills, as not all recent college graduates are tech-savvy and not all older librarians are tech-fearful. As the profession and technology move forward, it is left to be seen if this essay's discourse is a benchmark in time or a problem that will persist in the future.

13. Rare Books and Manuscripts Section, ACRL/ALA, and Task Force on Core Competencies for Special Collections Professionals, "Guidelines: Competencies for Special Collections Professionals," July 1, 2008, accessed July 12, 2015, http://www.ala.org/acrl/standards/comp4specollect.

14. "[M]any disciplines now encourage the inclusion of primary source work motivated in part by the broader interdisciplinary value placed on it in the Common Core State Standards." Franky Abbott and Dan Cohen, "Using Large Collections in Education," 10, accessed July 16, 2015, http://dp.la/info/wp-content/uploads/2015/04/Using-Large-Collections-in-Education-DPLA-paper-4-9-15-2.pdf.

15. At the 2015 midwinter meeting of the public services group, allowing people to copy entire collections was topic 3 in the meeting minutes, January 31, 2015, Chicago ALA midwinter minutes from the public services group, accessed July 15, 2015, http://rbms.info/files/committees/minutes/2015/pubservminutes15m.pdf.

16. Traister, "Public Services and Outreach," 89.

17. Davison, "If We Build It," 38.

18. See John H. Overholt, "Five Theses on the Future of Special Collections," 2013, 15, http://dash.harvard.edu/handle/1/10601790.

19. Encoded archival description and e-mail were both used in the early 1990s.

20. See Sara Snyder and Elizabeth Botten, "Websites as a Digital Extension of Reference: Creating a Reference and IT Partnership for Web Usability Studies," in *Reference and Access: Innovative Practices for Archives and Special Collections 3* (Lanham, MD: Rowman & Littlefield, 2014), 182.

21. A flipped classroom means "that students gain first exposure to new material outside of class, usually via reading or lecture videos, and then use class time to do the harder work of assimilating that knowledge, perhaps through problem-solving, discussion, or debates." C. J. Brame, "Flipping the Classroom," Center for Teaching and Learning, Vanderbilt University, accessed September 21, 2015. Examples of flipped reading room videos can be found on Youtube.com created by Harvard, University of Edinburgh, Minnesota Historical Society, and San Diego State University, to name a few.

22. Snyder and Botten, "Websites as a Digital Extension of Reference," 172.

23. See Sally W. Kalin, "What Skills Are Needed for the Next Generation of Librarians?" in *Reference Reborn: Breathing New Life into Public Services Librarianship*, ed. Diane Zabel (Santa Barbara, CA: Libraries Unlimited, 2011), 281–298.

24. For more information on this movement, please see the ACRL/RBMS-SAA Task Force on the Development of Standardized Statistical Measures for the Public Services of Archival Repositories and Special Collections Libraries, accessed July 30, 2015, http://www.ala.org/acrl/rbms/acr-rbmtfsm.

25. Kenny Garcia, "Librarians That Practice Critical Librarianship Strive to Communicate the Ways in Which Libraries and Librarians Consciously and Unconsciously Support Systems of Oppression," accessed July 23, 2015, http://www.ala.org/acrl/publications/keeping_up_with/critlib.

26. Davison, "If We Build It," 39.

27. See Jackie Dooley, "Ten Commandments for Special Collections Librarians in the Digital Age," *RBM: A Journal of Rare Books, Manuscripts and Cultural Heritage* 10, no. 1 (March 20, 2009): 51–60.

28. Davison, "If We Build It," 39.

29. For more information on the challenges MPLP implementation creates for public services, please consult the work of the Reference and Processing Collaboration Group of the Reference, Access and Outreach Section of the Society of American Archivists, accessed July 23, 2015, http://www2.archivists.org/groups/reference-access-and-outreach-section/navigating-minimal-processing-and-public-services-working-group.

30. This list is from respondents' concerns to digitization, but it works for public services generally as well. Dooley and Luce, "Taking Our Pulse," 69, accessed July 12, 2015, http://www.oclc.org/content/dam/research/publications/library/2010/2010-11.pdf.

31. Davison, "If We Build It," 47.

32. Abbott and Cohen, "Using Large Collections in Education," 20. While the Digital Public Library of America report is the most recent survey on users and metadata, readers interested in this topic should read Jennifer Schaffner's 2009 OCLC report, "The Metadata Is the Interface," accessed July 31, 2015, http://www.oclc.org/content/dam/research/publications/library/2009/2009-06.pdf.

33. Michelle Light and Tom Hyry urged the profession in 2002 to not omit "extremely important contextual information: the impact of the processor's work [on finding aid creation]" and "do not go so far as revealing our own impact on collections, leaving researchers to assume falsely that we have no transformative impact or to

guess about the nature of the work we have done." Michelle Light and T. Hyry, "Colophons and Annotations: New Directions for the Finding Aid," *American Archivist*, 65, no. 2 (2002): 216–230, accessed on September 10, 2015, http://digitalscholarship.unlv.edu/lib_articles/462.

34. Bradley J. Daigle, "The Digital Transformation of Special Collections," *Journal of Library Administration* 52, no. 3–4 (April 1, 2012): 244–264.

35. Ibid.

36. "SAA RAO Section Newsletter Winter 2015," accessed July 2, 2015, http://www2.archivists.org/sites/all/files/SAA%20RAO%20Section%20Newsletter%20Winter%202015_0.pdf. To see the bibliography created by the Reference, Access and Outreach section on access to electronic records, see http://www2.archivists.org/sites/all/files/saa_rao_aerwg_access_electronic_records_annotated_bibliography.pdf, accessed July 23, 2015.

37. Jackie Dean and Meg Tuomala, "Business as Usual: Integrating Born-Digital Materials into Regular Workflows," in *Description: Innovative Practices for Archives and Special Collections*, ed. Kate Theimer (Lanham, MD: Rowman & Littlefield, 2014), 159.

38. See for example, Laura Carroll, Erika Farr, Peter Hornsby, and Ben Ranker, "A Comprehensive Approach to Born-Digital Archives," *Archivaria* 72 (2011): 61–92; Laura Wilsey, Rebecca Skirvin, Peter Chan, and Glynn Edwards, "Capturing and Processing Born-Digital Files in the STOP AIDS Project Records: A Case Study," *Journal of Western Archives* 4, no. 1 (2013), accessed July 21, 2015, http://digitalcommons.usu.edu/westernarchives/vol4/iss1/1/; Chloe Edwards, Amy F. Brown, Meg Eastwood, Martha Tenney, and Kevin O'Donnell, "Processing Internal Hard Drives," *Practical Technology for Archives* 1 (2013), accessed July 19, 2015, http://practicaltechnologyforarchives.org/issue1_edwards/.

39. For a brief overview of emulation and migration as digital preservation strategies, see Clifford Lynch, "Preserving Digital Documents: Choices, Approaches, and Standards," *Law Library Journal* 96, no. 4 (2004): 609–617.

40. Jennifer Meehan, "Making the Leap from Parts to Whole: Evidence and Inference in Archival Arrangement and Description," *American Archivist* 72 (2009): 86.

41. Heather MacNeil, "Picking Our Text: Archival Description, Authenticity, and the Archivist as Editor," *American Archivist* 68 (2005): 272.

42. Carroll et al., "Comprehensive Approach to Born-Digital Archives," 84–85, 87.

43. "Virginia Memory: Look Under the Hood," Library of Virginia, accessed July 24, 2015, http://www.virginiamemory.com/collections/kaine/under-the-hood.

44. Researchers using large data sets at National Archives and Records Administration request copies of the files and then are "free to analyze the records on their own terms and with whatever computing hardware and software they had or had access to, retaining copies of the records indefinitely." Margaret Adams, "Archival Reference Services for Digital Records: Three and a Half Years Experience with the Access to Archival Databases (AAD) Resource," in *New Skills for a Digital Era: A Colloquium sponsored by National Archives and Records Administration*, ed. Richard Pearce-Moses and Susan E. Davis (Society of American Archivists and the Arizona State Library, Archives and Public Records: Washington, D.C., May 31–June 2, 2006), 96–97.

45. Dean and Tuomala, "Business as Usual," 149–161; Sudheendra Hangal, Peter Chan, Monica S. Lam, and Jeffrey Heer, "Muse: Reviving Memories Using Email Archives," *Proceedings of the 24th Symposium on User Interface Software and Technology* (Santa Barbara, CA), accessed July 31, 2015, http://xenon.stanford.edu/~hangal/dh2012.pdf.

46. *Lean In: Women, Work, and the Will to Lead* by Sheryl Sandberg was written in 2013 and explored why over 50 percent of the college graduates in the United States

are women but men still hold the majority of the leadership positions in society. The lack of women leadership in top executive positions means that "when it comes to making the decision that most affect our world, women's voices are not heard equally" (6).

47. Attending courses offered through the various rare book schools in the United States and overseas is one way of obtaining instruction specifically focused on the issues relevant to special collections and archives practitioners. Many of the courses, including Joel Silver's reference sources for researching rare books and printed Americana, can be beneficial to the practitioner, but these courses are limited, expensive to attend, and application based.

48. See Wendy Duff, Elizabeth Yakel, and Helen Tibbo, "Archival Reference Knowledge," *The American Archivist* 76, no. 1 (April 1, 2013): 68–94.

49. See George W. Bain, John A. Fleckner, Kathy Marquis, and Mary Jo Pugh, "Reference, Access, and Outreach: An Evolved Landscape, 1936–2011 (Session 406)," *The American Archivist* 74, no. S1 (January 1, 2011): 1–40.

50. Ibid., 9. At the time of this writing, SAA elected to offer a two-day workshop on reference in the Washington, D.C., area entitled Real World Reference: Moving Beyond Theory.

51. Bain et al., "Reference, Access, and Outreach."

52. Ibid., 5, especially since a 2011 survey of special collections job announcements revealed that reference and research were the most commonly found words in the duties sections of 39 special collection jobs. See Hansen, Kelli, "Education, Training, and Recruitment of Special Collections Librarians: An Analysis of Job Advertisements," *RBM: A Journal of Rare Books, Manuscripts and Cultural Heritage* 12, no. 2 (September 21, 2011): 110–132. Also of interest is Daigle, "The Digital Transformation of Special Collections," footnote number 17, where he says there has yet to be a formal study proving that digital content will increase use of physical materials and cites an article by Peter Hirtle from 2002 saying that digitization will lead to a decrease in use of paper originals. The OCLC survey results summarized in "Taking Our Pulse" state that "Even though more than 60% of respondents reported increased use of collections, staffing decreased in public services more frequently (23%) than any other area." Dooley and Luce, "Taking Our Pulse," 14.

53. Snyder and Botten, "Websites as a Digital Extension of Reference," 171.

54. See Constance Ard and Shawn Livingston, "Reference and Research Services in Special Libraries: Navigating the Evolving Riches of Information," *Journal of Library Administration* 54, no. 6 (August 18, 2014): 518–528.

55. "We offer so much content that it is hard for them [educators] to know where to get started and how to quickly assess the depth and breadth of available materials related to specific topics." Abbott and Cohen, "Using Large Collections in Education," 5.

56. See Valerie A. Harris and Ann C. Weller, "Use of Special Collections as an Opportunity for Outreach in the Academic Library," *Journal of Library Administration* 52, no. 3–4 (April 1, 2012): 294–303.

57. Ibid.

58. David Pearson, "Special Collections in a Digital Future," *Art Libraries Journal* 35, no. 1 (January 2010): 12–17. Pearson hypothesizes that "The net effect of EEBO [Early English Books Online] and ECCO [Eighteenth Century Collections Online] is more likely to be less use of early printed books in libraries, not more." At Stanford, the majority of special collections classes are focused on rare antiquarian books, some of which can be found either in EEBO, ECCO, Project Gutenberg, or Google Books. At the Teaching with Primary Sources Unconference that occurred in Ohio, a participant, Madeline Sheldon (Valparaiso University), asked, "Furthermore, we have a number of digital collections we'd like to promote and start teaching with. Faculty only seems interested in our rare book collection. How do we promote our digital

collections are good resources for our students?" accessed September 21, 2015, http://teachwithstuff.org/saa-2015-proposed-discussion-topics/.

59. "Seminar B: A Balancing Act: Collaborative Instruction in the 21st-Century Special Collection," June 24, 2015, RBMS Conference Oakland, accessed July 25, 2015, http://www.preconference15.rbms.info/programs/wednesday-june-24-2015/.

60. Athena N. Jackson, Hong Ma, and Laura Capell, "From the Reference Desk to the Inbox," *Computers in Libraries* 34, no. 2 (March 2014): 12–16, accessed June 22, 2016, http://bit.ly/28RlZpy.

61. Overholt, "Five Theses on the Future of Special Collections," 18.

62. Dee Ann K. Allison, *The Patron-Driven Library: A Practical Guide for Managing Collections and Services in the Digital Age* (Oxford: Chandos Publishing, 2013), 20.

Chapter 3
"Oh, Wow!": Assessment and Affective Learning in Special Collections and Archives

Anne Bahde

"Oh, wow!" "Awesome!" "Whoa!" "That is so cool!" Phrases such as these are delightfully commonplace in special collections and archives environments, and for librarians and archivists who teach with collections, they are a true pleasure to hear. In a classroom using original primary sources, these phrases can signal a moment of appreciation, connection, or discovery as a student encounters a compelling historical object. Enabling and witnessing those transformative moments are one of the particular joys of our profession. However, "oohs and ahhs" in the special collections classroom are now sometimes seen as one of the remnants of the show-and-tell era, and can be somewhat devalued as we move our pedagogical practices away from a focus on dazzling to an emphasis on active learning and purposeful engagement in the classroom.

Generally, we do not always look at these affective moments as something valuable to capture in our teaching and assessment activities. But as a principal site for powerful learning experiences that blend and synthesize emotion, intellect, and sensation, special collections and archives departments stand to gain significant benefits from strategic assessment of the affective learning experiences taking place in our classrooms. In this chapter, I will discuss the affective realm at work in special collections and archives, and the importance of paying attention to the affective domain in the special collections and archives instructional environment. Particular assessment strategies are suggested to demonstrate our instructional impact and unique contribution to institutional teaching and learning goals.

Libraries have increased emphasis on assessment in recent years, responding to trends following the economic downturn. Using evidence from both quantitative and qualitative assessment measures, administrators can strategize and make decisions related to departmental missions, staffing, programming, collections, and more; this evidence can also be used to show the library's impact and value for other stakeholders. For librarians and archivists who teach, assessment is an essential process that signals areas for instructional improvement and possibilities for deepening and extending one's pedagogical skills. Though classroom assessment can be challenging for many reasons, it is a necessary tool to gauge whether students are truly learning.

Researchers and educators have long found the affective domain to be challenging both to define and to assess. Bloom, Krathwohl, and Masia identified the affective, cognitive, and psychomotor domains as the three primary realms of learning in 1964 and defined the affective domain as the area of learning related to emotions, feelings, and attitudes.[1] Problems of definition have persisted ever since, including prolonged debate about whether this domain should consider the values and motivations of an individual as well as emotions and attitudes; but researchers have generally agreed that the affective domain comprises the emotions or attitudes a person experiences while in a situation or performing a task. A wide range of human emotional states are encompassed by the affective realm: excitement, worry, engagement, nervousness, annoyance, flexibility, willingness, shame, pride, diligence, persistence, impatience, curiosity, satisfaction, inspiration, disappointment, boredom, hope, and many more. Research has repeatedly shown that cognitive learning and affective states are closely intertwined; both negative and positive emotions strongly impact cognitive learning. If a student is anxious or bored, for example, it will be harder to remember or process information. To truly learn anything, a student must be well-disposed to learning and take an active interest in that learning. The affective domain, then, can be seen as the gateway to effective cognitive learning. But in pedagogical practice, the cognitive domain has long been dominant over the affective realm when it comes to teaching and assessing.

Learning experiences that combine the separate affective, cognitive, and psychomotor domains are especially effective. Object-based learning theory demonstrates that when sensory components from the psychomotor domain are combined with cognitive and affective elements, the learning experience becomes more memorable, successful, and valuable. The sensory aspects of learning have been overlooked even more than the emotional aspects, especially in higher education. It has even been argued that the college classroom is a "sensory deprivation chamber."[2] Though Bloom's division of learning domains has dominated educational theory and practice for the past 50 years, critics agree that the lines it draws between the domains are false, problematic boundaries, which prohibit an integrated, holistic view of education.

The special collections and archives classroom is a prime site for learning experiences that integrate and play with the constructed boundaries between cognition, affect, and sense. Original historical materials ignite emotional connections; engage sight, sound, touch, and smell; and invite new thoughts and inquiries. For example, imagine a student puzzling to decipher the marginalia penned in a manuscript made over 500 years ago, visually observing the artistry of the illuminator and touching the rough parchment, and feeling the thrill of connection with the people who produced it. In this experience, cognitive processing, sensory activities, and affective reactions are all combined in a meaningful, multidimensional learning experience. The sensory experience of the object opens the door to affective reaction, which in turn can positively influence cognitive learning of skills or information. Even strongly negative emotions and senses can ignite interest in cognitive learning. Imagine a student examining the typescript draft of a speech by a racist politician in the 1960s, reading his words, touching the deep impressions where words were harshly marked out in pen and made more hateful, and feeling the anger and frustration inspired by the unjust world in which this document was created. This student's negative experience is also a powerful combination of cognitive, affective, and sensory, and can spur his or her deeper interest into the fate of the document's creator within the events of the civil rights movement.

As integrated as the domains seem to be in our classrooms, there seems to be even more going on when students encounter authentic historical materials. What about the chemistry student who calls her encounter with a famous chemists' Nobel Prize "a religious experience"? Or the student who becomes tearful while exploring a particularly rare and beautiful fine press edition? Or the student who lingers over a handwritten letter from a survivor of the Holocaust, clearly touched and captivated by its content? Critics of Bloom et al. suggest that the definitions of the three domains do not encompass the full human learning experience suggested in situations such as these.

Of the many alternative learning taxonomies proposed over the years, one in particular stands out as being especially relevant to special collections educational experiences. In 1975, Foshay proposed a model comprising six dimensions: the intellectual, the emotional, the social, the physical, the aesthetic, and the spiritual.[3] Bloom's domains are clearly reflected here, but deeper experiences within the affective realm are also suggested. Foshay added the aesthetic, a dimension he defined as "the formal, technical, sensuous, and expressive response to an object of contemplation," and the spiritual dimension (later renamed the transcendent), which he defined as related to a learner's insights into his or her personal connection with time, space, the human realm, and beyond. The affective responses to historical materials we see in the special collections classroom correspond much more closely to these six dimensions because this more inclusive model of learning allows for a wider range of emotions and reactions. The moment a student exclaims "Oh, wow!" can signify a confluence of stimulating sensory data, aesthetic response, intellectual insight, and even spiritual illumination, coming together in a profoundly significant learning experience. But how do we effectively harness the power of that moment? How do we capture and convey the educational potency of our collections for faculty, administrators, and funding agencies?

The affective domain is notoriously challenging to assess, for many good reasons. The models of assessment that work well for the cognitive domain do not effectively translate to the affective realm. Under the Bloom, Krathwohl, and Masia paradigm, "affective learning" is characterized by a change of the learner's emotions and attitudes from a negative or neutral state to a positive state defined by the educator. The attitudinal change is marked by a change in the student's outwardly manifested behaviors. Krathwohl's taxonomy of this domain presents five levels of affective learning, progressing from receiving information to the highest stage of internalizing. As a value or an attitude is internalized by the student through the learning activity, it increasingly affects his or her outward behavior, which instructors must observe carefully in order to measure. Instructors are meant to create learning objectives to directly produce to this specific, observable affective behavior.

But emotions and attitudes can be mercurial, unreliable, and faked; many cultures and backgrounds discourage all expression of emotions or attitudes in public.

It is very difficult to identify the outward behaviors that would signal the affective change desired, and designing instruction for them, especially within just one instruction session, can be an almost impossible task. Foshay described the problems of behavior-based affective assessment well:

> The values and attitudes which underlie a [learning] objective are acquired slowly, as a cumulative result of a number of elements in the environment—not all of which are within the control of the instructional designer. The precise correspondence of objectives, instructional episodes and outcome measures which mark good instructional design in the cognitive and psychomotor domains usually is not practical in the affective domain.[4]

A further problem with this model of assessment is that the educator must define the positive state for the student to achieve, an action that many instructors rightly find too prescriptive and dominating. Defining this affective state; devising learning objectives that are "specific, unambiguous, and measurable";[5] and creating classroom activities and tasks that will produce a behavior-based attitudinal change in students can lead to a very contrived environment that remains difficult to assess.

Foshay describes an alternative method of affective assessment, more suited to the special collections and archives environment, focusing on identification and expression of emotion rather than on tasks.[6] In this model, personal analysis of the affective response becomes the springboard for cognition. Students are asked to explore and express their own emotional responses to the object or set of objects. Reflection on those responses is then used to bring cognitive understanding to the course content.

For example, imagine that a labor history class is due to visit special collections and archives to see documents related to labor tensions in the late 19th and early 20th centuries. The instructor and the special collections librarian select a variety of materials from the collections to use in the class session including government reports, leaflets and flyers, posters, radical newspapers, photographs, and oral histories and letters from both activists and industrialists. The instructor hopes that in addition to being exposed to the wealth of primary sources available to them, students will expand their developing primary source analysis skills. After a brief introduction to handling primary sources, students complete an in-class activity that begins by browsing the sources, choosing one, and answering a series of basic questions related to identification of a creator, purpose, and audience in a document analysis log. The very first question on the worksheet, before these analysis questions, is, "What feelings or sensations did this document evoke for you? What about the document prompted these responses?" Class discussion follows, and begins with an exploration of the different emotions that students may have experienced, which might include sympathy for the underpaid workers, enthusiasm for and identification with the labor cause, disappointment in the strikebreaker's actions, or keen support for the company owners' dilemmas. During this discussion, students share the details of their sources and introduce the answers to their questions, and the class discusses the role of the sources in the context of what they have learned about the labor movement in class lectures. After hearing about all of the sources, the instructor and the librarian turn the discussion to questions of bias: author bias within the documents themselves, the personal or cultural biases the students may be bringing to their interpretations of the documents, and how emotional response to the documents is related to this bias. The class concludes with a group dialog about the role of bias in historical analysis.

In this example, students are not asked to perform a task or manifest a specific behavior that is tied to an attitudinal or emotional change. Instead, they are simply encouraged to express their own emotional responses to the document in their own terms, whether positive, negative, or neutral. (Those students who do not wish to share their responses in public can still demonstrate their expression via responses on the worksheet.) Students' ability to reflect upon those emotions and articulate them is the only assessable behavior here, and that affective response is closely joined with a cognitive component. Robert Lagueux, who has experimented with this model in music history classes, argues the particular utility of this approach to affective learning:

> [W]hen we can marry this emotional response to intellectual reflection, we provide a scaffold on which to hang the cognitive "content" of a course. The critical thinking … becomes a way of cultivating genuine interest, because it is directed towards students' emotional responses.[7]

In this example, the integration of the emotional enhances understanding of the cognitive, and encourages active, reflective, intellectual analysis of both the student's own personal responses and the source itself. Integrating students' emotions and attitudes into a safe, nonjudgmental class setting can also increase the relevance of the content for them, and acknowledging their emotions can improve engagement and participation in both the class session and the overall course. This approach to affective learning, when paired with historical materials, encourages the development of historical empathy, may pique or sustain curiosity, and can quickly expand students' civic and social justice literacy. Lagueux also notes an effective enhancement to this method: he urges instructors to freely express their own personal reactions to the materials with students to promote a classroom dynamic of reflection and active contemplation. Librarians and archivists in special collections and archives environments have had their own powerful "Oh, wow!" moments with primary sources by sharing these unreservedly with students; by doing so, we can help them open to critical examination of their own affective responses.

Foshay's integrated dimensions model strongly complements this approach to affective learning. He suggested writing learning objectives for his proposed dimensions with attention to the types of response each dimension can produce; these are not based in a change of emotion or attitude, nor does each dimension have to appear in every lesson. In the labor history session example above, the learning objectives for each dimension might read as follows:

Intellectual: Students will identify and understand the major issues at the heart of the labor movement in the late 19th and early 20th centuries.

Social: Students will listen actively to others' opinions and interpretations.

Emotional: Students will identify and describe their personal feelings and biases toward the multiple perspectives of the labor movement.

Aesthetic: Students will recognize and express their own responses to labor movement design techniques, and evaluate the nature of their responses using what they know about propaganda from course content.

Physical: Students will handle fragile primary sources with care based on the document's individual needs.

Spiritual: Students will recognize how their personal belief systems shape their understanding of labor issues.

To effectively assess student learning for each of these objectives, librarians and instructors can employ the established assessment techniques they already often practice in classroom evaluation, such as observation and the creation of authentic learning "artifacts." But looking a little differently at these techniques may yield even more nuanced and useful data. As in traditional affective assessment, observation plays a key role. However, it is observation focused on the students' expressions of their own experiences, not necessarily on measurable behaviors that demonstrate a change from a negative state to a positive state. Librarians and archivists can become more aware of expressions of affect in the classroom simply by becoming more intentional in their observation techniques. Listening for these expressions from students and recording them within the situational context can, in time, yield patterns of affective response to collection materials or ideas that will improve item selection and session design according to course goals. Borrowing techniques from qualitative ethnographic methods, such as informal interviews, and adapting these to the special collections and archives environment may also prove useful for librarians and archivists. Brief interviews or short conversations with students can enhance librarians' understanding of how they respond to materials, how well librarians have integrated their selected materials with course content, and what and how students are really learning. Simply asking a student "What do you think of this item?" while walking around class during a browsing session can yield meaningful insights into how and why students are connecting to the content. Listening carefully to responses, asking follow-up questions, and taking notes about answers can deepen and augment that insight.[8]

Another assessment technique to employ for affective learning is the in-class creation of authentic learning products or artifacts. Defined as "research logs, reflective writing, 'think alouds,' self or peer evaluations, research drafts or papers, open-ended question responses, bibliographies, presentations, posters, performances, portfolios, worksheets, and concept maps,"[9] authentic artifacts of learning enable instructors to more deeply analyze and understand the extent of student learning. Affective learning might easily be gauged through in-class reflective writing, or through in-class self-reporting. Even simple worksheet questions such as "Which was your favorite or least favorite item? Why?" or "What did you think about the materials you saw today?" can yield responses that, when collated and analyzed, can show how students are responding emotionally to the materials, and whether those materials are the best choices to pair with course content. Creating authentic artifacts of learning can be difficult, however, when most sessions in special collections and archives instruction are "one-shot" single visits. In most cases, special collections librarians and archivists can diminish this issue by working closely with the course instructor to communicate assessment needs, and requesting the opportunity to review papers, presentations, or other course artifacts that may show how the visit to special collection and archives affected the student's learning throughout the course.

Following up with course instructors to share these products will also help librarians and archivists triangulate multiple methods of assessment.

Finally, special collections librarians and archivists should keep eyes and ears open for particularly important cases of connection and affective response, ones that may not have even been expressed during class. Watching social media for after-class mentions and descriptions can be a useful glimpse into emotions and reactions that students perhaps did not feel comfortable expressing in person, and can also deepen one's understanding of the emotions that were publicly expressed. We should also be open to developing longer-term relationships with students, beyond the class visit. Did the student who became tearful over the fine press book go on to become a book artist? Did the student who got very excited over the illuminated manuscript recently get his PhD in medieval studies? Does that chemistry student have her own Nobel Prize now? Though it may seem daunting to keep contact for the time it takes for these results to develop, nurturing and preserving these relationships can yield powerful stories of how the "Oh, wow!" moment can change lives.

Instructional assessment is an ongoing, iterative cycle of collecting, interpreting, and acting upon information, ultimately intended to result in the continuous improvement of instruction and assessment. At the programmatic level, the aggregate data can provide important information about what that program can offer to a variety of stakeholders, including faculty, administrators, and funders. But, as Megan Oakleaf notes, programmatic assessment can be very challenging in a library environment; it "requires librarians to aggregate information from multiple librarians, diverse student populations, and a variety of instruction offerings and approaches."[10] Too often, the particular instructional offerings and approaches of a special collections or archives instruction program are not included in that aggregate. To ensure that their unique contributions in the affective realm and beyond are represented in that programmatic picture, special collections librarians and archivists must work to craft clear, descriptive learning outcomes for and assessments of their class sessions, as well as to communicate these and build relationships within the organization. When they are folded into the larger structure of assessment and reporting, aligned and mapped within larger programs of instruction, the patterns of impact that emerge can give new, more significant meaning to special collections and archives' instructional work.

Over time, collecting the evidence of affective impact can result not only in improved instructional effectiveness, but also in the creation a powerful presence for a department's (or library's) instructional program. Using these stories of response within the classroom can spur new connections between students and staff. Hearing how others like them have responded to historic materials may help to pique students' interest. When working with institutional or library administrators, department directors can weave these narratives into quantitative data, illustrating how special collections materials and staff ultimately fulfill and enhance the institution's primary missions. Bringing the stories of affective response into the library's or department's outward-facing materials such as publicity brochures, websites, and social media will raise the profile of the department, and demonstrate the potential impact of working with authentic historical materials to a larger audience.

Special collections materials hold great potential for stimulating curiosity, cultivating empathy, stirring inspiration, and beyond. When we acknowledge the power of the affective domain in our classrooms, implement plans for assessing learning and impact, and plan for its potential to enhance and extend other dimensions of learning, we can truly demonstrate the transformative capacity of the special collections and archives classroom.

Notes

1. Benjamin Bloom, David Krathwohl, and Bertram Masia, *Taxonomy of Educational Objectives* (New York: David McKay, 1964).

2. Sarah Kuhn, "Coming to Our Senses: Thinking with Things in the Classroom," *The Atrium: A Journal of Academic Voices* (Spring 2013), http://nwi.ivytech.edu/atrium/site/archives/spring2013/kuhn.pdf.

3. Arthur Wellesley Foshay, "Toward a Humane Curriculum," in *Philosophers Speak of Aesthetic Experience in Education*, ed. Robert Leight (Danville, IL: Interstate Publishers, 1975).

4. Arthur W. Foshay, "An Alternative to Task Analysis in the Affective Domain," *Journal of Instructional Development* 1, no. 2 (1978): 22–24.

5. Ellysa Stern Cahoy and Robert Schroeder, "Embedding Affective Learning Outcomes in Library Instruction," *Communications in Information Literacy* 6, no. 1 (2012): 73–90.

6. Foshay, "An Alternative to Task Analysis."

7. Robert Lagueux, "Inverting Bloom's Taxonomy: The Role of Affective Responses in Teaching and Learning," *Journal of Music History and Pedagogy* 3, no. 2 (2012): 119–150.

8. These analyses should, of course, only be used for internal assessment and personal instructional assessment reflection; to use these analyses as formal research, review by an institutional review board is advisable.

9. Megan Oakleaf, "A Roadmap for Assessing Student Learning Using the New Framework for Information Literacy for Higher Education," *Journal of Academic Librarianship* 40, no. 5 (2014): 511–513.

10. Ibid.

Chapter 4
Developing K–12 Outreach Methods for Special Collections Centers

Amy Chen, Lisa L. Crane, Melanie Meyers,
Charlotte Priddle, and Abby Saunders

In 1998, Anne Gilliland-Swetland argued that "addressing the educational needs of K–12 communities represents an unparalleled opportunity" to increase the social impact of special collections, emphasize the role of the field's professionals within the broader field of cultural heritage institutions, enhance the likelihood of repositories acquiring grants, and even encourage young students to consider entering the profession.[1] But, in 2006, only one-third of surveyed special collections within the Association of Research Libraries accepted K–12 students into their reading rooms.[2]

Only in the past few years has the field begun to open special collections to K–12 students. To give a brief overview, in 2012, elementary and secondary instructional methods became the subject of a Society of American Archivists bibliography.[3] In 2013, at the American Library Association conference, Lori Dekydtspotter and Cherry Williams' poster on the topic received substantial attention, prompting them to write an article a year later on the subject, addressing both the use of primary sources in physical and digital surrogate form.[4] In 2014, Anne Bahde, Heather Smedberg, and Mattie Taormina's *Using Primary Sources: Hands-On Instructional Exercises* contained an extensive set of ideas for how to teach younger students.[5] And then, just a few months into 2015, the Cataloging Hidden Special Collections and Archives Symposium included a workshop on using special collections with K–12 students[6] and Kate Theimer's *Educational Programs* volume, from her series *Innovative Practices for Archives and Special Collections*, counts three chapters on K–12.[7] These bibliographies, papers, chapters, and presentations are an encouraging sign that younger audiences are now widely seen as an important demographic to reach, even if engaging elementary and secondary students requires new methods and networks.

The authors of this chapter came together to discuss K–12 outreach after Amy Chen asked a question regarding this demographic in a session at the 2014 Rare Books and Manuscripts Section conference. While we hold a variety of positions at our respective institutions, we share an interest in special collections instruction and feel strongly that educational opportunities using rare materials should not be limited to adults. Given that we are employed in different types of institutions, the methods we use must be adapted to our repositories' resources. Each locale has specific collection strengths, staff time requirements, and infrastructure challenges that come to bear on how we recruit K–12 students to come, see, and work with our materials. Access, security, and handling determine how special collections staff handle teaching or instruction sessions. Keeping an eye on material in a class of 25 undergraduate students can be difficult enough; watching what happens when there are over 50 six-year-olds in a room makes this task almost impossible. For this reason, by first reflecting on our institutions' particularities in each case study, we highlight how a wide range of institution types with special collections holdings currently are conducting K–12 outreach at a level that suits their capacity for engagement. Amy Chen served as the editor for these pieces and provided research to support our claims regarding the history of special collections outreach to K–12 students and the role of digital collections, while Lisa Crane, Melanie Meyers, Charlotte Priddle, and Abby Saunders provided case studies.

Lisa Crane, of The Claremont Colleges, explains how preexisting community and alumni connections can be the first step for repositories interested in K–12 outreach. Once these connections are made, she demonstrates how methods used for older students can be adapted to suit younger ones. Crane also describes the way in which the Museum of History and Art, Ontario, developed a one-hour unit to suit a grade's curricular needs, which made the unit easier for teachers to integrate into their lesson plans and more easily presented by anyone charged with educational duties—particularly useful if a variety of people in special collections, like the museum's volunteer docents, share teaching responsibilities. If your repository has a teaching collection, or is interested in creating one, Charlotte Priddle, of New York University's Fales Library & Special Collections, illustrates how teaching collections are a valuable resource to use with elementary students and why, if possible, taking materials to them is an important step to pursue. Then, if a variety of academic departments across campus are willing to work together, Abby Saunders highlights how the University of Southern California used the Cassady Lewis Carroll Collection as a jumping-off point to engage a variety of disciplines in K–12 outreach. Finally, if long-term, programmatic approaches are feasible, Melanie Meyers, from the Center for Jewish History, describes both her repository's Junior Scholars Program curricula and participation in National History Day. The Junior Scholars Program brings students into the repository for more extended engagement while National History Day provides a way to engage those who are not able to make it to campus. Together, these scalable approaches ensure that no matter a repository's level of commitment, K–12 outreach can be conducted successfully.

The Claremont Colleges, Special Collections and Libraries

The Claremont Colleges is a cluster of five undergraduate colleges and two graduate institutions located in Claremont, California.[8] The Claremont University Consortium (CUC) is the central coordinating and support organization for The Claremont Colleges. Originally established in 1925 as part of Claremont University Center, in July 2000, CUC incorporated as a freestanding organization offering academic, student, and institutional support services that meet the needs of more than 6,900 students and 3,600 faculty and staff.[9] Among these services is the Claremont Colleges Library, home of Special Collections and Libraries.[10] The Claremont Colleges' Special Collections and Libraries lack a formal educational program for K–12 education, but they have been successful in their occasional K–12 outreach activities due to strong community and alumni connections.

Evidence of the importance of developing these connections can be seen in the recent activities in Special Collections and Libraries. For example, a troop of eight-year-old Cub Scouts visited after a request by a Pomona College staff member; an eighth-grade field trip from a local charter school came by after a request by a former Scripps College student who is a teacher at the school; and a group of high school sophomores, juniors, and seniors participating in Pitzer College's Native American Summer Pipeline to College program also visited as a part of the college's program.

While these sessions are directed at younger patrons than Special Collections usually hosts, the librarians and staff have noticed that they spend no less time researching and selecting materials for these events than they would for a regular class visit from one of The Claremont Colleges. Discussions with the person requesting the event help identify important demographic information about the proposed visitors, such as age group, number of potential attendees, what type of group it is, any particular interests or subject focuses, and the desired outcome of the visit. Additionally, materials shown to younger students are selected specifically with their needs in mind; there are no canned program materials. As all sessions are tailored to the needs of the individuals attending, librarians and staff must consider rare books and materials through the vantage point of K–12 audiences who have little or no knowledge of the original context of such materials. Queries to colleagues regarding their experiences with children from a particular age group and the staff's extensive knowledge of special collections' holdings improve the potential for selecting materials that will connect with the target audience and enhance the overall experience for all. For example, Ulisse Aldrovandi's *Serpentum, et draconum historiæ libri duo* (1640)[11] was a popular item among the eight-year-old Cub Scouts due to its early modern era depictions of snakes and dragons, as were the historical Boy Scout ephemera and memorabilia.

Special Collections staff also realized that they must consider the spatial requirements of K–12 oriented sessions. Due to the lack of separate classroom space, these events usually are held in Special Collections' reading room, creating potential disruption for those undergraduates, graduates, and other researchers who are present. Furthermore, furniture and equipment are not scaled for some of the younger audiences. The Cub Scouts were not as tall as expected, so materials in book cradles on a reading room table surrounded by high-backed chairs posed viewing problems. The librarian resorted to holding up each item, which was difficult to do for some materials and caused the large number of scouts to clamber for an up close and personal view. In hindsight, it would have been a good idea to move the chairs away from the table and have the scouts sit in the chairs or on the floor.

Despite these challenges, Special Collections and Libraries at The Claremont Colleges will continue to pursue K–12 outreach as community and alumni continue to find these visits both exciting and educational. It is also rewarding to see the students' interest in and enthusiasm for historical materials. One eighth-grade visitor was completely flabbergasted when he realized he was holding an authentic version of George Washington's Farewell Address printed in 1811. For this reason, The Claremont Colleges enjoy facilitating young students' connection with history on such a personal level.

The Museum of History and Art, Ontario

The Museum of History and Art, Ontario, is located in San Bernardino County in Southern California[12] and houses and cares for over 25,000 artifacts and archival documents related to the history of Ontario and the surrounding region. Museum programs include permanent exhibitions on local history and a temporary exhibition program featuring five or six shows that rotate each year. The cornerstone of the museum's outreach program, Ontario History on the Go, is an educational local history program about the founding of the city of Ontario and the surrounding area and covers the period from the 1880s to the early 1900s. Ontario History on the Go is successful because it uses a combination of original and digital facsimile material to create a lesson designed to meet to state curricular requirements that can be taught by any trained docent in the classroom.

Both docents[13] and education volunteers present this one-hour program in local third-, fourth-, and fifth-grade classrooms. As the program follows a set format, anyone trained to perform the presentation is able to do so easily, making the instruction responsibilities more easily shared among a variety of staff. During the presentation, actual museum artifacts such as an antique sad iron,[14] original text books similar to those found in early Ontario grammar schools, and historical photographs are used as hands-on teaching materials. Maps, historical documents, and other fragile materials were digitized; their facsimiles are used in the classroom in lieu of the originals. Through a combination of lecture, role-playing, and games, students become engaged in the learning process. A packet containing postactivities for the class is presented to the teacher at the end of the program. Lastly, students are encouraged to bring their parents, siblings, and other family members to the museum later, as admission is free.

The Ontario History on the Go program was developed and marketed to address state curricular needs. The program satisfies history and social science content standards adopted by the California State Board of Education.[15] Though developed for third-, fourth-, and fifth-grade students, the program is flexible enough to be adapted for any K–12 classroom. Anecdotally, it appears that Ontario History on the Go programs lead to future classroom visits to the museum through school tours. Similarly, school tours at the museum lead to additional Ontario History on the Go programs in the classroom. Perhaps the most significant impact of History on the Go is that, with budget cuts and limited resources, area schools benefit by utilizing the museum's program as a means of supplementing reduced curricula in the areas of history, art, culture, and social studies.

New York University, the Fales Library & Special Collections

The Fales Library & Special Collections serves as the special collections for the arts and humanities at New York University, and comprises around

350,000 printed volumes, 11,000 linear feet of archives, and 90,000 media elements, ranging from cuneiform tablets to rare books to born-digital materials. Due to the difficulty of bringing younger students to campus on designated field trips and ensuring proper handling of rare materials in special collections once they arrive, it often works best to go to where the children themselves are, using a combination of a PowerPoint presentation and a teaching collection. This strategy also ensures that the audience are in their own comfort zone, rather than disturbed or distracted by being in a new place. Because the attention span of small children can be short at the best of times, anything that can prevent their focus wandering is helpful.[16]

Students need a bridge between previous concepts they learned and those needing to be introduced. In the case of Priddle's session with first graders, the learning objective simply was to give the students an introduction to how books were produced—an elementary history of the book. Priddle began by asking the children about the library in their school and how they used it, what kinds of books they checked out, and how they read them. Then, Priddle introduced the idea that she worked in a library without beanbags, reading nooks, and the ability to take the books home. This prompt lead into a discussion of why a library like this exists and the reasons these rules are enforced. At some point, one of the children is likely to suggest that the reason might be because of the material housed in her library—it contains "old books" or "special books."

Once students recognize that special collections contains different types of material, the conversation really began. Priddle augmented this moment in the discussion with a PowerPoint of images of different kinds of books, from tiny "thumb" Bibles to a book so large it dwarfed the student holding it, to spark students to ask additional questions. This PowerPoint, which did not contain any text, also provided a background to the props brought to the session, including a teaching collection of early printed books, and other items.

The teaching collection consists of duplicate materials that date from the 17th century upward as well as samples of leather, vellum, and other binding materials. Not everyone will be comfortable with children handling materials, but if children are invited to touch things, the items must be able to withstand such wear. The duplicates are sturdy books, mainly bound in stiff vellum, and able to withstand the fascinated touch of a group of elementary school children. Building a teaching collection does not have to be expensive or consist of only early materials. Ephemera, facsimiles, pieces of typeface, or early 20th-century materials can be used, so long as they can help tell the story being communicated and can be open to being handled more frequently and potentially more roughly than other items. However, during the session, Priddle noticed students innately acted carefully toward the books. They were fascinated by the gothic script of the books and by the sound the paper made; they were intrigued by how the cover felt and the stiffness of the boards. In contrast, the pieces of leather were sniffed, stretched, wrinkled up, crinkled, and stroked—perfectly acceptable practice toward scraps and samples.

Most children of this age are used to picture books or chapter books gauged for their age group; these books often are of a specific size, shape, and thickness. Allowing children to handle duplicates and scraps of leather give them the beginnings of an understanding, however small, of the world of materials that are out there for them and the importance of what their eyes, noses, and fingers can tell them about physical objects. It also necessarily teaches them that they already know certain things about the subject they are learning about and that their reactions have validity and worth, connecting them to a historical perspective that they may otherwise feel excluded from.

University of Southern California, Special Collections, Cassady Lewis Carroll Collection

The Cassady Lewis Carroll Collection at the University of Southern California (USC) Libraries Special Collections includes over 3,000 rare books, manuscripts, and objects created by or about the author of *Alice's Adventures in Wonderland*, Charles Dodgson, better known by his pen name, Lewis Carroll. Special collections receives a multitude of requests for fifth-grade-level tours from surrounding schools around Southern California, and the curator, Abby Saunders, works to expand the students' understanding of "Alice in Wonderland" beyond the contemporary film versions in order to foster a connection to the original 19th-century classic and its many adaptations across genres, media, and languages. Unique, multidisciplinary approaches and outside funding were needed to fully realize this goal for, as Alice says in the first chapter of *Alice's Adventures in Wonderland*, "What is the use of a story without pictures or conversation?"

By working with divisions across the campus and within the collection's community, special collections brought the Cassady Lewis collection to life for elementary schoolers. The USC Libraries, the Lewis Carroll Society of North America (LCSNA), and the USC School of Dramatic Arts partnered to create a unique pedagogical experience for 90 fifth graders from the 32nd Street USC Visual and Performing Arts Magnet School in Los Angeles. A dramatic reading from *Alice's Adventures in Wonderland*, in addition to class art and reading assignments from their teachers and a tour of the Cassady Lewis Carroll Collection in special collections, helped students understand the history and importance of this classic tale, which changed children's literature from primarily featuring lessons, moralistic tales, and fear tactics meant to scare and guilt children into behaving themselves to encouraging curiosity and discovery while fostering a love of reading. While requiring extensive collaboration, partnerships like this can create a larger impact than each division or group working independently.

For the spring 2013 LCSNA conference, USC Libraries Communications and Special Collections departments reached out to the 32nd Street USC Visual and Performing Arts Magnet School to hold the Maxine Schaefer Reading for their fifth-grade class, comprised of over 90 students whose curriculum focused on visual, performing, and cinematic arts. Before the reading, the school's art teacher created an assignment asking students to create Mad Hatter hats to wear to the event. Special collections provided digital scans of the original John Tenniel illustrations of the Mad Hatter tea party scene, and the students used these images as reference. In some cases, they even cut the images out and pasted them onto their hats! On the day of the reading, the students came wearing brightly colored hats decorated with original illustrations from the story.

Oliver Mayer, playwright and associate professor of dramatic writing from the USC School of Dramatic Arts, adapted the Mad Hatter's Tea Party scene from Carroll's original text to create the dramatic reading presented to the fifth-grade class. He cast students and professional screen actors from Los Angeles to play the characters. On the day of the performance, the

Dormouse's nose twitched and his sleepy voice made the students giggle, the Mad Hatter's animated antics and lively performance kept the students riveted, and they all shared in Alice's bewilderment at this absurd tea party.

Following the reading, August Imholtz, a member of the LCSNA, gave a brief overview of the history of the story of *Alice's Adventures in Wonderland* and conducted a question and answer session, providing a forum for students, now newly curious from the performance, to discuss the text with an expert in the area of Carroll studies. This exchange also allows the LCSNA members to view Carroll's tale through the inquisitive and imaginative minds of children. At the end of the event, the LCSNA and USC Libraries gave students their own copy of the book that could be signed upon request by the actors and members of the LCSNA.

The week following the reading, the students visited special collections to handle rare items from the Cassady Lewis Carroll Collection. The 90 students were broken up into three groups, rotating through different parts of the library to gain visual and tactile experiences. Saunders chose materials from the collection that not only linked to the students' experience with the story, but also challenged their preconceptions. For example, they saw production sketches and hand-painted film cells from Disney's 1951 animated film *Alice in Wonderland* and handled flip books to understand the mechanics of nondigital animation processes from the mid-20th century. Most of the students had seen the Disney film, but prior to this Alice event, they had not known it was a book. Saunders then showed them a photograph of Alice Liddell, the real-life girl who inspired Carroll's story, as well as a facsimile of the original manuscript, *Alice's Adventures Underground*. The connection of the story to a real person stuck with the students, as shown in their responses to the assessment survey at the end of the tour. Saunders also brought out a first edition of the story, and the students ran their hands over the marbled end papers and recognized Tenniel's illustrations from their Mad Hatter art project. To conclude the session, students visited the lobby of Doheny Library, where students saw an Alice in Wonderland–themed anamorphic sculpture by Hollywood-based sculptor Karen Mortillaro. They were handed a rolled-up reflective sheet in which to view the anamorphic sculpture and asked to identify certain characters from the story and guess which chapter the sculpture represented.

In order to gauge what students took away from these experiences, an assessment sheet was given to the class to fill out before they left. It asked the following four questions: What are two things you learned about the special collections and Lewis Carroll's *Alice's Adventures in Wonderland* today that you didn't know before? What was the coolest thing you saw today in Special Collections? What else do you want to know about Special Collections or *Alice's Adventures in Wonderland*? And draw your best *Alice in Wonderland* picture on the back of this page and sign your name. From the responses, USC Libraries learned that many of the students enjoyed seeing the miniature and pop-up books as well as the translations, sculptures, and Carroll's handwritten letters. Students were interested to learn that Alice was based on a real girl, how animated movies were made, and that Carroll was a math teacher. They also were surprised by how old the books were. Overall, the students reported a positive experience at Special Collections, and they walked away with a better understanding of Carroll and his work through their experience with the materials.

The Cassady Lewis Carroll Collection can inspire a variety of types of outreach methods geared toward late–elementary school students. Because these students are already familiar with the story of *Alice in Wonderland*, their knowledge was used as a springboard to discuss many other topics such as translations, manuscripts, artist adaptations, and film adaptations during each activity. Additionally, each activity and event informed the next and created a deeper understanding of the material. Students became familiar with the original illustrations through their art project prior to the dramatic reading, and this allowed them to connect to the first edition when they saw it later on the collection tour. The dramatic reading entertained the students and allowed for a better understanding of the 19th-century text through stage adaptation by a modern playwright. Finally, a tour of special collections holdings that include visual materials that span multiple genres, such as film, art, fiction, and poetry, suggested many different ways of connecting students to the story. By partnering with the professional organization, the LCSNA, as well as the USC School of Dramatic Arts, USC Libraries was able to bring this classic tale to life.

The Center for Jewish History

For many years, the Center for Jewish History (CJH), which is a five-partner consortium environment with one consolidated public services system to serve all five collecting bodies, has sought better ways in which to reach out to younger readers and encourage use of the collections by a wider audience than just experienced scholars. As a result, CJH developed the Junior Scholars Program to provide a more immersive experience for students who would be able to visit more than once and were motivated to do primary source work and began participating in National History Day to reach those who could not come to the repository on their own. The Junior Scholars Program represents the most intensive curricular engagement model for advanced and/or older K–12 students.

Created by the senior manager of Grants and Communications, Miriam Haier, and funded by the New York State Office of Family Services, the program is a fellowship whereby 10 to 12 high school juniors and seniors spend two weeks at the center, learning to interact with primary sources and doing group assignments using resources and materials. The application process requires submitting a personal essay and recommendations, which the CJH staff reviews in order to select the fellows from among the applicants. Academic transcripts are not required; the personal essay is the most important tool for evaluating applicants, although letters of recommendation also are a helpful tool for assessing the applications.

The two weeks the junior scholars are in residence give them the opportunity to tour the facilities and participate in a number of different activities; this program has been so successful that CJH is considering expanding the program to last for three weeks. During the current version of the program, junior scholars are shown the special collections reading room, the genealogy institute, and CJH's exhibitions. The students have a materials session with special collections staff, where they discuss a variety of different types of paper and printing methods; a processing session with an archivist who explains the process of preparing archival materials for use from start to finish, including the creation of finding aids; and a two-day long unit with the preservation and conservation laboratory, where they create preservation boxes. More advanced scholars—postdoctoral fellows or doctoral candidates —come in to run seminars, give lectures on topics in Jewish history, and participate in group discussions on topics like the book as object and artifact, provenance marks and their purpose, and the rise of Yiddish print culture in New York in the early 20th century. The junior scholars are given a final assignment of selecting one object from the collections, requesting it through the reading room, and then writing a paper that describes and contextualizes the object. After these papers are completed, the center holds an event for the scholars to present their projects, with their parents in attendance to see their work. In the coming year, the plan is to expand the time frame from two weeks to three weeks, as there are additional activities CJH would like to add to the junior scholars' schedule, such as having them curate an exhibition.

However, not all students can come to CJH for field trips or extended programs, so the center needed to think of ways to export its offerings. One fruitful outreach effort developed to meet this challenge was for CJH to participate in local events such as the launch reception for National History Day in New York City, which the center never considered previously. Participating entailed CJH creating a LibGuide specific to the theme of the year,[17] attending the event with a laptop and materials about CJH, and conducting reference work with the attendees for their projects. Meyers taught attendees how to search CJH's catalog for books and periodicals, what digital objects were and how to access them, and the basics of archival research, including looking at finding aids and what information they contain. After this event, CJH started seeing teens who had attended the fair start coming in to use the collections. Meyers also received a number of e-mails from parents, thanking her for their assistance and from students asking questions about using the digital objects. As participating in this event took very little preparation, and was very successful in terms of the results we saw, it has now become CJH's intention to participate in National History Day annually.

Using Digital Collections

The previous case studies concentrate on introducing K–12 students to understanding, appreciating, and even using original materials. However, digitization now is a widely accepted priority in many special collections, as it allows repositories to preserve materials while reaching out to populations that may or may not be able to visit the originals.[18] The National Archives and other national level repositories have generated K–12 curricula using digital surrogates. These repositories are models for what is possible when educational outreach builds from digitized resources. However, repositories need to customize content to suit their own collections and communities; additionally, the scope of projects at national-level repositories makes these sites unlikely to be reasonable guides for smaller institutions' goals. For these reason, the CJH offers a model of how a current digital project can be tweaked to include educational outreach to the K–12 demographic. Building on previously existing curated digital content allows repositories to showcase their collection strengths while limiting the number of websites that require maintenance to remain updated and useful as technology changes.

Many national models of how to combine digitized content with K–12 outreach exist. Among them is the Folger Shakespeare Library's Teaching Modules, which combine texts with lesson plans submitted by partnering K–12 teachers that are then curated by Folger staff before being displayed online.[19] However, these teaching modules are not connected to a specific digital exhibition but are built from Folger's Digital Texts. These Digital Texts are not digital surrogates of items within the collection; rather they are plain text (Moby Text) transcripts of Shakespeare's works.[20] Another example, DocsTeach from the National Archives,[21] pairs digital surrogates with community-sourced lesson plans. These surrogates also are not part of a specific online exhibition or digital humanities project. While Folger's Teaching Modules and the National Archives' DocsTeach are excellent models to follow when considering how to adapt digitized content to suit the curricular needs of K–12 students, both repositories' programs are at a scale unlikely to be matched at smaller institutions. Folger's Teaching Modules currently offer 20 lessons approved by the library; DocsTeach combines thousands of digitized pages made available to seven different activity-creation tools for five different historical thinking skillsets.

In contrast, the CJH supports an initiative that is a more realistic guide to follow when considering how to use digital surrogates for K–12 educational objectives. CJH boasts a robust digitization program supported by the efforts of the Gruss-Lipper Digital Lab and strategic partnerships with other institutions.[22] As a result, CJH hosts over 100,000 digital objects hosted in its digital asset manager, Digitool (http://search.cjh.org/). While these objects are accessible to the public through search.cjh.org, in the past few years, CJH has also been creating digital humanities projects for outreach and educational purposes, curating digital content more selectively, and adding context that may be lacking from the digitized item as a singular entity. While these digital humanities projects do not request, curate, or provide access to community-sourced lesson plans currently, this is an option that could be provided in the future.

One of the first examples of this exploration was an interactive map of provenance marks, drawn from the papers of Colonel Seymour Pomrenze, which can be found at bookstamps.cjh.org.[23] Pomrenze was the first director of the Offenbach Archival Depot, one of the collecting points for books being recovered from Nazi caches of stolen cultural heritage materials. When stores of stolen books were found, they were sent to Offenbach, where they would be sorted in order to facilitate their return to the country of origin when possible. In order to assist in this sorting process, the Offenbach workers created scrapbooks with pictures of provenance marks, sorted by country; these scrapbooks represent a breathtaking pictorial representation of Nazi looting and theft. Contained in Pomrenze's collection are copies of two of the Offenbach albums, volumes that represent Eastern and Western Europe.[24] These albums had already been digitized and were available for viewing through Digitool when staff at CJH and American Jewish Historical Society decided to collaborate on creating a digital map that would translate the provenance marks and add historical context.

The project got a great deal of attention,[25] including mentions in the *New York Times* and the *New Yorker*.[26] After the success of the initial project, which was hosted on Flickr, CJH then committed to additional funds and staff time to expand the project. As of this writing, CJH is preparing for the relaunch of the Offenbach map as a far more ambitious entity; it will still feature the map and provenance information, but will also contain additional content related to *The Monuments Men*, Colonel Pomrenze, World War II theft and looting, bibliographies and subject guides related to all of the above, and a large section on bookstamps and provenance marks as informational, artistic, and artifactual entities.

While wrestling with how to reconceptualize Offenbach and to scale the initial concept upward, CJH also started thinking about making the project accessible to the largest possible cross-section of users. Younger students were earmarked as a potential target demographic due to the difficulty in bringing them into the physical space. Revamping the Offenbach project would allow CJH to bring the content to K–12 students in their home institutions, thus removing the logistical issues surrounding field trips. As an institution, the CJH felt the map would greatly benefit from a more forceful emphasis on how to use it as an educational tool, not just as a way in which to imagine the scope of a collection.

Thanks to the innovative thinking of David Rosenberg, Reference Services research coordinator, an educational component has become an integral part of the reenvisioned map; the new project will include all the content listed above but will also include multiunit lesson plans for using the map in conjunction with classroom exercises. Rosenberg brought in an intern, Rachel Smith, who has a background in education. Smith created lesson plans for Offenbach, with units focusing on using primary sources, improving map-reading skills, and learning about bookplates and stamps. Activities include analyzing the map, thinking about how historians use artifacts to conduct research, and creating a custom provenance mark either in a group or on an individual basis.

These lesson plans clearly articulate the skills to be learned from the unit and activities, and are scalable, presenting the basic exercise with suggestions for customization for younger children or more advanced learners. The exercises are also congruent with the Common Core State Standards, so it can be used by the greatest number of teachers and students possible. CJH is planning to pilot the Offenbach lessons in the Junior Scholars Program in summer 2015, and, assuming the results are encouraging, the goal is to create more lesson plans using digital content going forward, utilizing Smith's templates to greatly enrich the value and potential usage of a formidable amount of aggregated digital content.

However, it is important to note that any repository seeking to provide K–12 lesson plans as a supplement to the content of a DH project or digital exhibition should consider the requirements for maintaining the site. Several early educational pages that sought to provide K–12 curricula based on special collections holdings stop updates after the project's original funding ended. For example, Territorial Kansas Online,[27] featured in Scott Walker's chapter for *Advocacy, Outreach, and the Nation's Academic Libraries: A Call for Action*,[28] was funded through an Institute of Museum and Library Services grant in 1999. The site has not been updated since 2004, although the homepage—as of June 3, 2013—does show its most recent modification dating to September 12, 2013. CSS *Alabama*, created by the W. S. Hoole Special Collections Library at the University of Alabama,[29] was one of the earliest digital projects of its type; it was built in 1995 after the division obtained support from the UA Capital Campaign Fund.[30] However, it also has not received a major update since it was created. Now, CSS. *Alabama* lingers online as an example of the fact that repositories must commit to ongoing maintenance of web projects, especially if they hope them to remain useful.

Digitization provides many exciting opportunities for enticing K–12 students, and their educators, to work with primary sources found in special collections. National-level repositories, such as the Digital Public Library of America, the National Archives, and the Folger Shakespeare Library, showcase a variety of ways curricula objectives can be met by pairing digital surrogates with specific learning goals. However, CJH's Offenbach project offers a more scalable model of how digital materials can be used to foster K–12 outreach. By adding K–12 lessons tailored to the content of preexisting digital exhibitions or DH projects like CJH did, repositories can restrict their invest-ment to already-digitized materials that presumably build on their current collection strengths. Additionally, by adding K–12 lessons to current projects, repositories should be more likely to be able to commit to maintaining these pages so that they remain updated.

Recommendations

Our case studies suggest there are three key factors to contemplate when creating a K–12 outreach program. First, the venue where the visits take place needs to be carefully considered. While special collections in aca-demic libraries are used to hosting college students in their own space, this venue may not be the most feasible or accessible for younger audiences. Field trips can be difficult to schedule as they require significant advanced planning in order to fit visits into school calendars, as Priddle discussed; may involve logistical challenges such as considering adult-sized infra-structure, as Crane noted; or the challenge of managing large groups, as Saunders observed. While alternative methods to bring students to campus exist, like the CJH's Junior Scholars Program or USC's Maxine Schaefer Reading, not all repositories will be able to make this type of extensive com-mitment to their outreach efforts. But going to the students, which solves transportation and timing problems, also poses different challenges. Either special collections instructors must secure permission to bring original materials outside of the repository—which, as Priddle observes, may be more easily done with duplicates within the collections rather than unique materials—or they will need to teach through facsimiles or digital editions. While reproductions generate less concerns regarding how to verify that transporting original materials will not pose a security or preservation risk and how to ensure that young students follow proper handling procedures, they do not offer the tangible traces of history that enthrall students no mat-ter their age.

Second, before selecting what items to showcase, special collections instructors should consider state- or national-level learning objectives for the grade level of the students. For example, Ontario on the Go found that identifying the curricular objectives visiting K–12 teachers were required to follow in their classes would help docents integrate their tours and discus-sions to the themes and skills explored during students' regular coursework. Docents at the Museum of History and Art, Ontario, are required to go through an extensive training program, in part because they are volunteers rather than employees. However, these types of discussions can be done informally too, as Crane notes in her summary of the Claremont College's outreach, provided both the elementary or secondary teacher and the special collections instructor can communicate well. USC's work with the art teacher of the 32nd Street USC Visual and Performing Arts Magnet School demon-strates how educational, and how fun, the result of such collaborations can be.

Third, by working from digital resources that have already been created, as seen in CJH's Offenbach map project, special collections can also choose to develop educational supplements to already-existing material. This strategy allows repositories with limited time to build from their current strengths, more quickly identify targeted grade(s), and generate resources that appeal to diverse audiences while also making it easier to consider the project's lifespan online.

In conclusion, while K–12 audiences are a relatively underserved demographic for special collections instructors to consider, working with younger students gives repositories the opportunity to reach an enthusiastic set of burgeoning scholars, while simultaneously offering schools the ability to show their charges the value of primary sources and how history can be exciting by interacting with materials in a way they would be unable to in a museum. Our case studies, which pull from a variety of special collections repositories across the United States, demonstrate the value of working with K–12 students and offer scalable suggestions on how outreach can be conducted for this demographic with both physical objects and digital surrogates. The materials that reside in many special collections—including research libraries, historical societies, and museums—often include not simply the representations of a homogenized general "cultural heritage," but also materials from what have often been historically marginalized groups, communities, and peoples. Sharing these materials with youngest students allows these stories to be told in new ways, and invites them to begin their own journey of discovery and education in special collections.

Notes

1. Anne J. Gilliland-Swetland, "An Exploration of K-12 User Needs for Digital Primary Source Materials," *The American Archivist* 61, no. 1 (Spring 1998): 137.

2. Michelle Visser, "Special Collections at ARL Libraries and K-12 Outreach: Current Trends," *The Journal of Academic Librarianship* 32, no. 3 (May 2006): 315.

3. Reference, Outreach, and Access Section of SAA, "Teaching with Primary Sources Bibliography," Society of American Archivists (2012), accessed April 20, 2015, http://www2.archivists.org/groups/reference-access-and-outreach-section/teaching-with-primary-sources-bibliography.

4. Lori Dekydtspotter and Cherry Williams, "Not beyond Our Reach: Collaboration in Special Collection Libraries," *Universal Journal of Educational Research* 2, no. 5 (2014): 432–436.

5. Anne Bahde, Heather Smedberg, and Mattie Tourmina (eds.), *Using Primary Sources: Hands-On Instructional Exercises* (Santa Barbara, CA: Libraries Unlimited, 2014).

6. Tamar Dougherty, "Using Special Collections for K-12 Students," Workshop for the 2015 Cataloging Hidden Special Collections and Archives Symposium: Innovation, Collaboration, and Models (March 12, 2015), accessed April 21, 2015, http://www.clir.org/hiddencollections/2015-symposium-unconference/schedule.

7. Kate Theimer, ed., *Educational Programs: Innovative Practices for Archives and Special Collections* (Lanham, MD: Rowman & Littlefield, 2015). Disclosure: Amy Chen is an author of a chapter included in this volume, but her piece is not about K–12 outreach; however, Melanie Meyers and Charlotte Priddle are coauthors, along with Janet Bunde and Andy Steinitz, of one of these three pieces. Their chapter is titled "Archivists Teaching Teachers: The Archives Education Institute and K-12 Outreach."

8. The Claremont Colleges include Pomona College (1887), Claremont Graduate University (1925), Scripps College (1926), Claremont McKenna College (1946), Harvey Mudd College (1955), and Pitzer College (1963) and they are on adjoining campuses. The Keck Graduate Institute of Applied Life Sciences (1997) is located on a nearby campus.

9. Adele B. Vuong, e-mail message to author, January 27, 2015.

10. Special collections and libraries offer a breadth of resources in the humanities, arts, sciences, and social sciences, with strengths including U.S. and European

history; California and the West; Claremont Colleges' archives; city of Claremont and the Inland Empire (San Bernardino and Riverside Counties); Asia; history of the book, book arts, and fine printing; religion; literature; music and performing arts; gender and women's studies; and the history of science and technology. From *Special Collections and Libraries*, Special Collections and Libraries brochure, Claremont, CA: Claremont Colleges Library, 2015.

11. Ulisse Aldrovandi, *Serpentum, et draconum historiæ libri duo*. Bartholomævs Ambrosinvs . . . opvs concinnauit . . . Sumptibus M.A. Bernie, Bononiæ, apud C. Ferronium, 1640.

12. The museum is a public-private institution operated by the city of Ontario with support from the all-volunteer, nonprofit group, the Museum of History and Art, Ontario Associates. The museum itself is a department of the city's Community and Public Services Agency. Located in Ontario's historic second City Hall constructed in 1937, the museum was established by City Council Ordinance in 1979 and opened to the public in 1981. A five-member governing board of trustees is appointed by the mayor and city council. For more information, go to "City Facts," City of Ontario, California, accessed April 21, 2015, http://ci.ontario.ca.us/index.aspx?page=783; and Museum of History and Art, Ontario Associates, *Museum Volunteer Manual* (Ontario, CA: Museum of History and Art, Ontario, 2004), 3.

13. The museum's inaugural docent training program began in January 2005 and is held every other year; annually effective in 2015. Trainees are required to attend two 90-minute training sessions per month for a total of six months where they learn about Native Americans in Southern California, Southern California in the nineteenth and twentieth centuries, Ontario history, learning theories, and other topics pertaining to school curricula, state standards, and teacher needs. Following training, docents must commit to participating in docent assignments a minimum of one day per month for two years. Education volunteers are similar to docents, but they are not required to participate in the six-month training program or make a two-year commitment. They may assist docents or museum staff with school tours and/or the museum's outreach program, Ontario History on the Go.

14. "Sad" is an Old English word for "solid," and the term "sad iron" is often used to distinguish the largest and heaviest of flat irons, usually five to nine pounds. Ontario is the home of an early manufacturing plant for Hotpoint and, later, General Electric irons.

15. The content standards, developed by the state of California in 1998, that Ontario History on the Go meets are as follows: 3.1. Students describe the physical and human geography and use maps, tables, graphs, photographs, and charts to organize information about people, places, and environments in a spatial context; 3.3. Students draw from historical and community resources to organize the sequence of local historical events and describe how each period of settlement left its mark on the land; 3.5. Students demonstrate basic economic reasoning skills and an understanding of the economy of the local region; 4.1. Students demonstrate an understanding of the physical and human geographic features that define places and regions in California; 4.4. Students explain how California became an agricultural and industrial power, tracing the transformation of the California economy and its political and cultural development since the 1850s; 4.5. Students understand the structures, functions, and powers of the local, state, and federal governments as described in the U.S. Constitution; 5.8. Students trace the colonization, immigration, and settlement patterns of the American people from 1789 to the mid-1800s, with emphasis on the role of economic incentives, effects of the physical and political geography, and transportation systems. See California State Board of Education, "History-Social Science, Adopted October 1998," Content Standards, California State Board of Education, accessed April 21, 2015, http://www.cde.ca.gov/be/st/ss/. Note: the PDF was created on May 18, 2000.

16. Group brainstorming about how to address the needs of young students can be quite helpful. One way archival professionals in the New York City area address their concerns about this demographic is by attending the Archivists Roundtable (ART) of New York's Archives Education Institute, which pairs archivists and special collections librarians with K–12 educators in order to learn how best to integrate primary sources into the primary and secondary school classrooms. As Charlotte Priddle and Melanie Meyers both participated in the 2013 ART session, their outreach efforts at their respective institutions came out of this valuable opportunity to generate methodologies for connecting special collections holdings to the needs and interests of K–12 students. For more information, read: Janet Bunde, Melanie Meyers, Charlotte Priddle, and Andy Steinitz, Archivists Round Table of Metropolitan New York, "Archivists Teaching Teachers: The Archives Education Institute and K-12 Outreach," in *Educational Programs: Innovative Practices for Archives and Special Collections*, ed. Kate Theimer (Lanham, MD: Rowman & Littlefield, 2015), 87–102.

17. "Leadership and Legacy," LibGuides, Center for Jewish History, accessed April 20, 2015, http://libguides.cjh.org/.

18. This point does not mean to conflate that accessing electronic versions of archives, rare books, and other special collections materials is a replacement for viewing the originals in person. For example, Matthew Lyons is an author who is positive about the role of digital surrogates in K–12 classrooms; he nevertheless notes that they are necessary substitutes rather than the preferred way for K–12 audiences to interact with special collections. See "K-12 Instruction and Digital Access to Archival Materials," *Journal of Archival Organization* 1, no. 1 (October 2008): 19–34.

19. View the Folger Shakespeare Library's community-sourced Teaching Modules here: http://www.folger.edu/teaching-modules.

20. For an explanation of Folger's Digital Texts, please see http://www.folger digitaltexts.org/?chapter=4.

21. Visit DocsTeach, provided by the National Archives, here: http://docsteach.org/.

22. The Center for Jewish History (CJH) is a consortium environment composed of six different institutional "partners." The center is the sixth partner, and provides support and library/archives related services to the other five. The five partners (American Jewish Historical Society, the American Sephardi Federation, the Leo Baeck Institute, the Yeshiva University Museum, and the YIVO Institute) maintain their own collections and separate collection development policies. For more information about the partners or CJH, please visit www.cjh.org.

23. The collection, P-933, "The Papers of Colonel Seymour Pomrenze," is held by the American Jewish Historical Society, and the society has graciously allowed the use of its materials for this project.

24. These can be viewed, in their entirety, on search.cjh.org, through the finding aid for the Pomrenze collection.

25. The work on creating the Offenbach map was the subject of two other articles and two short paper presentations at conferences, and was part of the Digital Projects showcase at the annual SHARP conference in addition to the pieces in the *New Yorker* and *New York Times*.

26. Sally McGrane, "What Became of the Jewish Books?" *The New Yorker*, February 28, 2014, accessed January 9, 2015, http://www.newyorker.com/books/page-turner/what-became-of-the-jewish-books; Jennifer Schuessler, "Online Exhibit Tracks Books Saved by the Real-Life Monuments Men," *New York Times*, February 11, 2014, accessed January 9, 2015, http://artsbeat.blogs.nytimes.com/2014/02/11/online-exhibit-tracks-books-saved-by-the-real-life-monuments-men/?_r=1.

27. Territorial Kansas Online can be seen by visiting http://www.territorial kansasonline.org/~imlskto/cgi-bin/index.php.

28. Scott Walker, "Advocacy through Engagement: Public Engagement and the Academic Library," in *Advocacy, Outreach, and the Nation's Academic Libraries:*

A Call for Action, ed. William C. Welburn, Janice Welburn, and Beth McNeil (Chicago, IL: American Library Association, 2010): 20–21, http://www.ala.org/advocacy/advocacy-outreach-and-nation%E2%80%99s-academic-libraries-call-action.

29. CSS *Alabama* can be viewed by visiting: http://www.lib.ua.edu/content/libraries/hoole/digital/cssala/main.htm.

30. Read more about CSS *Alabama* in Andrea Watson and P. Toby Graham's "CSS *Alabama* 'Digital Collection': A Special Collections Digitization Project," *The American Archivist* 61, no. 1 (Spring 1998): 124–134.

Chapter 5
Teaching with Special Collections: Alliances between Cultural Heritage Professionals

Maureen E. Maryanski

Introduction

Teaching with special collections has recently become a stronger focus for many libraries, as librarians assess the effectiveness of their participation with teachers and professors in introducing and teaching research skills to various levels of students. As evidenced by the work conducted by the Brooklyn Historical Society in its Teach Archives project, it is of the utmost importance for special collections librarians to seek more options for how classes can be structured, planned, and tailored to the education needs and goals of instructors.[1] Librarians can gain new skills and techniques from other established and evolving fields to help them develop, implement, and evaluate courses, class visits, and educational programs. One field of particular value to special collections librarians is museum education.

At first glance, it might seem that museum educators and special collections librarians have little in common. However, both cultural heritage professionals work with primary sources and assist students and other visitors with interpreting and analyzing these materials. Both share a commitment to life-long learning. Yet these two types of professionals rarely interact with each other or learn about each other's professions and best practices. An institution like the New-York Historical Society (N-YHS) with a unique organizational history that led to the development of a museum and a library offers valuable space and opportunity for these two fields to intersect.

As special collections librarians expand their teaching endeavors and explore new possibilities for developing classroom experiences and enabling students to access and work with special collections, colleagues in museum education can offer new perspectives for scaling, organizing, and assessing this work. Bringing together two professional disciplines offers new insights for both museum education and special collections librarianship. By focusing on what each field offers the other and emphasizing the common ground in the work we do with students, a more nuanced dialog can develop centered on how to enrich student experiences during museum and library visits and aid the educational goals of teachers and professors.

The New-York Historical Society

Founded in 1804 by prominent New York business and government leaders, including Mayor DeWitt Clinton and John Pintard, N-YHS is the second oldest historical society in the nation and New York's oldest continuously operating museum. Serving over 250,000 visitors annually, the society's museum collection features over 1.6 million objects, including historical artifacts, paintings, sculpture, decorative arts, and drawings. Prominent parts of the collection are world-renowned Hudson River School paintings, an extensive collection of Tiffany glasswork, and 433 of John J. Audubon's 435 original watercolors for *Birds of America*.

In addition to the extensive museum collection, N-YHS is home to one of the United States' most distinguished independent research libraries, the Patricia D. Klingenstein Library. The library's collecting strengths include the local history of New York City and State, colonial history, American military and naval history, religions and religious movements in the 18th and 19th centuries, the Anglo-American slave trade and conditions of slavery, and American art and art patronage. The collection features books and pamphlets; maps; broadsides; dining menus; sheet music; one of the finest early American newspaper collections; over two million manuscript items; nearly a million prints, photographs, and negatives; and the architectural collections of 12 prominent firms, including McKim, Mead, and White, Cass Gilbert, and George B. Post.

Education is one of the main goals of the society, as it is for most museums and libraries. N-YHS aims to reach as many audiences as possible through exhibitions, public programs, and group visits, from schools and colleges to the larger community. N-YHS Education Department is largely responsible for the thousands of students and teachers who pass through the institution's doors each year. Due to the scale of work done at N-YHS, the Education Department handles field trips for grade school through college courses, as well as outreach programs into school classrooms. An extensive teen internship program is also facilitated by the Education Department, offering opportunities for a selected group of high school students revolving around the work of museums. Other elements of museum education usually facilitated by an education department, such as public programs, family programming, and a docent program, are at N-YHS such extensive undertakings as to warrant their own departments.

N-YHS library also welcomes undergraduate, graduate, and community groups to visit for presentations and classes conducted by members of the public service staff. Most of these visits are show-and-tell presentations, offering an introduction to the library's collections, how to access them, and an overview of research skills. Groups have the opportunity to view and analyze multiple examples from the three library departments: Printed Collections; Manuscripts; and Prints, Photographs, and Architectural Collections.

In the past few years, collaborations at N-YHS have offered new opportunities for the Education and Library departments to coordinate in creating and crafting programs, providing chances for increased communication and cross-pollination between these professions. As the programming and volume of students who visit the institution through field trips and groups visits increase, so too does the level of collaboration between the Education and Library departments. The library's level of involvement in education programming has significantly increased over the last three years, partly due to a renovation project currently under way on the fourth floor of N-YHS building. This floor previously housed N-YHS Luce Center of visible museum storage, allowing a large percentage of the society's museum collections to be viewed by visitors and school groups. With the majority of these museum objects housed off-site for the duration of the renovation, the on-site library collections have become vital to ongoing Education Department programming. This partnership has led to in-depth conversations, program development, and an exchange of ideas, techniques, and skills between the Library and Education staffs.

Two questions have emerged from these collaborations that are worth considering. The first is what librarians can learn and borrow from museum education. The second is how collaborations between special collections librarians and museum educators can be mutually beneficial and influence the practices and experiences of all cultural heritage professionals. These experiences and observations, grounded in the work of N-YHS over the past few years, will assist special collections librarians in further developing thoughts and practices for teaching with special collections and prompt further inquiry and discussion through professional organizations and publications.

Collaborate, Communicate

A certain level of collaboration has existed between the Education and Library departments at N-YHS for several years. Documents, including maps, prints, photographs, and letters, have been utilized by the Education Department in its programs, with facsimiles used for both on- and off-site programming. The librarians' roles have varied, from assisting educators in researching and accessing materials (many of which have been reproduced for use in programs) to working alongside museum educators to create the content and objectives of a program. In the past three years, the number of programs involving a more active librarian presence has increased. Additionally, during the past year the library staff has begun to diversify its audience by age levels, collaborating and participating in programs for middle school children, in conjunction with N-YHS family programming department: the Dimenna Children's History Museum.

The Education Department predominantly initiates collaboration with the Library Department. Education staff identify a program or class that will benefit from visits to the library and/or use of library materials. Depending on the level of library involvement, a varying number of meetings take place between education staff members and the liaising librarian to determine how to proceed. For some programs, such as a semester-long Fordham University history course structured around four visits to N-YHS library and four visits to N-YHS museum galleries, several meetings are required to coordinate between the professor, museum educator, and librarian. For this class, library and museum items relating to four different time periods in American history are paired for students to analyze and explore in groups. Much work is required as the professor, educator, and librarian select these paired items. This class has run every fall for the past several years, and as it evolves, fewer in person meetings and more e-mail communication is used, unless a unit of the class requires a review, as when the closure of the Luce Center visible storage altered which museum objects were on display and available for use in the program, leading to rewrites.

Regardless, a combination of e-mail and in-person meetings are required when planning or revising programs. The key to successful programs, such as the summer Teen Scholars program begun in August 2014, is open and flexible communication. This program gives a select group of high school students the opportunity to research in N-YHS library over the course of six sessions, under the supervision of librarians and educators. It provides access to original materials that these students would not have unless accompanied by a parent or a guardian. The program benefited from communication between educator and librarian early enough in the planning to allow input from both parties. Communication should and does continue throughout the planning stages and program itself, as well as with post-program meetings to evaluate and assess its success, based on the goals and objectives determined during the planning stage. For example, a meeting to assess the program's first year led the librarian and educator to determine that a more focused end product was needed. Students were allowed to pick any topic to research, with the belief that they would write a short summary of their findings. Students became engrossed in research, and with no parameters clearly defined to limit their research, they had little time left for writing, and no summaries were produced. This observation led to adjustments in scope and focus to allow time for both research and writing in the 2015 program. The free exchange of ideas between educator and librarian on logistical feasibility and program content is vital for the program's smooth execution and assessment. The key is to communicate early and often.

Some programs and classes require fewer meetings. One of these was a week-long teacher professional development workshop entitled "New York City at War." The workshop culminated in the teachers developing lesson plans based on primary sources in N-YHS collections related to the American Revolution, the Civil War, or World War II. In order to introduce the teachers to potential sources, as well as how to search for and find such sources, the museum educator wished to bring the teachers to the library for two show-and-tell presentations. Because of the wealth of information the workshop would cover in one week, the educator planned to limit these presentations to materials on one war and in one format (a different format for each war). The materials were chosen based on consultations with librarians: broadsides for the American Revolution and photographs for the Civil War.

The idea for this teacher workshop was to offer a selection of the kinds of primary sources available for use in the classroom. It was not meant to be exhaustive, nor was it, as in the Fordham course, a very specific selection of individual items in the library collection. Thus, a degree of flexibility was allowed for the librarian to select materials, with a final meeting a week prior to the program for the educator to see the selected items, allowing time for any potential adjustments.

A by-product of the planning meetings between educators and librarians is the discussion of professional fields, standards, and techniques. In order for these two staffs to work together, mutual respect and understanding of how the other department operates, and what its objectives and procedures are, is necessary. The collaboration between these two departments allows the staffs of these departments to relate and find common ground as they work together to develop unique experiences for students and teachers. It is hopefully only the beginning of a continually evolving partnership. Library visits can be integral to education programs, but currently fit into a framework initially conceived and developed by museum educators. I would like to see a broadening of scope and more of a true partnership from conceptualization to execution. Doing so requires an understanding of both professional fields, as well as an exploration of what each field can teach the other.

What We Learn: Scale and Organization

As collaborations have evolved and expanded between the Library and Education departments at N-YHS, staff members in both departments have been able to observe and learn practices from their colleagues' training and fields of expertise. Broadly speaking, what librarians can learn from museum educators are methods for scaling and organizing class visits and programs. Scaling, or scale, of programs and classes has two meanings. The first concerns the number of programs that museum education departments develop and run. At N-YHS, the Education Department runs 150 discrete school programs, a number of enrichment programs, and a two-tiered teen internship program. In fiscal year 2014, these programs added up to 1,282 field trips of 32,840 students, teachers, and adults and 1,367 enrichment, art of history, and outreach programs serving 98,551 students and teachers in the New York City area. In comparison, the library welcomed 60 classes and groups, totaling 784 students and adults in the same time period, including collaborations with education programs. This discrepancy reflects differences between the size and scope of what the Education and Library departments do in their work with students.

The Education Department sends educators to school classrooms from grade school to college-level classes to discuss the work of historians and museums and to introduce how to analyze artifacts and documents. These class visits utilize facsimiles and reproductions. Library visits are all on-site events, limited by several logistical and practical matters, chief of which is space. Currently, N-YHS library does not have regular access to classroom space, which is prioritized for education school groups visiting the museum. Therefore, all class and group visits to the library must take place in the reading room while it is open to researchers. Groups must be limited in size, with a maximum of 20–25 individuals. Groups must also be kept to smaller numbers in the library due to the nature of these visits. Original documents and materials are brought out for participants to see and, sometimes, to handle. The reference librarian leading the visit must be able to monitor the use and treatment of items throughout the class. Librarians can learn how to streamline and work with larger volumes of classes and students, which is most helpful as the current numbers for fiscal year 2015 are showing significant growth: 100 classes and groups and 1,646 students, teachers, and adults.

The second meaning of scale is being able to adjust classes and programs for different age levels. The library predominantly deals with undergraduate- and graduate-level classes. By partnering with museum educators, librarians have been able to develop and contribute to programs for high school and middle school classes, thus learning how to tailor discussions of handling, research skills, and various historical topics to different grade levels and abilities. It has allowed the librarians to increase their influence by reaching a new and larger audience. Most significantly, librarians at N-YHS have worked with teen programs, including the summer Teen Scholars program and a middle school program called Camp History.

The Teen Scholars program offers high school students the opportunity to come into the reading room, learn how to access these materials, and conduct research in a special collections library. Students learn how to find sources for their research in the library's online catalog and finding aids. For many, this is their first experience viewing and handling manuscript documents, rare books, historic prints and photographs, and items from architectural collections. This tangible experience with library materials teaches students how to handle items of historical significance, inspiring them to join librarians in an effort to preserve cultural heritage.

The Camp History program allows middle school students to view some items from the library collection that are preselected for the age group. Students do not conduct their own research, nor do they handle library collections. The difference between the Teen Scholar and Camp History programs is an example of the scaling that museum educators must do to tailor activities and programs to specific age levels. The decision to scale in this manner for different age groups came from several conversations between educators and librarians regarding what could reasonably be expected from the age group, both in terms of dexterity in handling materials and in the cognitive ability to grasp sometimes-tricky search methods. The designation of preselected items for the younger age level was suggested and insisted upon by the librarians. While the scaling method is a staple of museum education, the way it is applied in library activities and involvement in programs is left to the discretion of the librarians after discussing the objectives and goals for the program as a whole.

The organization of programs run by the Education Department and the daily and weekly operations of the department are much different from those of the public service librarians. These differences are partly due to the size of the staffs: the Education Department has 9 full-time and 7 part-time office/support staff members in addition to 28 educators and teaching artists. The full-time Education staff members have divided responsibilities, with some handling the scheduling and marketing of programs and others handling the developing and writing of them.

For the library, six public service librarians and five senior staff members share the responsibilities for teaching and conducting presentations, with each librarian working on the checklists and preparation of their individual classes and presentations in consultation with the teacher or professor. All the library staff members involved in presentations and teaching have other job duties; these activities are not their primary responsibilities. One public service librarian coordinates the scheduling and logistics for all the groups, as well as acting as the liaison to the Education Department for collaborations.

Librarians can borrow from museum educators how programs are written and how they can be transferred between staff members. The programs and classes that museum educators conduct and lead are recorded in detailed outlines that provide background information about the goals and logistics of the programs, as well as information about each individual item used and what points need to be emphasized for the specific educational goals of the program. These are circulated to the museum education staff electronically, as well as in mandatory staff trainings that occur several times throughout the school year. Because of the large number of programs run through the Education Department, an equally large staff is needed to teach. That means that programs are documented so they can be easily transferred between people.

Typically in the library, the knowledge of what the goals and focus of a class were and what items were used resides with an individual person, not in a document that explicitly shares all this information. Checklists are typically kept by staff members, either in Word documents or generated from the Aeon circulation system, but at most these lists offer only the librarian's notes to themselves, which can vary greatly. Writing down, saving, and freely sharing contextual information on all items used and the class goals make it easier to learn about previous classes and develop them further. This method is especially helpful if there is much staff turnover. It streamlines the entire process of preparing for class visits, saving time, energy, and frustration.

In addition to having written program goals and outlines, the Education Department also has a slate of established programs and classes that it can offer teachers and professors. Programs are written to correspond to each current exhibition in the museum, as well as various topics of American history and art that are well represented by N-YHS collections. This practice is another staple of museum education that can be borrowed and adapted to special collections librarianship. Often teachers and professors contact the library, asking for an overview or introduction to the library's collections and conducting research. Some teachers and professors have very definite topics they want covered in classes, but others do not. If special collections librarians could write class outlines focused on specific collection strengths of their libraries or specific research skills, these options could be offered to potential classes and teachers in a menu-like format. This would help with librarians' workload, as they could start from a template when preparing for classes, a template they could adapt and adjust for the needs of each individual class. It would also allow librarians to share their expertise, so that a librarian specializing in photography could design a class outline for an introduction to photography that could be delivered by other staff less familiar with the format and subject matter. Some special collections libraries do utilize such a system, yet it could be a more widespread technique in the field to facilitate smoother organization and communication among colleagues.

What We Share: Life-Long Learning

The exchange of ideas and thoughts between museum educators and special collections librarians during collaborations has a mutually beneficial effect. One of the most common requests from educators at the beginning of these collaborations is to offer students the opportunity to view and interpret original primary sources and possibly gain experience with hands-on handling of these materials in the library. At minimum, educators, and indeed those teachers and professors who contact N-YHS library independently, want students to be able to see original and unique documents that can be analyzed and explored. Why is this experience so unique and valuable to students? How is it different from the majority of museum-centric programming created by the Education Department?

The teaching and interaction that occur in special collections libraries are different experiences than those central to museum education, which is focused on artifacts and documents in exhibitions or on the use of facsimiles. Materials on exhibit are in cases or behind glass, protected from any damaging handling by the public, yet still available for students to analyze and investigate. Facsimiles allow educators to utilize documents and objects not currently on display, broadening the scope and content of their classes and lesson plans. Facsimiles such as touch objects, reproductions of historical artifacts students can touch, are used in museum education to allow exploration without the fear of damaging originals. Reproductions and transcriptions of publications and documents are routinely used in classrooms, both in museum education and in the broader education field. Students read a modern reprint copy of *Pride and Prejudice* in the classroom, not a first edition, though they are studying the same text. The same is true of reproductions utilized by museum educators in their programming. What makes a visit to a special collections library unique, if students can access like items in exhibitions, facsimiles, and reproductions? Why should students be exposed to original documents?

On a surface level, class visits to a special collections library are viewed as a "cool experience" for teachers or museum educators to incorporate into their lesson plans. It can be an enrichment, a supplement, to the main objectives and goals. However, can these experiences go beyond enrichment? What impact can these experiences have, and how do they compare to experiences interacting with facsimiles and reproductions, including digital surrogates? On a practical level, teaching with original materials in special collections libraries allows other aspects besides content to be studied and learned. For example, facsimiles and reproductions focus on the words and ideas, the text, of a book. However, a book is also the leather binding, the marbled endpapers, the handmade paper, the impressions left from a handpress printing press, an inscription from father to son, a name and date on the inside front cover, and marginalia. The physical nature of a book can provide just as much information into the study of the past as the words on the page. These physical features and traces tell how it was created and used; they connect us to the people who created and used it. It is no longer an inanimate object, but a living, breathing link to people long dead, who left a piece of themselves in the materials left behind.

Broadly speaking, special collections library visits offer students unmediated (but monitored) access to library materials. They make the items real for students and allow them to connect with materials from the past on both an intellectual and a visceral level. While the same analysis of a text or image can be made as with a facsimile, the physical format and details of an item can convey something much more intangible and valuable. As one N-YHS educator put it, "Students continually express the significance of viewing 'actual' archival materials and are struck by the 'humanness' of these documents—their understanding of history is significantly informed by this access." Having access to collections in special collections libraries can change students' assumptions and opinions about the people who created and used these items. These visits and classes create an environment in which students can gain insight and connection to the past, and these introductions to original documents and artifacts can challenge habitual modes of thinking.

Moving Forward

These collaborations between museum educators and special collections librarians at N-YHS do not offer all the solutions for others hoping to develop similar working relationships. As stated before, these initiatives are constantly evolving. More often than not, librarians and museum educators are aiming at the same thing. They share the same goal. They teach students, of various age and experience levels, how to find and analyze primary sources. That is the simplest form of what they do. Regardless of the discipline the class is studying, or whether a painting, a letter, a rifle, or an architectural drawing is being investigated, the core of what they do comes back to teaching how to access and work with these unique materials. Each field uses different terminology and techniques to describe these processes. In recognizing the similarities and common aims that exist between the museum and library fields, a first step can be taken toward enriching and broadening student experiences. The goal should be to constantly evolve, to improve the experiences of students, and to broaden horizons.

The most important next (and ongoing) step is communication, not just at the institutional level, but at the local, regional, and national levels. Hopefully the type of collaboration at N-YHS will spur more discussion between the museum education and special collections library fields. At the local level, professional organizations such as the Metropolitan New York Library Council and New York City Museum Educators Roundtable would be excellent forums for discussion. Seminars, workshops, and roundtables could be organized to bring members of both professions together and facilitate conversation and exploration. The Archivists Roundtable of Metropolitan New York is also an excellent idea for a professional organization to facilitate such events, especially considering its recurring K–12 Archives Education Institute, which brings together teachers and archivists to facilitate the introduction of primary sources into K–12 curriculum. At the regional and national levels, presentations, papers, and workshops at conferences can add to the conversation, and hopefully prompt new questions and avenues of inquiry.

A third component of collaboration should also be added to the discussion. Teachers and professors are vitally important to any ongoing conversation. So much of what each of these three fields does is interrelated. Free and open communication is necessary: about the educational goals and objectives for classes and courses, the roles that museum and library visits play in these goals, and the individual goals of the museum educators and librarians. Several questions are raised about goals and objectives through collaborations, such as: What goals should we always have? What is the minimum that students should walk away with at the end of a class? How do the goals of teachers, museum educators, and librarians fit together to make a cohesive whole? As more questions are raised, it becomes clear that more discussion, analysis, and inquiry is necessary at all levels to help answer these questions, find solutions, and benefit the people whom all this teaching is for in the first place: the students.

Note

1. Brooklyn Historical Society, TeachArchives.org, accessed September 15, 2015, http://www.teacharchives.org.

Chapter 6
Legacy, Leadership & Collections: Programming in a Congressional Archive

Audrey McKanna Coleman

The Robert J. Dole Institute of Politics is an inspiring place to run an archive. Situated in the West District of the University of Kansas (KU) campus, it is infused with the D.C.-esque energy and drive of civic-minded young people ready to make a difference. These students have their favorite causes, they think big, and they work hard; the institute's leadership, visiting fellows, and program guests aren't slouches either—a power mix of emerging, tested, and visionary leaders in professions in government, politics, business, journalism, nonprofits, and others, from local to international in influence. All of these come together in service to the Dole Institute's mission to promote political and civic participation as well as civil discourse in a bipartisan, balanced manner.

The Dole Institute's claim to these values is rooted in the leadership legacy of U.S. senator from Kansas, Bob Dole (U.S. House 1960–1968, U.S. Senate 1969–1996), who himself is still an active professional based in Washington, D.C. The papers of Senator Dole came to the KU in the mid-1990s, in an initiative lead by then-chancellor Robert Hemenway. At the time, Senator Dole had served over three decades in Congress, and was contemplating his run for the presidency. Were the outcome of the 1996 U.S. presidential election different, the Dole Institute would have become Dole's presidential library. Following that model, the Dole Institute of Politics is the physical home to Dole's historical collections, in the department of the Robert J. Dole Archive and Special Collections.

The Dole Institute is an asset not just to students at KU, but the public at large. The 100-plus public programs each year, crowned with accomplished professionals discussing issues across subjects and political perspectives (all free of charge), draw thousands of attendees annually. Dole's personal papers—that is, his "Congressional collections" or "working papers"—are all housed on-site, and commonly understood to be the foundation of the Dole Institute. However, the expansive meaning, value, and application of these special collections are only beginning to be realized.

The Nature of Congressional Collections

What is a congressional collection? Frank Mackaman, director of the Everett Dirksen Center in Pekin, Illinois, describes it succinctly as "the artifact of the Congressional office," a body of records that reflects unique member personalities as well as idiosyncrasies of process and management, but with commonalities of function found across collections; it consists of records relating to a member's representational role, such as casework and constituent mail; records relating to lawmaking, such as files of legislative assistants and reference files; and records pertaining to the member himself or herself, such as appointment books and schedules, newspaper clippings, photographs, administrative records, and communications files such as press releases, speeches, audiovisual materials, and campaign and political files.[1] Richard A. Baker, U.S. Senate historian emeritus, in his reflection on congressional history enhanced understanding of the personal nature, volume, and the significance of congressional papers by quoting Vernon Ehlers of Michigan in March 5, 2008, as House Resolution 307[2] was passed, contrasting the form of the day's records—"the scourge of clutter"—with their content: "threads, that, when woven together, create the fabric of our democracy."[3]

It is through a similar array of documents that the Dole Archives documents the life and career of Bob Dole. A native of Russell, Kansas, Dole attended KU before enlisting in the U.S. Army and serving in World War II. As a replacement platoon leader, Dole suffered grave injury on a battlefield in Italy on April 14, 1945. Initially paralyzed from the neck down, he persevered through a grueling recovery, including infections that brought him near death. Before the war, he had hoped to become a surgeon but his acquired disability required him to reassess his career path and, considering the contemporary perception of people with disabilities, prove himself against low societal expectations. During law school, he served one term on the Kansas House of Representatives, and upon graduation was elected as county attorney in his home county. He served in that role during the 1950s, and was encouraged to run for national office by area Republican officials. His election to the U.S. House in 1960 lead to a 36-year career in Congress including five terms in the U.S. Senate, ending when he resigned to pursue the presidency. The collection also documents Dole's chairmanship of the Republican National Committee, 1971–1972; his campaign activity both for House and Senate, as well as for the Republican presidential nomination in 1980 and 1988, and his presidential campaign in 1996; the papers of the Dole Foundation for the Employment of People with Disabilities; and personal and family papers.

Dole is the longest-serving Senate Republican leader to date, at 11 years (Sen. Mitch McConnell is poised to usurp this title). Senator Dole's legislative career culminated in the 1980s, by which time he had achieved national recognition and seniority in the Senate at large but also in key committees such as Agriculture, Nutrition, and Forestry; Finance (for which he was chair during 1981–1983); and Judiciary. It was in the 1980s that Dole earned his reputation as a master of bipartisan negotiation—one of the key values upon which the Dole Institute is based.

Congressional collections are maintained in various types of environments. Many become the purview of "political papers" collections in university libraries and special collections departments, where they are administered with the academic research collections or as a subset of these. There are many centers for politics and public policy in university and communities nationwide with affiliated collections, some in the form of "congressional centers"; many of these have administrative affiliations with academic programs.[4] The Dole Institute of Politics is a relative rarity in that the Dole Archives collections are administered on-site, sharing both space and an institutional identity with noncollections-based programming, without an administrative relationship to an academic department. The institute's director reports to the chancellor of the university, an intentional arrangement that both elevates the profile of the institute and fosters programming development for public audiences of all ages, in addition to university students and academics.

In the past, congressional collections have, due to both volume and cataloging logistics as well as tradition, frequently been subject to long-term closures and restrictions imposed by donors. In line with practice throughout the rest of the archival profession, the institute now resists accepting donations with lengthy or perpetual restrictions. With guidance from the former senior archivist, in the mid-2000s Senator Dole agreed to amend his original deed of gift and allow for the opening of his papers incrementally upon completion of their processing (as early as 2004 for House of Representatives papers, and 2009 for his Senate papers). Thanks to intensive processing work on the part of Dole Archives staff, which was supported with a grant from the National Historical Publications and Records Commission (NHPRC),[5] processing and online finding aids were completed for 1960–1996, with selections of digitized material also online. About 1,700 linear feet is open for public research. Because the Dole Archives is a part of a larger organization that does not identify explicitly as a collecting institution, the department has kept with a relatively narrow collecting focus, prioritizing materials from Senator Dole and his associates (including staff, colleagues, and constituents) that fill in the story of Dole's legacy, and emphasizing instead building programming and visibility.

We as U.S. citizens have a generation of archivists and historians, working together with allied legislators, to thank for the acquisition and ongoing maintenance of congressional collections. While federal laws implemented in the post-Watergate era mandated the preservation and collection of presidential personal papers, the personal records of members of Congress, and records of their offices, remain the property of the individual member.[6] A member may dispose of working papers at any time; with the closure of an office, records of all types may be dispersed or destroyed. It is only through sustained advocacy that these records of the legislative branch of government are collected and preserved.[7] Many of these professionals are members of Society of American Archivists' Congressional Papers Roundtable and/or the Association for Centers of Studies of Congress.

Senator Dole, for his part, wished explicitly that the Dole Institute of Politics not become a "personal monument." The gift of his papers is an expression of his appreciation and reverence for the history and democracy of the U.S. During the 100th Congress (1987–1988), Dole delivered nearly 300 "Bicentennial Minutes," typically at the beginning of the Senate's daily session. These minutes focused on "significant people, unusual customs, and memorable events" in the Senate's first two centuries.[8] In this spirit, Dole's collections document the U.S. Senate and are a window into the behind-the-scenes business of U.S. democracy. But they can also do much more, and appeal to a broad constituency of users—as researchers or other nontraditional consumers. As Raymond W. Smock, director of the Robert C. Byrd Center for Legislative Studies and former historian of the U.S. House of Representatives, stated of congressional collections in remarks made in April 2014:

> We can use the records of Congress to create a portrait of the collective political, social, economic, and cultural situation through the papers of the members who have served. Congress may best be studied by turning the mirror around and not looking for a single face, but the face of this nation at any given time as seen through the records of Congress . . . Congressional history is not just politics . . . It has dimensions of every subject imaginable that relate to American history and world history.[9]

Dole Archives: Roles and Strategies

As a department, the Dole Archives also has an expanded role to play supporting the administrative functions of the Dole Institute. In the same sense that a corporate archive supports the brand image of a parent company, so too the department provides materials that support marketing of events and programs, as well as institutional values. As an organization dedicated to promoting Dole's "brand" of leadership, bipartisanship, and public service, we garner our unique and authentic claim to do so as the holder of his documentary record. Over the last three years, we have made ongoing efforts to build connections internally with our marketing and communications team, and are preparing to implement an institutewide digital asset management (DAM) system to manage our digital material more efficiently as well as facilitate archival asset and institutional records use by marketing and development staff, in addition to our web-based searching designed for research access by the public. It is possible that a public-facing version of the DAM may one day supersede the Archon interface.

The Dole Archives also functions as an institutional archive of the sort described by Barbara Haws, archivist for the New York Philharmonic; she characterizes archivists as "the keepers of the memories of the most powerful and influential in their community . . . both past and current,"[10] emphasizing that "an archivist should always begin by favoring the living."[11] We foster connections with people who are likely to care about our collections most, often because our materials document their own legacies and communities. For the Dole Archives, the community has many layers: most immediately, the "Dole Alumni" group, including Dole's own close friends and colleagues, staff, and volunteers and their families. More broadly, we can consider our "community" to be Dole's Kansas constituents, as well as his supporters across the nation, particularly those involved with his primary causes, such as veterans and people with disabilities and their advocates. We as an archive are able to nurture these relationships to build connections with the collections and the Dole Institute, supporting collection, programming, and financial development.

Lastly, the Dole Archives is a classic special collection, a rich resource of information for researchers of all ages and credentials (graduates and academic researchers but also K–12, undergraduates, and the general public). It is a Swiss-army knife of resources, useful for studying history—cultural, social, economic, and political, at the local, state, national, and international levels, over several decades—as well as communication, rhetoric, media, and American studies. We can teach not only historical research methods and information literacy, but also skills related to communications, leadership, civic engagement, and problem solving.

In fall 2014, Dole Archives departmental staff engaged in a semester-long strategic planning session in which they attempted to define the scope and vision for their operations, and how they related that to the stated mission of the greater Dole Institute of Politics beyond being the keepers of biography or stewards of a Senate history collection. We are not a separate entity with an exclusive set of goals: the Dole Institute's mission statement is "to promote political and civic participation as well as civil discourse in a bipartisan, balanced manner." The Dole Archives "supports the mission of the Dole Institute of Politics by acquiring, preservation, interpreting, and promoting the use of unique collections that document Senator Bob Dole's life, career and far-reaching legacy"; the department's vision includes serving as "a facilitator of teaching, learning, and research" to be a "key resource across subjects and academic disciplines, including history, government, politics, leadership, democracy, and the broad American experience."[12] This broad interpretation of content value of collections leads us to connect with values shared not just with collecting institutions (archives, special collections, libraries, and museums) but also humanities disciplines and social sciences, and organizations that promote these values. For example, the National Endowment for the Humanities' The Common Good: The Humanities in the Public Square[13] initiative announced in April 2015 to "bring the humanities into the public square and foster innovative ways to make scholarship relevant to contemporary issues" is a natural lead-in to a discussion of how our political and congressional history has influenced where we are now as a society in any number of ways.

What better place to start training our future leaders, than by engaging them with the records of those who have been there and done that—emphasizing both their humanity and their process? This is an angle familiar to social studies teachers in K–12 settings nationwide, and one that congressional archives should explore.[14] And in our physical and institutional setting, the Dole Archives is also developing in this area. Over the last three years, the Dole Archives has demonstrated the flexibility and appeal of the congressional collection—using it as both a window and a mirror—in order to position ourselves more readily for larger-scale initiatives and move toward broad impact in the civic spaces of humanities, community identity, and leadership.

Outreach to Interdisciplinary Academic Programs

Building relationships with interdisciplinary programs for freshman here at KU has been our campus outreach priority—each of these are a conduit to a network of instructors who have a specific interest in connecting KU freshmen to on-campus resources. One of these programs is KU's top-rated Undergraduate Honors Program, comprising about 1,000 students for each graduating class. Of the requirements to complete the honors curriculum, each student enrolls in a 1.0 credit hour seminar their first fall; with over 30 sections of the seminar each fall, connecting to the program means engagement with as many faculty and staff conveners across disciplines.

Each section is limited to 8–10 students and 1–3 student assistants, upperclassmen in the honors program.

While the initial intent was to provide instruction opportunities to existing seminars, we were also encouraged to convene one of our own. The course introduced in fall 2014, entitled "American Idol: Legacy, Leadership, & Collections," reflects the broad vision for the relevance and application of the Dole Archives and promotes involvement in the student culture at the Dole Institute by introducing students to the student advisory board and mentoring programs. The course is founded upon basic exposure to Senator Dole's biography and career chronology, as well as his leadership legacy, introduced via Dole Institute programming, our own archival collections, and complementary collections at area special collections and museums. The course's final project is to create an annotated bibliography around a topic of the student's choice—perhaps even a policy issue relevant to their area of study—using research and resources from our and others' collections. Through studying the archival collections, students gain an appreciation for the complexity of policy development and lawmaking, seeing for themselves the nuanced perspectives on any given issue that a Senate leader faces, and understanding that the information and communication landscape is even more complicated today. Mindful to incorporate professional advocacy, we also discuss the meaning and value of archives and heritage collections, and what they offer our society in a crowded field of public priorities.

The time investment is not insignificant; seminar instructors also have an advising role. However, we as a department learn a lot about the perspectives of today's college students and their baseline familiarity with museums and special collections, the role of liberal studies in their undergraduate and future professional lives, and their tendency toward civic engagement—not to mention the effectiveness of our online finding aids and digitized resources. This is a great opportunity for us that helps us determine the thrust of other programming for this age group. Additionally, if they remain active with the Dole Institute at large, these students bring their "archive culture" to the cohort.

In fall 2014, we initiated a relationship with KU's department of First Year Experience (FYE). Itself a young department, founded in 2012, the FYE hosts First-Year Seminars (3.0 credits) developed around diverse special topics and 45 UNIV 101 (2.0 credit) sections, which are KU orientation seminars. One UNIV 101 course, entitled "Sport, University, and You," has visited the Dole Institute several times and made use of the museum gallery exhibits and collections as they examined the connection between sports and politics. The FYE department also hosts the KU Common Book program, a community-reading initiative; 2014's Common Book selection, *The Center of Everything*, afforded direct overlap with the Dole Archives' collections. *The Center of Everything* by Laura Moriarty is a coming-of-age novel about a disadvantaged girl growing up in rural Kansas in the 1980s. The thematic ties were too strong to ignore, and under this aegis we contacted the department with hopes for a thorough integration. We created a themed guide to our collections, and hosted UNIV 101 seminar sections. The novel was also integrated into the Dole Archives honors seminar, with students comparing its social themes to issue-based press releases from the 1980s.

The Dole Archives does host history research and methods classes, but we find that, due to our physical location and perceived limited scope, the Dole Archives are of secondary preference for these sessions; most of these courses visit the centrally located, and much larger, Kenneth Spencer Research Library on the main campus. We cast our net widely because we have to, and look to build a meaningful and sustainable relationship with large-scale campus initiatives where our goals are a subset of their goals. Other examples of this include connecting to the KU 150 sesquicentennial celebrations in 2015 (we created a small display of Dole KU-era letters and memorabilia), the campus World War I centennial commemorations, and an established interdisciplinary Food Studies Work Group; discussions are in the works with integrating our collections into a spring 2016 Food, Feminism, and Philosophy course in the Women, Gender, and Sexuality Studies department, based on our collection's strength in food policy.

"Your Story, His Story, the Legacy" Program Series

By 2012, the archives department had an established claim to at least one large-scale Dole Institute public program each year, in the form a visiting fellow, who discussed issues related to archives. Previous guests included Richard A. Baker, historian emeritus of the U.S. Senate, and David Palkki, deputy director of the Conflict Records Research Center at National Defense University. The first visiting fellow we selected was Amy Herman, creator of the Art of Perception program, which uses art museum collections to train FBI agents, first responders, CEOs, military special forces, ER docs, and others to sharpen their visual analysis and communications skills.[15] By featuring Ms. Herman and her unique collections-based program, the Dole Archives hoped to challenge perceptions of the use-value of collections in general and emphasize their potential impact in a professional setting.

Though this effort was intriguing and successful, it was determined that this annual program take a different form if we were really going to promote understanding and appreciation for our own collection resources. In spring 2014, with the support of our Friends of the Dole Institute coordinator, we began a partnership with the KU Alumni Association (KUAA). We knew we would be able to create some kind of program based on Dole's personal or political connections to KU (he attended KU for 1.5 years, but did not graduate from KU), but what we zeroed in on was a passing comment made by the local KUAA chapter chair, recalling a memory of a Dole visit to KU, "sometime in 1966." Dole was a congressman at the time, and his records of that period, while well maintained, are significantly less in volume. After a classic frustrating search, we found the clipping documenting the visit (dated 1965, of course!).

The newspaper clipping was from the local newspaper, and featured Congressman Dole speaking with five KU students, identified in the caption, at a recognizable campus landmark. More digging revealed newsletters from the KU College Republicans announcing the visit, itineraries, and volunteer lists. A letter from then-Congressman Donald Rumsfeld (IL) touted Dole's KU campus tour (one of several campuses he visited that trip) as a model for Republican outreach to young people. We had found our hook—a "discovery," an inspiration from a personal story, a great glimpse at student life of the era, and also in line with the popular interest in the "Mad Men" era at the time. We wondered if we could track down the students pictured, presumably KU alumni, or others who had volunteered, to assess their recollection of the meeting in the program; we received three enthusiastic responses.

The final program was a big experiment: hybrid panel discussion, live oral history interview, and a primer on archival collections.[16] We wanted the participants to describe their memories of that day, KU life at the time, and Dole's ongoing influence in their life—the legacy of that encounter as they experienced it. It was a way to discuss Dole in a personal context, with a fixed sense of place that only could have been done in our place, with these people—and with *our* collection. The "treasure hunt" was part of the story—so I used a document camera and a few preselected boxes, files, and documents to attempt to give attendees a visual experience similar to researching an archive, realizing that most would never do it themselves.

The program model has continued. We also moved regular scheduling of the archive program to October, in honor of American Archives Month, sponsored by SAA. Fall 2014's installment of the series covered the 1974 U.S. Senate race in Kansas, Dole's closest and most hard-fought Senate campaign. Interviewees included Bill Roy, Jr., the son of Dole's campaign opponent, Congressman Bill Roy, and Dole's campaign manager, Dave Owen. We did not include the "live searching" of the archival material but did incorporate images of documents (including contemporary photos of the interviewees) and audio/video clips, which interviewees reacted to. Preceding the event was our Friends of the Dole Institute annual reception, and invitees included those who worked on either the Dole or the Roy campaigns, many of whom have been and are active in politics today, regionally and nationally. The nature of the subject matter, and the head-on take on the events of the day, helped underscore the Dole Institute's bipartisan values. In summer 2015, Congressman Roy's son contacted me on behalf of the family and donated a large collection of Dr. Roy's campaign materials, including records and many audio recordings of events in 1974. We were gratified that the Roy family would honor our repository in that way, giving us a fuller picture of the 1974 race and entwining the two men's legacies in our collections.

Commemorate ADA: A Project Becomes a Program[17]

Original content-based programming takes a lot of work—not just in research but in creating interpretive content and managing projects and relationships. However, if they come together as much as possible, around a unified theme, the work is done once and repurposed in multiple ways for different audiences. Our first full-scale effort was launched in summer 2015, as the Dole Institute commemorated the 25th anniversary of the 1990 Americans with Disabilities Act (ADA), called "the last civil rights act of the 20th century," the passage of which Dole himself has called his proudest achievement.

In 2011, the Dole Institute had received a financial gift from General Electric (GE) company to support students and efforts to commemorate the ADA's milestone. Among the funded programs were monies for student research in areas related to the ADA, archival and otherwise. With some internal discussion we were able to tap into this fund to support the in-house development of an exhibit related to Dole's disability advocacy, as an accompaniment to public programming series that unfolded in installments in fall 2015. The entire series was branded as commemorateADA, which began with a public exhibit opening on July 26, 25 years to the day that the ADA was signed into law. We also registered our events with the ADA Legacy Project,[18] a national clearinghouse for ADA history and education, and branded our exhibit and events accordingly. Four research grants were awarded, two based on archival research, the GE Archival Fellowship and the GE Curatorial Research Fellowship. Fittingly, the programming series closed with a two-week visit by our GE Archival Fellow in December 2015.

Our GE Curatorial Research Fellow, whose research focus is on veterans and disability, was based at KU and cocurated the exhibit, "Celebrating Opportunity for People with Disabilities: 70 Years of Dole Leadership," which was developed as two-dimensional graphic panels and an online web portal. We launched the project effort in January 2014, convening an exhibit committee comprising allied professionals on campus (director of museum studies graduate program, campus ADA coordinator, humanities specialist in Kansas history, our GE Curatorial Research Fellow, our own Public Education Coordinator, and later, the Dole Institute marketing coordinator). The concept was not for the exhibit to be of archival documents per se, but to let the documents "speak" as part of an interpretive narrative that told the story of Dole's leadership as only an archival collection can—not only in terms of seminal moments, or highly technical ins and outs of legislative history but also showing how work is done day to day, over a long time, and how that sustained vision and investment lead to meaningful change. Logistical challenges included our desire that the exhibit have a traveling program, when we had no existing traveling infrastructure (administration, marketing, or managed site contacts), the condition that any exhibit in the Dole Institute would be constrained to two-dimensional display in highly trafficked and relatively open environment, and the fact that this type of project had never been undertaken at our institution before. We also were especially conscious that an exhibit about disability issues be designed with accessibility in mind, as is good practice in any context.

We navigated the project through many limitations: departure of key staff, time of the volunteer committee members, and the limits of our own time and experience. The project changed scope and direction: the traveling portion of the exhibit was taken out, and integrative social media also proved too much for this time frame. However, the physical exhibit, which was designed on two-dimensional graphic panels, lent itself well to an experimental, open-source web platform; we were able to supplement the exhibit (physical and web) with over 12,000 pages of scanned archival material, digitized and searchable online; we enriched relationships with KU's Council for Social Studies, a student group of preservice teachers, and forged a new one with the Kansas Audio-Reader Network, which supplied us, in the last weeks of the project, a descriptive audio narration of the full exhibit.[19] We were able to arrange a promotional partnership between ourselves and Independence, Inc., a local organization that was the primary sponsor of a community ADA25 celebration at the local public library. Instead of competing with one another, we planned our events as a package weekend, and shared marketing exposure in print, online, and radio. Many of those from the disability community who attended the Saturday event at the library turned out the following Sunday afternoon at the Dole Institute for our exhibit opening, fulfilling the intention that the exhibit be an opportunity for disability advocates today to come together.

Our entire department, and most of Dole Institute staff, contributed to the production of these exhibits. The strategic choice of ADA and disability advocacy gave us all the opportunity, through collection research, to learn more about our collections' strengths in documenting disability advocacy, issues, policy, and leadership over the last half of the 20th century. The narrative we created and the analysis of collection materials have "fed" our other functions, including multiple class visits on subjects related to disability across departments (including Honors, History and American Studies), and laid the groundwork for an installment of "Your Story, His Story, the Legacy: The 1990 Americans with Disabilities Act," featuring Maureen

"Mo" West,[20] Senator Dole's legislative assistant for disability issues during the lead-up to the ADA, whose extensive efforts are well represented in the archives. Our GE Curatorial Research Fellow continues his work in our archives; he has also cross-promoted our exhibit with an ongoing seminar on disability studies conducted at our campus humanities center. The slate of formal commemorateADA events concluded with his visit in the fall of 2015 and a Friends of the Dole Institute coffee and conversation event with both GE archives researchers. The exhibit remained on display until July 2016, supporting academic, public, and K–12 programming on an ongoing basis. The effort we invested this year will continue to pay dividends for us. The relationships we built (and will continue to maintain) as a department and institution with KU faculty who are working on disability and accessibility issues, as well as the disability community in Kansas, have provided personal connections to follow up on for oral history, collection development, and potential reformatting/marketing of the exhibit as traveling pieces.

Political Programming

An extensive congressional collection could become the basis of an archives' public programming agenda, with the ability to reach multiple audiences on a near-limitless variety of subjects from the historical to the contemporary. Demonstrating this, however, will probably require stepping outside of one's comfort zone, as the emphasis shifts from connecting researchers to information resources to interpreting the resources for a general audience. An additional layer of complexity is added if within an active political or commemorative context—when general interest is likely to be high, but so too is risk to the "neutral" archives environment.

This risk is worthwhile. Continued funding for historical collections relies on the public's understanding and appreciation for, if not their use of, the content of our records. Most of the general public—not to mention university students—will never be sustained users of archival resources, online or on-site. We cannot attract new audiences without providing some context for what they are, what they mean, and how they can be used. A congressional collection reflects the concerns, the constituency, and the vast network of the individual member; it is a capture of society during a specific time, and its contents are both fascinating and relatable. In the Dole Archives we have many excellent commemorative opportunities in the coming years to replicate this community-based programming model, using the archives to connect with the public at large as well as Dole alumni: the 1976/1996 presidential campaigns, politics in the Vietnam War era, Dole's 1988 campaign for the Republican nomination, and policy areas of special interest to Senator Dole.

Programming of this sort is an investment, certainly, though not necessarily one of extensive financial resources. It takes time to identify, develop, and nurture partnerships, as well as the interpretive narrative context. In the case of the latter, we prioritize the collection itself as the central player—what we have drives student assignments, exhibit structure and content, and a program's participants and line of questioning. We attempt to "transmit" or "amplify" the material, rather than interpret it; to implement a journalistic approach versus an academic one; and to begin from a place of curiosity rather than expertise. As the steward of Senator Dole's documentary legacy, the Dole Archives serves a popular legacy in a popular way, and strives to make a programmatic impact proportional to the man whose life's work we preserve, at the institute named for him.

Notes

1. Frank Mackaman, "Congressional Collections: Where the Mundane Becomes Compelling," inn *American Political Archives Reader*, ed. Glenn Gray, L. Rebecca Johnson Melvin, and Karen Dawley Paul (Lanham, MD: Rowman & Littlefield Publishing Group, 2009), 419–427.

2. 110th US Congress, H.R. 307: "expressing the sense of Congress that Members' Congressional papers should be properly maintained and encouraging Members to take all necessary measures to manage and preserve their papers." On June 20, 2008, the Senate joined the House in approving the resolution. Richard A. Baker, "Reflections on the Modern History of Congressional History," in *American Political Archives Reader*, ed. Glenn Gray, L. Rebecca Johnson Melvin, Karen Dawley Paul (Lanham, MD: Rowman & Littlefield Publishing Group, 2009), 1–2.

3. Baker, "Reflections on the Modern History of Congressional History."

4. Repositories holding congressional collections can be identified from an index prepared by the Center for Legislative Archives, which is extensive but not exhaustive: http://www.archives.gov/legislative/repository-collections/. Professionals engaged in the preservation of congressional papers can be found in the membership lists of the Association for Studies of Congress, http://www.congresscenters.org/; and the Congressional Papers Roundtable of the Society of American Archivists, http://www2.archivists.org/groups/congressional-papers-roundtable All sites accessed on January 12, 2016.

5. http://www.archives.gov/nhprc/about/, retrieved January 12, 2016.

6. The working papers of Supreme Court justices are also the property of each individual justice. A great discussion of this can be found in the December 1, 2014, issue of *The New Yorker* magazine: Jill Lepore, "The Great Paper Caper," accessed January 12, 2016, http://www.newyorker.com/magazine/2014/12/01/great-paper -caper.

7. Official information products of Congress, such as the *Congressional Record*, are produced and preserved by the U.S. Government Printing Office. The Office of Art & Archives, under the Office of the Clerk of the House, and the Senate Historical Office document the institutional history of Congress. The National Archives & Records Administration preserves official House and Senate and committee records and records from legislative branch organizations and commissions in the Center for Legislative Archives. https://www.archives.gov/legislative/.

8. The Bicentennial Minutes were compiled in a published volume. Robert J. Dole, *Historical Almanac of the United States Senate*, ed. Richard A. Baker and Wendy Wolff (Washington, D.C.: U.S. Government Printing Office, 1989).

9. Raymond W. Smock, "Resources and Perspectives" remarks from a panel discussion the State of Congressional History, delivered on April 5, 2014, at the Annual Meeting of the Society for History in the Federal Government, published in *Federal History Journal*, no. 7 (2015): 77–81.

10. Barbara Haws, "Advocating within the Institution: Twenty-Five Years for the New York Philharmonic Archives," in *Many Happy Returns: Advocacy and the Development of Archives*, ed. Larry Hackman (Chicago: Society of American Archivists, 2011), 192.

11. Ibid.

12. Robert J. Dole Archive & Special Collections, "Identity Statements, Version Nov 2014" (working paper, Dole Institute of Politics, Lawrence, Kansas, 2014).

13. More information available at http://www.neh.gov/commongood/about.

14. Truman Library's White House Decision Center is one example of a successful leadership program based on historical documents; accessed January 12, 2016, http://www.trumanlibrary.org/whdc/.

15. Dole Archives 2014 Visiting Fellow program, "Innovation in Plain Sight: Transforming Our National Security Landscape with Museum Collections" with Amy Herman, May 2014; accessed January 12, 2016, https://www.youtube.com/watch?v=3upZ4RLGbmk&list=PLaTmc9U0F6DbgnlLqhHmFRR01ZZqvCaiq&index=19.

16. "Your Story, His Story, the Legacy: Snapshots in Time from the Dole Archives," March 24, 2014; accessed January 12, 2016, https://www.youtube.com/watch?v=Pg-IKX90GEQ&list=PLaTmc9U0F6DbgnlLqhHmFRR01ZZqvCaiq&index=7.

17. Digital Project, Dole Archives: "Celebrating Opportunity for People with Disabilities: 70 Years of Dole Leadership," http://dolearchivecollections.ku.edu/collections/ada/. In September 2015, the website received a Technology Award from the Kansas Museums Association. From launch date in late July to December 15, the site garnered 1,355 web hits. The site is also a featured link on the website of the Kansas Commission on Disability Concerns; https://kcdcinfo.ks.gov/disability-history/national-events.

18. The ADA Legacy Project, www.adalegacy.com.

19. In July 2016, the Dole Institute and the Kansas Audio-Reader Network received the American Council of the Blind's 2016 Audio Description Achievement Award in Museums/Visual Arts/Visitor Centers for their shared "outstanding contributions to the establishment and/or continued development of significant audio description programs in each of three areas: media, performing arts, and museums."

20. "Your Story, His Story, the Legacy: The 1990 Americans with Disabilities Act" with Maureen West, October 7, 2015, https://www.youtube.com/watch?v=s-g_vyTZTwY.

Chapter 7
Collecting Printed Books in a Digital Age

John Overholt

Librarians are all too familiar with the cry of the budget-cutter: "What do you need libraries for? Isn't everything online now?" We know quite well that this isn't true at all, most especially in the realm of special collections. But what about when it *is* true—at least for some specified subset of "everything"? The set of surviving printed books from the handpress era is large, certainly, but it isn't infinite. I don't expect everything in that set to be available digitally within my lifetime, but it will happen eventually, barring societal collapse to the point that the study of the past is no longer pursued. (Such a scenario lies outside the scope of the present chapter.)

When that moment comes, will we simply close the reading rooms, and stride out into the sunshine of a blissful postprint future? I don't believe that, and I doubt anyone reading this does either. Print collections will continue to have important uses in scholarly research. This is a critical moment, however, to consider what those uses will be. If any profession ought to pride itself on taking the long view, surely special collections librarianship should. Our collections span centuries, even millennia, and are the product of conscious choices about what to preserve for the future.

Books have many uses, but fundamentally they exist to transmit texts, and it's that use that is most readily supplanted by digitization. I work in a large special collections library situated next door to one of the world's great research libraries. I have books in profusion, steps away from my desk. Yet when I want a text merely for text's sake and for quick reference if not prolonged reading, I usually check to see if it's online first. Am I lazy? Possibly, but I don't think I'm *exceptionally* lazy, and in any event I'm not on trial here.

Since the first book was digitized—arguably since the first book was microfilmed—what we might call the "business case" of a special collections library as a repository of texts has been on the wane. Every year that passes will bring fewer patrons through the door in search of a text they can read no other way than through a printed book paged to a reading room.

Special collections libraries are expensive beasts to maintain, and the funding they need to survive will evaporate if we don't adapt to changing circumstances. We demonstrate our relevance in lots of ways, of course, but one of the most fundamental is putting researcher posteriors in reading room seats. I don't expect this to change as a crucial benchmark of the usefulness of special collections.

What, then, are the qualities of a book that future researchers will find compelling enough to continue to trek to our libraries and use our collections? How can we prioritize those qualities in our acquisition practices in the hope of "future-proofing" our collections? What is our best guess about what scholars of 50 or 100 years from now will need from us? It can only be a guess, but collecting is about making choices, and those choices will be better the more they are intentional and well-informed.

Variant Texts

The conventional account of the advent of printing as the great standardizer of texts tends to obscure the extent to which early books are handmade objects, and bear all the hallmarks of the fallible humans who made them. Within the press run of notionally identical books, it is frequently the case that errors are corrected, errors are introduced, controversial passages are softened or removed, late-breaking discoveries are inserted, shifting political fortunes necessitate a change in dedicatees, or some damn fool knocks all the type onto the floor. Each of these incidents, however great or minor, provides invaluable, and otherwise unobtainable, evidence about the process of printing a book. They tell us about the specific factors that added up to the text by which we know a great work, but they also enrich our understanding of the general conditions under which all books were produced in the past. Hardly any books of the handpress period have been examined with the scrupulousness of Hinman's study of the First Folio, and our collections hold uncountable pieces of this evidence yet undiscovered.

Provenance

Most books in a special collections library have had multiple owners before they reach our shelves. While not all owners leave behind a bookplate or inscription as a record of their ownership, those who do allow us to trace the life of a book in the hands of its readers. Intense scholarly attention has long been devoted to the production and sale of books—so much so that the point at which they begin to serve the function for which they were intended feels comparatively understudied still. Understanding who buys a book and why is crucial to understanding the role that book plays in culture, both at the time of publication and in the years following. In the aggregate, too, books flow through an ecosystem of owners, booksellers, auction houses, and libraries that can only be understood and described by recognizing and recording the traces left behind by each stage of the process.

Annotations

Every book can be thought of as a conversation between an author and a reader. Annotated books preserve the otherwise ephemeral traces of the reader's half of that conversation. Having one's words preserved in print was historically a privilege available to relatively few; annotations capture a much greater diversity of voices than would otherwise be available to scholarship.

A particularly compelling example of this is in Houghton's collections: the annotated books of Hester Thrale Piozzi. She and James Boswell were rivals in their friendship with Samuel Johnson during his life, and rivals for control of his biographical legacy after his death. Boswell decisively won the battle of biographies, and his dismissive account of Piozzi could easily be the dominant view today. But the quick wit and fierce intelligence that shine out from the margins of her books have been crucial to a richer understanding of her life.

Artifactual Value

The printed book was the most important medium of intellectual exchange over the course of half a millennium. Regardless of what the future holds for the book, its importance in that period will never change. We cannot fully understand the culture of an era without physical copies of its books to study. Digitization imposes a sameness on books that obscures crucial information. Is this book large or small? Was it beautifully made or hastily made? Was it expensive to its owner or cheap? I hesitate to invoke the cliché of the smell of old books, but in fact *every* physical quality they possess is a potential piece of historical evidence. That evidence situates a given book within its milieu and helps us comprehend what it meant to the people who created it, and to the people who read it.

Qualities That Resist Digitization

The kind of photograph taken by a digital lab is more a mug shot than a portrait. Its goal is to represent the object as neutrally as possible, which is as it should be, but it can often be a pale comparison with seeing it in person. You can see a hundred pictures of a Kelmscott Chaucer printed on vellum and still not be prepared for the wallop of opening the real book. The contrast between the luminous page and the dense profusion of deepest black ink radiates an energy that simply doesn't translate into a photograph.

Iconic Value

Two of the printed books at my institution that have the highest circulation are perhaps surprising in the light of our usual presumptions about the works consulted at special collections libraries. One is the first edition of the Book of Mormon, and the other is a book bound in human skin. The thing these books have in common (and to be clear I mean to draw no other comparison between them) is that seeing them in person demonstrably offers an experience that cannot be had any other way. Adherents of the Church of Jesus Christ of Latter-day Saints visit the book as an act of pilgrimage. Those who come to see the human skin binding are seeking the thrill of a transgressive, taboo object. Images of both these books are available online, but in neither case do the images satisfy this desire to see and touch for oneself. These visitors are not typical of those who most frequently come to our reading rooms, but perhaps that makes them even more interesting.

Promotional Value

I am a firm believer in the power of exciting acquisitions to draw attention to the ongoing work of special collections to existing users, and help demonstrate what that work is to potential ones. Attention is a scarce and finite resource, and special collections libraries can make savvy use of exciting new acquisitions to command it—they provide an excellent "news hook" in a way that existing collections may not. I base my acquisitions decisions first and foremost on their long-term value for my library, but it's always worth pausing to ask "Who will be excited to hear that we have this, and what's the best way to reach them?" I use my and my institution's social media presence, and the relationships I've built with news media on campus and off, to share information about the interesting books I'm buying.

I don't expect that any of these reflections will feel individually revelatory. I have, however, found that articulating them here has helped to inform my own thinking about the books I acquire for my institution, and I hope that it can perform the same function for others. So often, the things that seem to go without saying are the things that need to be said as frequently as possible. To acquire books for an institutional library is to make a commitment that will likely last far beyond our own lifetimes. Every purchase is an opportunity to reflect on the nature of that commitment, and on what benefits will derive to the future from the decisions we make today.

Chapter 8
Digital Acquisitions and Appraisal

Sarah Barsness and Anjanette Schussler

Introduction

By now, most institutions have acquired some kind of digital material for their collections, but few institutions have developed a system for working with such materials that is as efficient as their processes for analog collections. Instead, digital materials are approached on a case-by-case basis, relying heavily on the work of one or two digital specialists to shepherd the collection from acquisition to access. This ad hoc, specialist-based model has generally sufficed for many years, but it is hardly sustainable in light of the ubiquity of digital files in our everyday lives. This chapter seeks to help institutions consider how they might better improve their processes for digital acquisition and to propose a programmatic approach for dealing with digital materials that leverages existing processes and lessens institutional reliance on digital specialists or project-based committees.

It is no longer in doubt whether or not the kinds of materials we as information professionals collect will become digitally based: that has already happened. Nearly all the contemporary materials our institutions collect, from government records to correspondence to book manuscripts, are now created digitally and later converted to an analog format. Rather than a matter of *if* our world will become digital, it is a question of *when* it will become impractical to collect materials in anything other than their native digital format. It is doubtful that we will ever stop collecting paper materials, but our society's increasing comfort and fluency in the digital realm mean that more and more significant evidence of our culture exists digitally, often in formats that cannot fully be captured in an analog way. Even materials that can be saved on paper are increasingly impractical to convert because of their complexity and volume.

These materials pose unique challenges to staff who care for and preserve digital objects, but there is a dedicated and talented class of digital preservationists who are working hard to develop increasingly sophisticated and long-term answers to those challenges. Institutions, consortia, grant projects, and even informal social networking groups dedicated to digital preservation serve as places to develop skills, ask for advice, address problems, and develop industry-best practices; several such resources are outlined at the end of this chapter. Groups such as these have developed countless tools, standards, and guidelines that are available for anyone working with digital materials to use, and cover the ingest process all the way to long-term preservation. We have also established best practices and preferred preservation formats for the vast majority of the digital materials that walk through our door. The area of digital curation is still growing and changing, but all told, our field has the knowledge we need to deal with these materials; we simply lack the infrastructure to efficiently and programmatically apply that knowledge within our individual institutions.

Instead of avoiding digital acquisitions altogether or leaving electronic materials unprocessed and unpreserved, one way many staff in institutions choose to work around this lack of infrastructure is to rely heavily on digital specialists. However, such a workflow is inefficient and highly demanding of everyone's time, particularly the specialist's.

This system, of course, relies on an institution's ability to devote most or all of the work time of a digital specialist to addressing digital collections. More often, institutions have a de facto specialist, someone who is more comfortable (or perhaps even just the person who is least uncomfortable) with digital collections; this de facto specialist is then faced with the impossible task of keeping up with a field that is complex and fast moving, in addition to the everyday demands of other, nondigital work. Situations such as these often leave the de facto specialist overwhelmed, with little time to work on preserving and keeping up with digital materials, causing the integrity of the materials to be called into question.

Instead, a more sustainable approach is to help *all* staff gain enough digital fluency to allow them to do their normal work with any collection, regardless of whether it is digital or analog; this would free up specialists to consult on special cases, help build the institution's digital infrastructure, and increase and improve the institution's ability to preserve an increasing range of digital materials. And if hiring a specialist isn't a possibility, educating and training staff in basic digital preservation will allow them to do the work that needs to be done, instead of letting it, and the files, languish and become slowly unusable.

In particular, the areas of digital appraisal and acquisition could benefit greatly from such an approach: if staff members who appraise and acquire have a basic understanding of some of the core issues pertinent to acquiring digital materials, they will be better able to work with creators and dealers to bring materials into the institution with little need for input from a digital specialist. Unfortunately, there is very little professional literature dedicated to addressing the appraisal and acquisition of digital collections; one of the best examples of this limited field is the excellent Council on Library and Information Resources report "Born Digital: Guidance for Donors, Dealers, and Archival Repositories."[1] Even this report, abounding in sound advice, suggests workflows that rely on digital specialists for nearly every stage of the acquisition process.

As we seek to build truly sustainable digital appraisal and acquisitions processes by increasing the confidence and digital fluency of acquisitions staff, it helps to think of digital acquisition as a subset of acquisitions more generally. Many of the same considerations and concerns arise when thinking of a digital accession as an analog one: content, provenance, condition, and potential access restrictions, all play a role when choosing to acquire any kind of collection. Purchasing digital collections from dealers, as with analog collections, requires careful investigation of ownership, the dealer's ability to transfer copyright and other intellectual property rights, and risks associated with unknown and/or unguaranteed condition of materials. Other universal considerations take on new complexity and urgency when working in the digital realm specifically; privacy, ownership and rights, and preservation of media require special attention. These issues are inherent in the work of making collections of historical significance publicly accessible; through careful and well-informed appraisal and processing, we can lessen the legal and reputational risks to our institutions. In the following sections, we will discuss each of these areas, including what acquisitions staff need to know in order to confidently appraise born-digital materials.

Issue One: Privacy

Effective management of the publicly identifiable information that could be found in a digital collection is an important consideration during appraisal and acquisition. Imagine that your computer or smartphone is one day donated to a research institution; one would suppose there is a good amount of material on it right now that you'd rather not be accessible to the public, such as browser history, downloads, photos, and financial data. And the material that you would want donated is probably not particularly well organized. An archivist or a librarian receiving such a device for preservation would have a difficult time providing access to the useful information on it because of its state of disarray. This is a scenario that can be avoided with a bit of predonation meeting time with donors whenever possible, so that they can be in control of what they donate and that it is organized in a way that makes sense.

Just as a paper collection could contain documents with such information as social security numbers, criminal records, medical information, financial data, and more, digital materials could also contain these sorts of records. The difference is they can be much harder to find, given the size and level of (dis)organization of many digital accessions. Instead of being able to, for example, easily identify and pull out a folder marked "taxes" or "health information" from a box of paper records (if you're lucky and the records have been organized by the donor), digital records often aren't as well maintained or weeded very much, if at all.

Digital records management can seem tedious, and with a seemingly infinite amount of storage space available, there often aren't compelling reasons to do it. Most people likely don't do it all that much in their personal lives, and when transferring their materials to a repository, copying and pasting documents from one folder onto a flash drive takes much less time. It's easier to leave the weeding to the archivist, after all. As much as an archivist would love to sift through millions of digital files one by one (or perhaps not), this just isn't feasible. While there are some computer programs that can search for specific pieces of data in a set of digital files, such as social security or credit card numbers, the risk of private, confidential data remaining in a digital collection waiting to be discovered by someone is quite high.

Potential donors need to be aware of these risks before they hand over their data. While the occasional donor is up to date on digital privacy, it is more likely that you will receive collections from people who haven't thought about this issue at all. We believe that, as information professionals, we have an ethical imperative to inform people about the potential risks of donating digital materials so that they can make fully informed decisions, and also that there aren't any surprises that pop up during or after the process. Reaching donors before a transfer occurs and assisting them with basic management of their digital records will go a long way toward making them feel more secure, strengthening relationships with your institution, and lessening any future liability issues that may arise.

The level of scrutiny that should be placed on digital collections depends on what sort of material is being collected; it's important to first be familiar with any statutes or federal laws in place that affect access to data. For example, in Minnesota, adoption records are private for 100 years after the date that the adoption was granted,[2] unless someone is granted a court order. Private medical data are similarly protected, and staff in repositories need to keep that in mind when determining whether a collection is open to the public or should in some way be restricted. If you're working with a collection that may contain any information that is protected, it is especially important to communicate with the donor about this, and look through the materials very carefully, to make sure laws are being followed and privacy is being protected.

Aside from legal restrictions, there may also be ethical considerations, such as information that, while not legally required to be kept private, is still sensitive or potentially revealing. For example, does the content of an acquisition feature details about people who are still alive and who may or may not know that researchers will have access to information about them? This issue often comes up in donations of diaries and journals or correspondence; donors may decide to restrict access to such materials for a certain period of time, such as 75 years after donation, to ensure that the immediate people involved are no longer living, or to at least provide a generous buffer of time before the collection becomes public. There may also be items that the donor just wouldn't want other people to see, such as tax documents, browser history, document drafts, and other transitory pieces of information. This is a decision that we should assist donors in making, as it may not be something they have considered, but it has the potential for embarrassment or negative reactions to occur. There will always be situations, such as with purchased collections, where we are responsible for making decisions about privacy and security on the behalf of creators; as with paper collections, we must strike a balance between our ethical obligations to both the creator and those represented in their materials and our obligations to researchers.

While we can and should walk donors through legal and ethical issues to think about, there is bound to be a gap in terms of publicly identifiable information screening between what is possible for us to do and what is feasible. Only so many precautions can be taken, especially if the information isn't very well organized and can't be thoroughly screened. Discussing these situations with donors will help them to make fully informed decisions about what exactly they want to leave behind, and how to provide the most appropriate access. As the saying goes, an ounce of prevention is worth a pound of cure; by taking in only what you want from a particular collection, processing, describing, and providing access will be that much easier, which means that researchers can use the collection sooner and more easily, without compromising the donor's privacy.

On the other hand, there can be legitimate reasons to provide comprehensive access to someone's digital collections, as in digital humanities research. If a researcher in literature or the social sciences wanted to be able to get a complete picture of how a person worked and what a person's digital life was like, being able to access that person's entire computer or set of data would be the best way to go about it. Sometimes the most interesting information to a researcher in these cases isn't the content itself but rather the thought processes of the creator, how that person worked, what a draft versus the final version of an essay looked like, and the like. Weeding out too much material can hinder such paths of inquiry; it is up to the archivist to strike an appropriate balance between researchers' needs and donors' privacy.

A notable example of this is the Salman Rushdie archives, which include four computers and a hard drive, at the Manuscript, Archives, and Rare Book Library at Emory University. Researchers use an emulator to view the desktop of one of Rushdie's computers on the last day he used it, minus some personal files that were deleted before this was made publicly accessible.[3] Another example is the Susan Sontag archives at the University of California, Los Angeles (UCLA). In addition to paper materials, there are also digital components, and another *New Yorker* article, from January 30, 2014, discusses how UCLA provides access to them. "The machines themselves are not in the library, however: future researchers will consult the material on a laptop in the reading room with software that displays it as Sontag would have seen it. This is to protect the physical files."[4]

Issue Two: Ownership and Rights

Establishing ownership and ensuring that rights are properly transferred with the deed of gift are key steps in the acquisition process with any accession, as they form the legal basis on which the institution preserves and provides access to the materials. In the digital realm, these matters take on new urgency, because of both increased complexity and the increased risks associated with the heightened exposure that comes with providing online digital access.

When considering a digital accession, it is particularly important to work with donors/dealers to establish ownership of the materials being transferred. In many cases, this can be quite straightforward (for example, an author's drafts of a book or a business's staff newsletter), but it can also be quite complex (like sorting a musician's home recordings from studio tracks that have different ownership from commercially purchased music, all stored on the same device). Collaboratively created works (correspondence, documents with multiple creators, and so forth) represent one problem, while files created using software with terms of use that affect ownership pose another. Each type of software or service used by the creator (for example, cloud storage service, social media platform, and so forth) should include information about intellectual property and copyright in their terms of service; if a collection has a large quantity of items that were created using a given service or proprietary software, it is worthwhile to do further research to ensure that there are no complications with providing public access to these materials. Collections that are purchased should have a clearly documented chain of ownership if possible to establish both provenance and ownership rights that can be transferred through the sale of the materials.

Another issue common to both analog and digital appraisal is the clarification of what rights and permissions are retained by the donor. With analog materials, this frequently takes the form of special access or waived copy/usage fees. Digital materials complicate matters somewhat because they are so easily duplicated and disseminated without any sort of generational loss; for all intents and purposes, there is no difference between a digital original and a digital copy. Many donors may wish to retain a copy of their materials for personal or business purposes. It is, therefore, important to work closely with them to establish what rights and permissions they retain and for how long, and to ensure they understand the rights they are giving up by completing the transfer. Such frank discussions can help to clarify expectations and responsibilities all around and ensure that the donor is comfortable with all aspects of the gift.

One area of digital ownership that varies significantly from analog is when hard drives or entire computers are accessioned, as such collections will almost always contain materials the donor does not own but which are vital to the operation of the device and the accurate rendering of the digital objects on it. Frequently, operating systems and software are licensed to individuals for use, not owned as such analogous nondigital frameworks might be. The terms of the license frequently limit the ways in which the licensee can use the software; donating a copy of the software, preserving it, or providing open online access to it may not be allowed under the terms of use.

Frequently, licensed software can easily be excluded from an accession, but other times the digital objects included are fundamentally dependent on a licensed product; this is true of architectural, CAD, and other similarly complex design files. In such instances, it is helpful to refer to a technical specialist and/or to conduct your own further research to determine what options exist for access and preservation. Are there other migration formats available that would faithfully render the digital object? What would it cost to get the proper permissions to emulate the software? Weighing the value of digital objects against the costs of maintaining them may well lead you to decide to exclude certain items from an accession entirely. Such preweeding work, while time-consuming, will ultimately improve the quality of the collection and ensure that what comes into the institution is able to be legally preserved and put online for researchers.

After working with donors/dealers to check the materials' ownership and to ensure that all parties are in agreement about the terms of the gift, the final piece is to ensure that these details are fully and explicitly outlined in the deed of gift or other legal transfer form. Some institutions have adapted their existing standard forms to include born-digital accessions, while others have developed a special form specifically for these materials. Most institutions, however, lack forms that can address these digital rights and privacy issues. When the standard form is insufficient, staff and donors should work together to amend and expand it with addenda that cover privacy, rights, and ownership of both digital objects and the physical media that house them.

Issue Three: Physical Media versus Digital Items

Unlike paper collections, digital donations can arrive in many different forms, including flash drives, external hard drives, or burned CDs; they can be transferred via FTP or e-mail attachments; or a donor could supply access to the institution's cloud storage service. No matter what media are used to transfer the materials, all of these methods are likely to transfer *a copy* of the materials to the institution, rather than *the original*.

Paper collections generally include any final versions of documents, such as the official copy of a report; someone transferring such a collection would realize that the official versions were now a part of a research institution, meaning that the donor would no longer have a copy. The donation process with digital files is different; it is not so much a transfer or donation of records as it is providing duplicate copies of records to an institution for preservation and access. Digital files are able to be copied endlessly, and establishing which version of a document is official or most complete can be very difficult if it is not well labeled, especially if more than one person worked on the same file.

In addition to being aware of issues with file versions, there is an increasing need for institutions to accept postcustodial digital donations, and these require more work for the information professional than traditional donations. Instead of making arrangements for the pickup and delivery of boxes of records, and putting them in storage until there is time to work on them, digital donations require communication in advance between you and the donor/dealer about how and when the files will arrive. While some digital collections may come on a medium that the institution can keep, such as a flash drive, some donors may prefer to have storage media returned. Perhaps a donor is interested in using a file-sharing site to make digital files available for download, and the provided link to access them will only be active for a certain amount of time. Such transfers of digital files will need to get done quickly: it is important to ensure that transfers are accurate and complete, and that all of the files that were agreed upon were received. Additionally, after the transfer, appropriate backup copies and checksums of the files will need to be done right away for preservation purposes.

Working carefully with donors ahead of such a transfer helps to establish a donation timetable and security protocols. It's possible that digital collections you receive may contain malware or other unknown security risks, so it's important to take appropriate precautions to make sure your network stays secure and isn't compromised when you're working with a new digital acquisition. For example, some institutions have a dedicated unnetworked workstation for processing digital collections, so that any malware in a digital collection doesn't infect the whole network. You will also need to make sure that any remote transfer methods used by the donor are trustworthy and secure, as well as free and easy to use, meaning that no paid software or subscription is required. Ideally there will be as few obstacles to donating as possible. The goal is to make this an easy process for the donor. There may be donors who are more aware of security issues such as these, and they may want to know about how you and your institution will handle their digital collection and what security protocols are in place.

Another item to consider is the ownership of both physical media and digital files; will you provide a hard drive for transfer of digital collections, or will the donor? If the donor provides it, will the donor want, for instance, the 2 TB external hard drive returned, or is it okay if your institution keeps it for future use? Is the hard drive password protected? This can be an easy issue to forget, but it's very simple to address and it keeps the transfer process smooth from start to finish. If the media is to be donated, it's a good idea to address personal security with the donor, such as, will the hard drive be kept and reused? How will the donor's data be securely erased, so that no one else will be able to access it? If the media is destroyed, how will that be done and by whom? Securely disposing of media is recommended particularly if it held confidential or sensitive data; merely deleting files off of a hard drive does not mean that the information is actually gone.

Used hard drives that were not sanitized correctly often contain residual data that digital forensics experts will be able to recover. There are many examples[5] of this on the ForensicsWiki Web site,[6] including a particularly notable instance from July 2013, in which a branch of the United Kingdom's National Health Service was fined[7] after one of its hard drives, which had been improperly disposed of, turned up on eBay; it had 3,000 patient records that the buyer was able to restore using data recovery software. The drive was supposed to be recycled by a third party, but the contractor sold the hard drives online instead. A similarly disturbing statistic from the United Kingdom's Information Commissioner's Office in 2012 found that 1 in 10 used hard drives contains personal data that can be recovered by digital forensics software.[8] These examples may seem extreme, but they illustrate why it is important to securely dispose of digital collections; given enough time, it is possible for an individual with the right tools and skills to recover virtually anything.

It's a good idea to talk about the possibility of your institution obtaining copies of digital files in the future, in case a mishap occurs and something is accidentally deleted, or if you're working with a corrupted drive of some kind and can't retrieve the data from it. Ideally, a digital collection would be backed up onto a server as soon as it was received, but realistically, it may be some time before the files can be pulled off of the media they arrived on, such as if your department needs to wait until a new fiscal year to purchase more server space. Another scenario may be that by the time someone is able to work in it, the media will have failed; Will you or a colleague be able to get second, identical copies of everything from the creator? Discuss these possibilities with the donor.

Some institutions have already done work in this arena and have compiled information and transfer forms specifically for digital records, including the Washington State Archives. There is a significant amount of information on its Web site[9] on how state agencies should transfer digital files and e-mails to their collection; it has a "transfer information plan,"[10] which covers everything from identifying the records and potential restrictions, future additions to the donation, the method of transfer, converting donations into other formats, contact information, and image formats. Its transfer form/transmittal agreement[11] covers access to the files being donated, and specifically states, "Public access to records may be provided through the Digital Archives Web site, with the exception of those identified by the Partner on a Transfer Information Plan (TIP) as confidential, privileged, or exempt from public disclosure."

Addressing ownership of media and its secure disposition, future access to digital donations, and copyright issues in a deed of gift may seem unusual or cumbersome, but doing so can be very important. It is generally painless to do, and it will demonstrate that you take security and access concerns seriously. Taking care of all of this in the beginning of the process is much easier than quickly trying to figure out if the collection can be put online, who holds the copyright of a file, and what should be done with donated media when it is no longer needed.

Future Directions

As we have considered the process by which we acquire and appraise digital materials throughout this chapter, several themes have emerged; these themes serve as core directives to guide our local practices as we seek to move our institutions toward an increasingly digital future. By emphasizing communication, improved documentation, and sustainable workflows, we can build our institution's capacity to effectively and programmatically appraise and accession digital materials.

Effective communication with donors and dealers of digital collections is a vital step, though it may occasionally be a time-consuming one. Many donors lack technical expertise on digital issues, but they are subject experts on their own materials. By educating donors, archivists not only fulfill their ethical imperative to be honest with donors about their materials, but are also better able to gain information and context from the donors to help all parties make informed decisions.

A successful digital records transfer depends not only on communication between donors/dealers and archivists, but also on fully documenting the materials and the entire transfer process. Archivists should make sure donors/dealers have completely documented their materials before starting the transfer process. Documenting materials to be excluded, institutional responsibilities for protecting private information, rights transferred to the institution, rights retained by the donor, and legal transfer of both digital objects and the media on which they reside will generate a robust and reliable legal document that is useful for both the donor and the institution for years to come.

Lastly, collaborative and sustainable workflows that mirror existing processes for analog materials can help institutions to increase their ability to efficiently take in digital items by taking advantage of the expertise of appraising archivists and, if available, utilizing digital specialists only where needed. Such an approach may seem intimidating to staff who are less comfortable in the digital realm, and it can be tempting to leave everything to a digital specialist, but the reality is that many institutions cannot afford such a staff person. Additionally, digital collections will continue to be a bigger and bigger part of what we collect, and blended digital/paper collections will become the norm, if they haven't already. This is why it is especially important for everyone who works on collections in your institution to be familiar with the issues raised in this chapter. It's entirely acceptable to have one person who works on digital collections more often, but it's also important to recognize how everyone else works or will work with digital collections at some point in the life cycle of the collection, beginning with seeking donations, following through to processing collections, and doing regular preservation work on them. Nonspecialists and specialists alike in digital collections will need to work together throughout the donation process.

Digital collections shouldn't be seen as a specialized category that inhabit their own silo, separate from everything else; they are integrated into everything we do, so it's important to be nimble and know how to work with them and the people who wish to donate them. Additionally, there are very few instances of purely digital collections; most have an analog component that must be considered alongside the digital objects, which is much easier to do if the two sets are not artificially separated. Everyone working on the acquisition of collections in general needs to have basic digital literacy and access to resources and assistance in order to continue to be effective and responsible collectors. Building, maintaining, and expanding our digital skills is best done by keeping up to date with what's going on in the world of digital curation, forensics, and archives—new projects and advances in the field are happening all the time, and we can learn from each other.

Selected Resources and Further Reading

Digital Curation Basics

Digital Archives Specialist (DAS) Curriculum and Certificate Program.
http://www2.archivists.org/prof-education/das.
The Society of American Archivists' DAS (Digital Archives Specialist) curriculum's foundational-level courses address knowledge and skills that are essential for working with digital records.

"Digital Preservation Management: Implementing Short-Term Strategies for Long-Term Solutions." Digital Preservation Management Workshops and Tutorial. 2003. http://www.dpworkshop.org.
The online tutorial offers a well-rounded introduction to the core issues of digital preservation. Accompanying workshops are also available.

Digging Deeper

Redwine, Gabriela, et al. "Born Digital: Guidance for Donors, Dealers, and Archival Repositories." October 2013, http://www.clir.org/pubs/reports/pub159/pub159.pdf.
The excellent CLIR report offers an in-depth look at many of the issues surrounding digital acquisition and appraisal, and deeply informed the formation of this chapter.

Corrado, Edward M., and Heather Lea Moulaison. *Digital Preservation for Libraries, Archives, and Museums.* Lanham, MD: Rowman & Littlefield, 2014.
This volume provides an in-depth look at the digital preservation field, covering concepts and practices in more depth than some of the other resources listed here.

Digital Preservation Outreach & Education. http://www.digitalpreservation.gov/education/index.html.
The Library of Congress uses DPOE to educate professionals globally using a curriculum that divides the large and unwieldy world of digital preservation into six phases that closely mirror core archival functions.

The Open Preservation Foundation. http://openpreservation.org/.
The OPF is an organization that aims to serve the digital preservation field. Its members are frequently developing new tools and standards for the field, making them a good resource for both knowledge and for specific tools.

The Signal: Digital Preservation. http://blogs.loc.gov/digitalpreservation/.
The Signal is a blog that marries approachable language with exciting work on the cutting edge of the digital preservation field.

Resources for Practitioners

Community Owned Digital Preservation Tool Registry. http://coptr.digipres.org/Main_Page.
The COPTR is a wiki-style resource that helps practitioners identify tools to meet specific digital preservation needs; the site can be searched or browsed in various ways.

DigiPres Commons Community-owned Digital Preservation Resources. DigiPres Commons http://www.digipres.org/.

The DigiPres Commons is a community-owned collection of resources aimed at helping fellow practitioners build stronger and more robust digital preservation programs by linking out to other helpful projects, including some of the other resources in this section.

Digital Curation Google Group. https://groups.google.com/forum/#!forum/digital-curation.

The Digital Curation Google Group is a technically minded and digitally focused take on the classic professional forum / listserv. Common topics include news about conferences, announcements of new tools, job postings, and collaborative troubleshooting of commonly used software.

Digital POWRR Digital Preservation Research. http://digitalpowrr.niu.edu/.

The POWRR project is a grant-funded effort from a consortium of Illinois institutions with the original aim of collecting a list of digital preservation tools and evaluating them through the lens of an institution with few resources to devote to a digital preservation program. Since then, the project has expanded to include more in-depth evaluations of specific tools and to nationwide workshops to help institutions with practical, hands-on instruction.

Digital Preservation Q&A. http://qanda.digipres.org/.

The Digital Preservation Q&A site, moderated jointly by the Open Preservation Foundation and the NDSA, offers an informal, searchable forum where practitioners help each other address questions from the general to the specific.

National Digital Stewardship Alliance. http://www.digitalpreservation.gov/ndsa/.

The NDSA uses working groups, awards, case studies, reports, and other projects to connect digital preservation professionals, identify issues in the field that require further development, and connect practitioners with new tools and resources.

Notes

1. Gabriela Redwine et al., "Born Digital: Guidance for Donors, Dealers, and Archival Repositories," October 2013, http://www.clir.org/pubs/reports/pub159/pub159.pdf.

2. Minnesota State Revisor of Statutes, "259.79—2014 Minnesota Statutes," accessed August 6, 2015, https://www.revisor.mn.gov/statutes/?id=259.79.

3. Dan Rockmore, "The Digital Life of Salman Rushdie," July 29, 2014, http://www.newyorker.com/tech/elements/digital-life-salman-rushdie.

4. Benjamin Moser, "In the Sontag Archives," January 30, 2014, http://www.newyorker.com/books/page-turner/in-the-sontag-archives.

5. "Residual Data on Used Equipment," last modified December 4, 2013, http://forensicswiki.org/wiki/Residual_Data_on_Used_Equipment.

6. "ForensicsWiki," last modified June 16, 2014, http://forensicswiki.org/wiki/Main_Page.

7. John E. Dunn, "Hospital Fined £200,000 after Hard Drive Full of Patient Data Bought on eBay," July 14, 2013, http://www.techworld.com/news/security/hospital-fined-200000-after-hard-drive-full-of-patient-data-bought-on-ebay-3457470/.

8. Sophie Curtis, "InfoSec 2012: One in 10 Second-hand Hard Drives Contain Personal Data," April 25, 2012, http://www.techworld.com/news/security/infosec-2012-one-in-10-second-hand-hard-drives-contain-personal-data-3353817/.

9. Washington Secretary of State, "Washington State Archives," accessed August 6, 2015, https://www.sos.wa.gov/archives/.

10. "Washington State Archives, Digital Archives (WADA) Transfer Information Plan (TIP)," November 3, 2009, http://www.digitalarchives.wa.gov/State/Washington/StaticContent/Transfer_Information_Plan.pdf.

11. "Washington State Archives, Digital Archives Transmittal Agreement," January 10, 2011, http://www.digitalarchives.wa.gov/State/Washington/Static Content/Transmittal_Agreement.pdf.

Chapter 9

Documenting Ferguson: Collecting Current Events in Archives

Meredith R. Evans, Shannon Davis,
Jennifer Kirmer, and Sonya Rooney*

On August 9, 2014, Michael Brown, an 18-year-old African American, was fatally shot by Darren Wilson, a white police officer, in Ferguson, Missouri. This event spurred impassioned community reactions in the St. Louis region and across the country. Protests, rallies, community meetings, and memorials were soon being organized through social media. In the Ferguson area, witnesses posted online almost minute-by-minute photographic accounts of what was happening outside their doors. According to the PEW Research Center, the story of Michael Brown "emerged on Twitter before cable."[1] The use of social media captured national attention quickly, and the momentum brought together activists who spent significant time reporting the story. Within weeks, local activists created Facebook pages and websites devoted to organizing what became a national social movement. An analysis of the PEW report suggested that citizens concerned about the issue had to legitimize the story with massive public activity before it was deemed worthy of national broadcast. "The digital content was especially powerful when compared with coverage of the case in the popular media vis-à-vis the reactions shared via Twitter from the general public and protesters on the ground."[2]

While this event would have been significant anywhere it occurred, it happened only a few miles from the campus of Washington University in St. Louis (WUSTL), affecting university staff members personally and professionally. With a charge from university librarian Jeffrey Trzeciak, a group of library personnel and faculty created a plan to preserve both local and national material surrounding Brown's death, including information related

*The authors would like to acknowledge the input of Makiba J. Foster, who also contributed to this chapter.

to citizen protests and rallies, community reactions, meetings, and memorials.

Staff in the Washington University Libraries rapidly responded, knowing that this collecting initiative would reflect the fast change in events from a local perspective and would not fit neatly into their existing collecting policies and procedures. Creating a repository for the public to upload content that will be preserved was the libraries' solution to supporting the local community as well as ensuring that scholars around the world would have access to content generated in real time by the local community.

The project that resulted is called Documenting Ferguson[3] a new type of undertaking for Washington University Libraries. For the first time, the libraries are archiving events as they unfold, gathering community-generated digital content, and collecting and preserving born-digital files captured on temporal media like cell phones. The project is different from the media's undertaking because its intent is to represent the unedited voice of the people of St. Louis and to create a repository built by them for them. The project is edited neither by the national media nor by anyone else. It is much like the Twitter accounts that chronicled the events; its content cannot be deleted or blocked and will be organized/curated in a way that the content can be retrieved easily. While mainstream media outlets picked up the story of Michael Brown, coworkers, neighbors, and friends were active participants supporting protesters and police officers in a variety of ways. The project has presented unique challenges requiring the expertise of staff from many different units of the libraries. The Documenting Ferguson team consists of subject librarians, staff from the Scholarly Publishing and Special Collections units, members of library administration, staff from Washington University's Center for Diversity and Inclusion (located in the university's main library), and one faculty adviser. Members have contributed expertise in the areas of project planning, digital project development, collection development, teaching and research, community outreach, preservation (both digital and analog), and copyright, among other areas. When the group was first called together, it was charged with creating a website where visitors could contribute digital media related to the events in Ferguson as well as with setting up a process for archiving social media. Within 48 hours, the initial infrastructure for the project was in place, employing Omeka and the Internet Archive's Archive-It as the primary tools. As the repository formed, a subject librarian created a LibGuide. The Resource Guide on Policing, Community Protest and Unrest[4] is a foundation for high school lesson plans and assists educators in using the repository and teaching about the events of Ferguson.

The libraries' Scholarly Publishing unit has been using Omeka digital exhibit software for digital image projects for some time; as a result, Omeka's contribution plug-in was tested during previous projects. It is the optimal solution for collecting digital media and metadata from contributors to the Documenting Ferguson project because it has already been proven to work for the libraries. In addition, there is precedent for using Omeka with community-sourced projects. The team benchmarked the following projects: The September 11 Digital Archive: Saving the Histories of September 11, 2001;[5] Hurricane Digital Memory Bank;[6] and Our Marathon: The Boston Bombing Digital Archive & WBUR Oral History Project.[7] The intent of these archives was to collect the "instant" history, to preserve cultural memory like a memorial. They all have a teaching or research initiative as well. However, unlike Documenting Ferguson, they all transitioned content to Omeka from another platform, partnered with more than one cultural institution, and/or provided public access after having a certain amount of content. There have been critiques of these projects as well that have often reviewed them based on the amount and quality of content and on the story that they tell. David Lowenthal notes, "Archival records came to be valued as reliable repositories of truth, seedbeds of unabridged and veracious history. Open to inspection by all and preserved for all time, archives promised an authentic, untampered-with past."[8] The libraries sought to follow this theory. The uniqueness and perhaps weakness of Documenting Ferguson is that the libraries didn't begin with any seed content. They actively solicited and accepted whatever came their way. Their ambitious choice to collect in the now was intended to capture unbiased, raw, real-time footage that the public wanted preserved, but it also resulted in poor images, minimal metadata, and unexpected content such as a zine dedicated to black women who have been killed by law enforcement.

Using Omeka, Scholarly Publishing created a form for individuals to use to contribute images or information to the Documenting Ferguson site. The form requests minimal metadata, an associated media file, and an agreement to the project's terms and conditions. Contributors also have the option of submitting a large number of files with corresponding metadata through a file-sharing cloud storage platform. The submission process is intended to be low barrier to encourage participation. Because Omeka is an access interface and not a preservation solution, Scholarly Publishing also ingested the metadata contributions into a Fedora repository and copied media files onto the Washington University Libraries' servers with standardized filenames to ensure the longevity of the content.

The second method of collecting digital content also drew on an existing platform entitled Archive-It, a subscription-based web-archiving service. This platform was selected since most of the content was documented online in social media, in blogs, and in the news. Although Twitter was the main source of data and correspondence among activists and participants, there were not adequate staff or resources to capture the feeds daily. Therefore, the team reached out to Archive-It to collaborate with their staff to collect web-based content that documented the events and reactions to Brown's death. Archive-It content is available publicly via its website, which made it a strong partner in building a robust digital repository of content. Washington University collaborated by dedicating archival staff time to researching and providing URLs to be tracked by Archive-It. In addition, the Documenting Ferguson project team publicized the Archive-It links for capturing content within the libraries and within the Washington University academic community. A link to "Contribute Web Content" on the Documenting Ferguson website further promotes submissions to Archive-It's main website. The Documenting Ferguson team assisted in the collection of more than 100 links to Archive-It, and over 900 total links to content were collected.

Many pieces of web content specifically document the Washington University community's responses to the Ferguson events. The libraries' digital archivist has been submitting these links to Archive-It for inclusion in its collection, and these links are additionally captured in the "Official University" collection therein. By adding the subject terms "Ferguson, MO" and "Campus Dialogue" to the relevant URLs, the team is making these links discoverable from the Ferguson angle and making them part of the larger documentation of WUSTL's official online presence. Some of these links include WashU Voices: Ferguson and Beyond,[9] a website created by Washington University Public Affairs to allow the community to reflect and engage, as well as web pages advertising discussions and events on campus relating to Ferguson.

Collecting and preserving physical materials related to Ferguson and making them accessible to viewers is another aspect of the project. The team is collecting physical materials directly connected to activities participated in by the Washington University community, as stated in its Collection Policy. The materials include student group fliers and posters, student newspaper articles covering Ferguson, and event fliers from WUSTL-hosted discussions. These materials will be made available to researchers, students, and the public to supplement the digital content.

Other cultural institutions nearby are also collecting physical material. Maintaining a narrow scope makes this project more manageable for current staff and strengthens existing partnerships with cultural institutions in the surrounding area. The Library and Research Center of the Missouri History Museum and the Ferguson Historical Society are collecting artifacts, including large pieces of plywood painted with protest slogans that were used to board up broken windows in Ferguson, the remnants of businesses left desolate by protest activities, and photographs of walls painted with countless murals.

Collection Development Challenges

Archival collections that chronicle events and social movements often consist of print materials that were collected at the time by a participant and donated to a repository months or years later, sometimes by chance and sometimes by request. As with Occupy Wall Street in 2011, with Documenting Ferguson, the sense of urgency to capture original content from protest participants and/or bystanders was more important than waiting for edited material from traditional news media, or waiting months for remaining or hidden items collected in the aftermath. The documentation of Occupy Wall Street made it clear that there was no shortage of information, but rather a challenge to archive that information consistently.[10] The information also remained in the hands of the creators, not the repository. "The work of Activists Archivists with the Occupy movement illustrates the importance of getting an archivist involved early in the life cycle of an important event, if possible," due to issues with rights, large quantities of "user-contributed" content, quality control, and preservation needs.[11] Like Occupy Wall Street, the events surrounding Ferguson should be credited to a Twitter-generated social movement, uniting strangers around the country under a common cause.

The most significant difference in collection development between the Documenting Ferguson collection and a typical archival collection is in the amount of time the project team had for planning. The process was a mix of "collect everything now and weed later" and making quick choices that would benefit the longevity and quality of the materials. With events in Ferguson unfolding rapidly, the team had to decide immediately about what types of digital content should be captured and what the best sources of materials might be. The team also had to determine which organizations it could collaborate with quickly and how to build relationships with those involved in the events. Informing the immediate and surrounding community about these choices and about the solicitation of content was a crucial part of the process.

With competing demands, collecting in real time made it difficult to deliberate about the best ways to develop and curate the collection and to decide who should lead the initiative. The team also had very little time to consider what the project would cost in staff time and resources. The time span for planning this collection development verged on days, sometimes hours, and involved a diverse team of archivists, librarians, digital humanities specialists, and academics. The ramifications of the planning meant that appraisal was limited and at times nonexistent and that the project committee was solely reliant on the individuals who chose to upload content into the Omeka instance. This method does not allow archivists to appraise or determine whether the content uploaded has permanent value or is of high enough quality to ensure longevity, replication, or reproduction prior to submission. In addition, the content uploaded is not reviewed or censored before making it available to the public. The team continuously discusses if and how evaluation and curation of the material should be done. The lens of evaluation for this work does not fit traditional collecting policies. The project has shifted the culture of the libraries beyond the walls of the university and its usual constituencies. To document these events, we have formed new relationships and have adopted a new way of thinking to ensure that content is captured and will continue to be added to the collection to meet the needs of our users and our new community audience. Appraisal decisions are based on several factors, including the original order of the documents upon donation, authenticity, reliability, comprehensiveness of content to "tell a story," preservation condition, costs, and intrinsic value. Because the intent is not to deaccession any of the submissions, Documenting Ferguson materials will be evaluated based on the key priority of meeting the needs and interests of researchers, site contributors, and persons directly involved in activities that followed Michael Brown's death. Professional staff will review the content from this viewpoint to determine what can be used and how the material can be used for research and teaching purposes, a goal that drives a university's collection policies. The staff will also ensure that the website is easy to use.

Typical collection development includes input from different individuals, for example, archival staff, faculty, and donors. Together, these individuals evaluate the collection's content within the framework of the institution's collection development policy and appraise it for research use. An example of this is the Washington University Archives' work on a collection from the Danforth Center for Religion and Politics. As a first step in the process of development for this collection, the university archivist and the digital archivist met with the Danforth Center's staff and discussed the kinds of material to be preserved in the archives. The center's staff described its material, and an agreement was reached on what material would be included in the collection. Then the center's staff sorted their content and transferred only the files that were agreed upon. All of the material was created at least a semester before the transfer. The center agreed to transfer similar content on an annual basis.

The archival collections at the Washington University Libraries grew out of the Washington University Archives. Events and social movements are reflected in the papers of organizations, institutions, faculty, alumni, and other related individuals. These collections were not formed as events occurred. There are records of the Urban League of St. Louis from 1914 to 1986, with reports and clippings on race relations, employment, and health and housing that provide insight into the effects of the 1917 riots in East St. Louis and into the impact of this organization on the Freedom Movement. There is supplementary material, such as correspondence, interviews, and archival footage from *Eyes on the Prize*, the definitive documentary of the civil rights movement, from the collection of Washington

University alumnus Henry Hampton. Never before has the libraries' staff created a collection from scratch, with limited connections to the participants involved.

Soliciting materials from various individuals and organizations with no affiliation to Washington University is another difference between typical collection development and the Documenting Ferguson project. This type of solicitation, combined with the rapid pace of events, gave the project an air of collaboration, both within the university and out in the community. The collaborative approach helped the team identify who should be contacted and which of the team members should develop particular relationships and solicit contributions to the collection. It also led to supplementary projects that enabled the team to gain more material quickly to complement the existing digital repository. These projects have been collaborative works with faculty and students such as conducting oral histories and exploring ways to capture the social media that continues to sustain the communication of what were single events and now form a social movement.

The public's use of social media to capture the events in or related to Ferguson presents a unique method of documenting episodes of historical significance and presents archivists and others who build primary source research collections with a challenge. The libraries' method of collecting digital images of the events in Ferguson, as well as the impact of social media as the main means of organizing and reporting the protests, transforms the appraisal, collection, preservation, and discovery of this type of research data. Omeka was workable for creating a digital portal where the community could upload content such as photographs, music, and poetry, but it did not capture the Twitter feeds that documented decision making and the organizing of the events. A team of information specialists is exploring ways to collect, preserve, and access Twitter feeds and the images attached to them for future research opportunities.

The fact that the members of the Documenting Ferguson team were collecting materials about events taking place in their own community also made the project unique. The members of the team worked during the day to set up the methods of collection and the collaborative framework. At night, they watched the protests—some from a distance and others up close. The protests were 12 miles away from the Washington University campus but only minutes from the homes of some team members. Protests took place in neighborhoods where colleagues, students, families, and friends live or work. The immediacy of the events was especially felt by staff located at the West Campus of Washington University, where demonstrations at the St. Louis County Courthouse just a few blocks away could be seen and heard.

Materials acquired in a collection from a donor or an organization may have a personal impact, but rarely will they have the immediacy of the events taking place in Ferguson. Materials from such a collection are also in a format that is much easier to transport, decipher, and preserve. The bulk of the content for the events in Ferguson is digital. To fill in gaps, the team decided to pursue oral histories in a variety of different ways. Oral history has been used successfully by scholars in a wide range of disciplines, such as history, sociology, and anthropology. Oral histories improve the scholarly and public understanding of a historical moment by recording the experiences, perspectives, and voices of the people who have been closest to it. Oral history is a valuable tool for journalists, activists, civic leaders, and ordinary citizens. Because the activists in Ferguson have a critically important role to play in helping remember and interpret the events that have unfolded in their community since August 2014, oral history is a particularly appropriate tool for the Documenting Ferguson project.

The libraries' staff led and collaborated with faculty and students to conduct four oral history projects to complement the digital community portal.

- Project One: Staff members assisted a student with interviews of Washington University student leaders who participated in different expressions of protest. The student documented meetings and recorded related social media as well.

- Project Two: Three members of the Documenting Ferguson team (one subject librarian and two staff members from special collections) partnered with a professor and worked with a class interviewing Washington University employees who live in the city of Ferguson.

- Project Three: Special collections staff and two faculty members formed a partnership in order to interview two groups: (1) faculty from different area universities, who were asked what information they were most interested in; and (2) local activists who had organized and led protests in the area.

- Project Four: Special collections staff set up a booth at the annual conference of the Organization of American Historians to hear reflections from conference attendees about the shooting of Michael Brown and the events that followed to learn what their research questions were.

All the projects aimed to introduce students to the diverse avenues of fostering historical memory and to note perspectives about the events from different constituents. The libraries' staff hosted an oral history workshop that provided training in creating quality questions, developing interview techniques, and utilizing oral histories as a research methodology and documentation strategy. The students were also taught basic and technical metadata descriptors to support access to the digital audio recordings. The Documenting Ferguson team members located WUSTL interviewees, and the students conducted the interviews. The students then added the audio-recorded interviews and metadata to the Documenting Ferguson repository. In addition, the interviews were added to the Washington University Archives Oral History Collection, bringing another dimension to an archive that consists of interviews with students, alumni, and current and past staff about their experiences at Washington University. The team plans to conduct more of these interviews and put them in both collections.

Assessment and Future of Project

Choosing to supplement the repository with additional data like oral histories and partnerships with Archive-It and other cultural institutions implies that there is some discomfort with having an uncurated digital community portal as the only representation of archival material. It is a big responsibility and risk to solicit and collect digital content as activities unfold and commit to preserving it for future generations. Unlike social media, our collection is not at risk of losing content when individuals delete their accounts. There are not many aspects of this project the libraries would have done differently. However, it remains to be seen if the libraries will pursue other projects of this kind. With a better understanding of why similar projects had seed collections prior to going public, the libraries remain committed to increasing the amount of material, and we are strategically seeking additional content. The library staff struggled with marketing the repository and often discussed whether or not the community trusted the institution enough to submit. There are opportunities for assessing the use and reasons for submission. At programs and meetings, when attendees are asked if they have submitted or would submit content, the anecdotal responses have often been that people didn't know about the project. The low visibility has led to the development of a stronger marketing strategy to possibly include radio ads and going to Ferguson and surrounding community venues, such as libraries, churches, and stores, to help people upload content from their phones.

The libraries have identified technical barriers that may have hindered use of the site. These barriers are being corrected, and the team continues to rely on grassroots efforts of word of mouth to encourage submissions. Documenting Ferguson is a community collection that will remain a part of the Washington University Libraries. Submissions have been received by faculty from different disciplines, and based on reference queries it is evident that Documenting Ferguson is being used in various ways from providing material for presentations to an examination of a chronology of events. Two faculty members, one in the Art department and one in Gender and Women's Studies, have used images from the collection to encourage discourse about civil rights and visual literacy. Documenting Ferguson is the subject of research as well. Notably a doctoral studies project on human/computer interaction looked at Documenting Ferguson with the intent of exploring human participation in crowdsourced digital community archives.

Documenting Ferguson remains a work in progress. As the anniversary of the death of Michael Brown approaches, the Washington University Libraries are actively promoting the repository and remain engaged with the community. Project team members and other library staff will continue to distribute flyers, and work in and with the community to add content, develop instructional information, interview with local media outlets, and serve on panel discussions around St. Louis. The libraries actively seek submissions to the repository that represent all sides of the issue, hoping that all involved will upload material. Activists and residents in the city of Ferguson continue to embrace the project. For the long term, the Washington University Libraries are working to foster an open dialog with the archival community so that individuals can provide feedback on the collection and other endeavors. In addition, the libraries are working to create a collective environment in which other institutions doing similar work can come together to share best practices, challenges, and successes.

The libraries continue to view this project as a form of activism and have written a public joint statement with other institutions to show their commitment. An excerpt reads:

> The work of libraries and cultural heritage institutions is often entrusted by their citizens to steward the intellectual and creative capital of their communities. It is our hope that the people of the surrounding areas who are engaged in the creative and social justice work of this movement see our spaces as places that inspire confidence when entrusting on collection practices. Joined together as a collective of institutions made up of individuals from different St. Louis communities, this collecting initiative exemplifies that we all have a stake in making sure that our individual

and collective stories are represented in all of their diversity and complexity. We collect, preserve, organize, and make accessible to the larger community that which has been shared with us, continually enhancing its ability to serve as an evolving public record.

The project team didn't know what kinds of content would be uploaded nor by whom, a risk more archivists should take to ensure the preservation and enduring value of evidential content that informs written history. It was important to encourage contributions while fresh in people's minds so as not to lose content or have people think images and documents of such activity are unimportant or not worthy of permanence. It was also critical that the media not be the only lasting evidence of a community's ordeal. Documenting the public sentiment of an event in real time is as valuable as the facts that unfold. The Documenting Ferguson repository does not serve as a jury or impose judgment. While it is the evidence of a community's reaction and the evolution of a social movement, related documents such as grand jury testimony, evidence, and the United States Department of Justice report have been uploaded. Although these reports did not confirm any wrongdoing in the Brown case, they do speak to past injustices, the militarized response, and the community's outrage. This repository can be and will be used for teaching and research.

Like the hashtags in Twitter feeds (#Ferguson, #BlackLivesMatter), the repository content is dominantly the expression of feelings experienced in response to the shooting, and the protests and events that followed. If the impact of the events surrounding the death of Michael Brown on the local community can be seen and heard beyond the broadcast by the national media, our intent for a community-driven digital repository has been realized.

Notes

1. Paul Hitlin and Nancy Vogt, "Cable, Twitter Picked up Ferguson Story at a Similar Clip," PEW Research Center, August 20, 2014, http://www.pewresearch.org/fact-tank/2014/08/20/cable-twitter-picked-up-ferguson-story-at-a-similar-clip/.

2. Jules Bergis, "Documenting the Now: #Ferguson in the Archives," April 8, 2015, *On Archivy*, https://medium.com/on-archivy/documenting-the-now-ferguson-in-the-archives-adcdbe1d5788.

3. Documenting Ferguson project, accessed August 1, 2015, http://digital.wustl.edu/ferguson.

4. Resource Guide on Policing, Community Protest and Unrest, accessed August 1, 2015, http://libguides.wustl.edu/communityresource.

5. The September 11 Digital Archive: Saving the Histories of September 11, 2001, accessed August 1, 2015, http://911digitalarchive.org.

6. Hurricane Digital Memory Bank, accessed August 1, 2015, http://hurricanearchive.org.

7. Our Marathon: The Boston Bombing Digital Archive & WBUR Oral History Project, accessed August 1, 2015, http://marathon.neu.edu/about.

8. David Lowenthal, "Archives, Heritage, and History," in *Archives, Documentation, and Institutions of Social Memory: Essays from the Sawyer Seminar*, ed. Francis X. Blouin, Jr., and William G. Rosenberg (Ann Arbor: University of Michigan Press, 2006), 193.

9. WashU (Washington University) Voices: Ferguson and Beyond, accessed August 1, 2015, http://voices.wustl.edu.

10. Michael D. Conover, Emilio Ferrara, Filippo Menczer, and Alessandro Flammini, "The Digital Evolution of Occupy Wall Street," ed. Matjaz Perc, University of Maribor, Slovenia, *PLoS ONE* 8, no. 5 (2013): e64679, doi:10.1371/journal.pone.0064679.

11. Mike Ashenfelder, Activist Archivists and Digital Preservation, October 1, 2012, http://blogs.loc.gov/digitalpreservation/2012/10/activist-archivists-and-digital-preservation/.

Chapter 10
Dance Companies as Living Archives: Protecting the Future by Preserving the Present

Supriya Wronkiewicz

In many respects, when we think of archives and archival records, it is usually in the sense that we are documenting the past, referring to materials that are considered inactive by the organizations or individuals that created them but that retain historic value. The creation of an archive often occurs when an organization ceases operations, upon an individual's retirement or death, or when inactive materials are transferred to a repository. In the case of organizations and individuals specializing in various forms of performing arts, much can be lost if archival intervention occurs at this stage, rather than while the organization and individual are active in their work. Active performing arts companies (dance, theater, music) are essentially living archives. Their archival holdings are working collections.[1] These archives consist of seminal documentation of practice and performance. Companies cannot simply shed documentation, even if they so desired, because active, functional applications for the materials exist. Simultaneously, these collections have external value to researchers, such as educators, scholars, and students, who wish to access the documentation to learn and/or to teach.

While the issues and concerns addressed in this chapter can be applied to various kinds of arts organizations, I focus on dance companies and independent choreographers. This chapter cites experiences with various projects with the Dance Heritage Coalition (DHC) and the Museum of Performance + Design (MP+D), a DHC founding member organization,[2] and discusses the importance of building connections with dance companies and choreographers while they are active and the benefits of the metacollections (collections of collections) that are created from these collaborative efforts.

As a result of many dance companies and choreographers operating independently and across a wide geographic range, their collections are essentially hidden. Some materials, such as audio and video recordings, may be on vulnerable, at-risk, and/or obsolete formats, requiring time and resources the companies may not have on hand to make available. In general, dance recordings are rarely commercially viable, resulting in limited, if any, access. The nature of these companies compounds access issues: access to a company's works may be only available at a site on or near their base of operation, and due to factors like limited resources and other organizational priorities, the creation and subsequent maintenance of archives may be problematic for many companies and choreographers. Thus, it is important to establish relationships with companies while they are still active.

In contrast, working with "dead" collections containing unprocessed materials without input from the artist can be complicated at best. At worst, there is the risk of loss of vital information or context. This scenario is compounded when working with the collections of a little-known company or artist where there may be little to no information available for research, causing a higher likelihood of the archivist being forced to make guesses, educated or blind, about the various components of the collection. Another benefit of early intervention with these companies' and choreographers' living archives is generating opportunities for their legacy to continue when operations may cease and/or upon the choreographer's death. If relations are already in place and work with the collections has occurred or is in process, higher likelihood exists for smaller and more obscure companies and choreographers to have their collections acquired and made ready for access, or for on-site access already in place to continue.

As DHC's mission is "to preserve, make accessible, enhance and augment the materials that document the artistic accomplishments in dance of the past, present, and future," the organization pursues its mission "by encouraging, initiating, and developing collaborative projects among the dance communities, library and archival fields, scholarly institutions, and individuals in four essential areas: access to materials, the continuing documentation of dance employing both traditional methods and developing technologies, preservation of existing documentation, and education within and beyond the field of dance."[3] To help bring together archival professionals with companies and choreographers, the DHC partners with dance companies and independent choreographers to help preserve their archives and protect their documentation and media, as well as enable scholarly access for learning about and from these companies through various grants and initiatives.

Both the company and researchers need to contribute to the preservation of a dance company's data and media. I will use as an example work done with the Joe Goode Performance Group (JGPG)[4] and its archives between 2010 and 2014, focusing on two specific projects: the DHC Archive Assessment Project, where I surveyed and assessed the JGPG holdings, and subsequent work participating in the Dance Preservation and Digitization Project (DPDP). The DHC in collaboration with MP+D used present and evolving standards to address the challenge around living archives such as JGPG that are not ready to donate their collections, but need help preserving their audio and video materials, and whose work needs to be made available for study. The DHC was able to bring several dance organizations/individual choreographers and archival professionals from multiple member organizations together, creating two metacollections (collections of collections). The DPDP highlights the benefits of collaboration between representatives from dance companies and archival professionals. The process brought together content creators, performing arts archivists, moving image archivists, digital librarians, technology specialists, and other contributors.

From 2009 to 2011, through a grant from the Andrew W. Mellon Foundation, DHC conducted outreach and archival assessments for several small to mid-size dance companies and individual choreographers, including, but not limited to, the Joe Goode Performance Group (San Francisco, CA), Margaret Jenkins Dance Company (San Francisco, CA), Dance Theatre of Harlem (New York, NY), Eiko and Koma (New York, NY), Lar Lubovitch Dance Company (New York, NY), Garth Fagan Dance Company (Rochester, NY), and David Gordon's Pick Up Performance Co(s) (New York, NY).[5] Through this funding, an early-career archivist with experience working with performing arts was assigned to each company to work closely with a company-assigned content specialist to develop a detailed survey and report, assessing what records and media were on hand and how they were organized and used, building on preliminary surveys already done by the DHC.[6] A detailed survey is essential, as many companies do not have a full inventory of their materials, crucial for establishing priorities for records retention and preservation. The survey was enhanced by a scholarly assessment to identify seminal works of the company/choreographer, contributions made to their field of dance, and a description of how the archives documented these contributions. This scholarly assessment also described the possible impact of making these materials available for future scholarship. While helpful for future accessioning by an archival repository, these assessments also help these companies and groups with fund-raising for work on their archives, as they document collection value. While many have some sort of informal records-keeping process out of necessity, companies strongly benefit from the kind of organization an archivist can offer to their records and objects. Manageable and sustainable archival work allows the companies to build from the work done, rather than have the materials examined once without effective follow-up. Working directly with the companies helps tremendously.

These assessment surveys were conducted according to established standards. For each collection, an inventory was created using a spreadsheet developed by Rebecca Hatcher of Yale University's Beinecke Library in collaboration with the DHC.[7] Each spreadsheet was divided into separate inventories for moving image materials, sound recordings, nonaudiovisual/paper-based documents, photographic materials, and, if needed, three-dimensional objects, such as artifacts and costumes. The nature of these living archives is that they all have multiformat collections; paper records, photographic materials, posters, oversize materials, audio materials, video materials, and born-digital materials may comprise, in combination or total, a collection. Following the survey of the physical and/or digital items and necessary interviews with key personnel, companies participating in the project received a copy of the survey-generated inventory, a written report summarizing the contents of the inventory, and recommendations for specific preservation needs, along with a separate scholarly assessment.[8]

Taking advantage of resources offered by MP+D, I worked with JGPG's designated contact specialist Maia Rosal (then JGPG's managing director) to conduct a survey of JGPG's holdings in 2011. Working closely with Rosal, I interviewed Dave Archuletta, then JGPG's executive director, and surveyed JGPG's primary work and performance space in San Francisco and the company's warehouse storage space in Oakland, California. Some boxes of video and audio materials were brought over to MP+D and surveyed there due to space concerns. Over the course of three months, I surveyed 664 video items,

334 audio items, 71 linear feet of paper-based materials, and 14 linear feet of photographic materials. Almost all video materials and the majority of the audio materials were inventoried at the item level. Paper and photographic materials were inventoried at the box level or folder/container level as appropriate.[9] Having direct access to a representative with intimate knowledge of the company and its working practices proved invaluable. In several cases, Rosal was able to identify obscure materials, provide insights into how records were maintained by JGPG, and help guide the survey process. Rosal was also able to start on the process of following through with some of the preservation recommendations for specific items, such as rehousing fragile paper-based items and/or audiovisual objects.

Because this assessment was being conducted for an active company, records that the company needed for daily operations needed to be distinguished from what a repository would keep following the donation of the company's records. These needs are not going to necessarily align perfectly. Collaborating with Rosal helped me to make this distinction as needed following the survey process; at several points, it affected my recommendations. For example, the company might have different redundancy and duplication of material needs than a repository. JGPG has a significant amount of redundancy in its video holdings for use in grant applications and promotion. A repository may choose to discard some of the derivative copies (such as if a videotape was duplicated for more than one grant application), whereas these likely would not be discarded while the organization is active, as they may be needed for future applications. It is also necessary to make a distinction between redundancy and exact duplication: some tapes may be multiple recordings of the same performances, while others may be recordings of the same work on different nights and/or venues. Based on value judgments or practical constraints, the company may decide that not all versions are to be kept. It needs to be taken into account that the works may change or evolve. While not the case with JGPG, dance companies may also have to deal with duplicate materials related to union regulations.[10] Adherence to collective bargaining agreements and issues that may arise require a unique set of records management practices that may only be applicable while the company is active and/or while the association with the union is current.

Having access to Rosal and JGPG staff was especially helpful with audiovisual items where it was not clear from attached labels if an item was a master copy, if two videotapes of the same performances were truly duplicates, or if one was from a date/time different from the other. Individual moving image recordings were identified in accordance to a schema established by the Jerome Robbins Archive of the Recorded Moving Image at New York Public Library of the Performing Arts for describing originals, preservation masters, viewing copies, and so on. This helps with making decisions on preservation priorities such as digitization that JGPG must contend with, especially the possibility of having master video and audio recordings in obsolete formats that cannot be easily played. This information is also valuable for repositories surveying the collection with the intent of purchase or acquisition. Extra copies of programs and posters can be repurposed for grant applications, fund-raiser items, and giveaways, which explains why a company would want to hold on to them while active (space and practical considerations permitting), but a repository might cull them down to two to three copies maximum.

Active companies like JGPG also benefit from learning that these items have long-term historical value and that two or three copies should be placed aside in a manner in accordance with archival best practices.

Doing assessment in a vacuum, without consulting with representatives from the active company, leads to sound recommendations for an archival collection in a repository, but not a living archival collection in current use. Ideally, the companies should be able to continue the work started by these assessments as they continue to function. A properly tailored assessment allows for a higher chance of follow-through. Oversight on the project as a whole maintains standards across different companies. Little is accomplished by providing funding for archival supplies with only cursory instructions and then walking away. Working with a representative and truly learning how the company functions also allow the archival professional to make recommendations and offer solutions in a way that applies specifically to that company's needs, and can allow for moving past the archival assessment "into a program with sustainable and continued work."[11]

Oversight from DHC provided the assurance that while the individual needs and institution cultures were being taken into account, the work of the archival professionals was being held to the same standards across the board. This management also created a support system allowing for guidance, collaboration, and the sharing of information, as needed, across the companies and archivists involved. Performing arts archives of all kinds will have similar types of materials. One of the lessons learned from tracking metrics for this multicollection project is that it is beneficial to have individuals with the different skillsets working together to develop robust records retention schedules and other guidelines.

Efforts stemming from the assessments can also work toward preparing for possible future accessioning of the company's archives by a repository: a museum like MP+D, an academic institution like the Harry Ransom Center at University of Texas at Austin, or a research library such as the New York Public Library for the Performing Arts. Many of these institutions have existing guidelines on what can be accepted into their collections. An inventory that can be updated and awareness of possible preservation issues can be strong assets in placing the collection, either while the company is active or following the company's closure.[12]

As part of the Mellon grant funding the assessments of JGPG and the other companies mentioned earlier, the inventories, narrative reports, and scholarly assessments were combined to create a facsimile of a finding aid for each of these collections. These finding aids included fields such as biographical/organizational historical notes, scope and content notes, collection organizations, restrictions if applicable, and inventory sections, which were broken down into series, each with an individual scope and content note. The complete inventories were not added as part of a container list because the contents of the inventories are likely to change. These finding aids were subsequently encoded using Encoded Archival Description and were posted to the DHC Finding Aids Database (FADb).[13] The FADb contains finding aids from over 12 DHC member institutions pertaining to their dance collections. While most of these institutions have access to their finding aids on their own site or other consortia, such as the Online Archive of California, the DHC FADb allows a portal focusing specifically on dance collections from these institutions, with the ultimate goal of becoming an one-stop shop for accessing these hidden archival dance collections as the database continues to grow and evolve. These organizations and their archival holdings are now visible in a way that may not have been possible before.

The work done also assisted with other projects. Following the archival assessment, I became involved with JGPG's participation, along with other local dance companies, in the DHC DPDP, an ongoing DHC initiative "[creating] preservation and access solutions for the dance field's moving images."[14] The materials digitized as part of this project would be uploaded to DHC's secure media network (SMN). The SMN consists of a searchable database of moving images and catalog records of "films, analog and digital tapes, and digital files—held by dance libraries," the majority of which have only been privately accessible. Access to the SMN is restricted to on-site viewing at DHC member institutions, so that moving image materials can "be delivered to libraries and centers for teaching and research without danger of unauthorized copying or distribution."[15] Due to the number of participants and restrictions on funds for the project, companies like JGPG made curatorial decisions on which works to send. For example, works on formats that were at risk of no longer being able to be played back therefore received a higher priority. As part of the pilot phase for the DPDP, 10 video recordings were chosen in 2012. Additional funding allowed for 11 more to be added in 2015. Information from the survey and the scholarly assessment provided by DHC helped JGPG determine which specific works, and which specific video formats, would be sent to a designated DHC digitization hub, or "digihub."

Many of the companies DHC worked with through the DPDP face serious issues: lack of funds, resources, physical and digital space, and/or staff. As the work from the assessments indicated, these companies have multiformat active collections. Both analog and digital materials, especially audiovisual items, have unique conservation concerns. Analog video recordings (u-matic 3/4", VHS, S-VHS, and Hi-8 cassette tapes among others) have complications associated with magnetic media, such as susceptibility to unique forms of physical degradation that can result in permanent data loss.[16] As a result, dance companies need to take precautionary measures as soon as possible to preserve the most important items in their audiovisual holdings, specifically, video recordings. In a report to the Andrew Mellon Foundation, DHC justifies this stance by stating:

> Dance itself . . . is intangible. Only its artifacts, such as programs, photographs, costumes, and set designs live on in a tangible form. While still photographs can capture some aspects of performance, dance movement could only be captured when the technology to record it became available.[17]

This need to preserve the dance performances resulted in the formation of the DPDP. As part of a Mellon Foundation grant–funded project in 2004, DHC took steps to determine a standard for reformatting analog videotapes to create digital masters. This work led to the concept of the digihubs, stemming from the idea that, according to past DHC executive director Elizabeth Aldrich:

> Funding must be secured so that the larger repositories may begin the work of reformatting their holdings; funding is also necessary to maintain digital files. Hubs need to be established so that independent choreographers and dancers as well as smaller organizations can avail themselves to this technology.[18]

Since Aldrich's 2004 report, several large institutions developed processes to manage their multimedia holdings, but less so with smaller organizations and individual choreographers.[19]

To address this issue, digihubs were established in San Francisco at the MP+D in 2010, in New York City at the Dance Notation Bureau in 2011, and in DHC's main office in Washington, D.C., in 2012. As of the time of this printing, digitization work continues at all locations. Schmitz explains that the digihubs model "brings a community archives ethic to the preservation of moving images in dance." Schmitz notes: "digihubs provide an opportunity for dance organizations to make a vital contribution to dance scholarship by helping to fill the void in available primary research materials in dance."[20] At each location, along with local DHC member organizations contributing moving image material to be digitized and uploaded, DHC and member organization staff engaged in localized outreach to companies and choreographers. Significantly, DHC learned that offering resources like the digihubs and other tools can only work as intended if appropriate outreach efforts are made to the dance companies and choreographers, who may be unaware of the resources available, and are likely to need assistance preserving their at-risk video recordings.

During the outreach process, especially with companies not actively taking preservation into consideration, another challenge arose. Preservation practices may be considered counterintuitive as dance performance can be considered an ephemeral art.[21] This philosophy assumes a performance can only be experienced in the moment, and therefore cannot be held onto.

Dance celebrates the need to be there for a live, ephemeral performance experience. Clarifying how the archival profession used the word "ephemeral" was necessary, especially in terms of long-term preservation, since the word "ephemeral" can be interpreted in a completely different and unintended way.[22]

Among dance companies and individual choreographers, multiple methods beyond video are used to document performance, including dance notation, such as Benesh Movement Notation, and the creation of dance scores. Given the varied nature of dance performances, there is no universally accepted, established standard or methodology to document or preserve dances. Artists also disagree whether or not works should be performed following the death of their creator(s). However, most companies and individual choreographers care deeply about their legacy.[23]

In conclusion, one of the biggest lessons learned from the creation of the metacollections, whether through the DPDP grant–funded project or the archival assessment grant–funded project, is that we cannot do this alone. Our preservation efforts must be a present, not a future, action for both archival professionals like those associated with the DHC and dance companies and individual choreographers with active working collections.

The archival assessments show the benefits of taking the time to come up with a plan while the company is still running and/or the individual choreographer is still producing new works. They allow dance companies to see exactly what records they have, and provide useful information for establishing priorities based on staffing, space, time, and funding issues for the future. The assessments are only of value if they adhere to existing archival and preservation standards *and* presents recommendations and solutions in such a way that are feasible and sustainable by the organization. Bringing multiple organizations together such as the DHC member organizations to work with dance companies of varying sizes, but especially smaller companies and individuals, allows for the creation of a vital support system. Bringing together these organizations not only allows for the SMN to truly serve as a strong and viable resource for dance videos for scholars and researchers, but also allows current dance companies' living archives the opportunity to be preserved in the present to ensure access for the future.

Lastly, while this chapter has focused exclusively on dance archives as living archives, much of what was outlined above can also apply to other performing arts organizations. Several members of the DHC, such as MP+D, also specialize in the preservations of archives for other forms of performing arts, such as theatre, opera, and music performance. DHC's efforts can be made relevant to almost any kind of performing arts groups, especially small companies and individual artists who may not be thinking of the long term, either due to lack of time, funds, workspace, or any number of factors. The work done with the FADb and the SMN can serve as a template for online databases with collections involving various forms of the performing arts. Companies with multiformat collections—especially audiovisual materials in any format must address preservation in the present with the qualified assistance of an archival professional, so these materials can remain accessible for all current and future uses.

Notes

1. Imogen Smith, Judy Tyrus, Kat Bell, "Adapting Traditional Processes to Nontraditional Collections: Putting the Dance Theatre of Harlem Archives Back Together" (presentation, Amigos Online Webinar "Preservation: Back to Basics," September 19, 2013, http://www.slideshare.net/danceheritage/bell-smith-tyrusamigos presentation-26472430).

2. For more information about the DHC and MP+D, please visit the following Web sites: www.danceheritage.org and www.mpdsf.org.

3. Dance Heritage Coalition, "DHC Mission," accessed April 1, 2013, http:// danceheritage.org/mission.html.

4. For more information about Joe Goode Performance Group, please refer to http:// joegoode.org/about/.

5. As part of my work for the DHC, I created finding aids surrogates combining the final products created for these companies. These can be accessed at http:// findingaids.danceheritage.org.

6. Imogen Smith (DHC Project Manager), e-mail message to author, May 22, 2015.

7. Elizabeth Smigel, telephone conversation with author, May 20, 2015.

8. Dance Heritage Coalition, "Archive Assessment," accessed March 23, 2015, http:// danceheritage.org/assessment.html.

9. The finding aid-like document created from the inventory and scholarly assessment can be found here: http://findingaids.danceheritage.org/xtf/view?docId=finding aids/Dance%20Company%20Finding%20Aids/JGPG.xml.

10. American Guild of Musical Artists, American Federation of Musicians, and the International Alliance of Theatrical Stage Employees, Moving Picture Technicians, Artists and Allied Crafts of the United States are among one of several unions dance companies may associate with.

11. Smith et al., "Adapting Traditional Processes to Nontraditional Collections."

12. Collection Development Policy at the Harry Ransom Center: http://www.hrc .utexas.edu/collections/pdf/Collection_Dev_Policy.pdf; NYPL Policy on Gifts of Materials: http://www.nypl.org/help/about-nypl/legal-notices/policy-gifts-materials; Elizabeth Smigel (DHC executive director) and Imogen Smith (DHC project manager), in discussion with the author, April 24, 2015.

13. The finding aids created for JGPG and the other institutions mentioned earlier can be searched for at this site: http://findingaids.danceheritage.org/xtf/search.

14. Dawn Schmitz, "The Dance Preservation and Digitization Project: The Technology Summit and Beyond, a White Paper for the Dance Heritage

Coalition" (DHC White Paper, 2015, http://www.danceheritage.org/dhc_whitepaper _preservation_digitization.pdf).

15. Dance Heritage Coalition, "DHC Secure Media Network," accessed March 23, 2015, http://danceheritage.org/securemedia.html.

16. Library of Congress, "Magnetic Tape 'Sticky Shed' Research: Characterization, Diagnosis, and Treatment," accessed March 23, 2015, http://www.loc.gov/preservation/ scientists/projects/sticky_shed.html.

17. Media Matters LLC, "Digital Video Preservation Reformatting Project: A Report" (presented for the Dance Heritage Coalition to the Andrew W. Mellon Foundation, June 2004).

18. Ibid., as quoted in Dawn Schmitz, "The Dance Preservation and Digitization Project: The Technology Summit and Beyond—A White Paper for the Dance Heritage Coalition."

19. Dawn Schmitz, "The Dance Preservation and Digitization Project: The Technology Summit and Beyond—A White Paper for the Dance Heritage Coalition," http://www.danceheritage.org/dhc_whitepaper_preservation_digitization.pdf.

20. Ibid.

21. Within this context, it is helpful to consider that the term "ephemeral" can have multiple meanings depending on the perspective of who is using the term. According to the Society of American Archivists glossary, "ephemera" means "Materials, usually printed documents, created for a specific, limited purpose, and generally designed to be discarded after use" (http://www2.archivists.org/glossary/terms/e/ephemera). A document of ephemeral value means "Useful or significant for a limited period of time" (http://www2.archivists.org/glossary/terms/e/ephemeral-value). In the context of a performance, "ephemeral" means "lasting a very short time; short-lived; transitory" and "ephemera" can also mean "anything short-lived or ephemeral" (from Dictionary.com).

22. Elizabeth Smigel (DHC executive director) and Imogen Smith (DHC project manager), in discussion with author, April 24, 2015.

23. Imogen Smith (DHC project manager), e-mail message to author, May 22, 2015.

Chapter 11
Success with Donors: Practical Approaches That Work for All

Sheryl Williams

Introduction

Our success in building and acquiring significant special and archival collections depends on our ability to work with potential donors. The dynamics of this activity have received surprisingly little attention in archival and special collections literature over the years. Sessions that deal with these topics at library and archival meetings are well attended, elicit lively discussion, and reveal the need for more to be published in this area. The building blocks for success are rooted in practicality. Some are intuitive; all can be learned. The newcomer to building collections can rest assured that taking some practical steps will help to build confidence and expertise in this area.

In addition, working with potential donors for personal or organizational papers or for collections is closely allied with the need to raise money to process and care for these collections. It's not an area that librarians and archivists often feel comfortable with. We haven't been trained in the art of "the ask." Approaching donors, where appropriate, for funds to care for their collections or to support other initiatives is something that needs to be more consciously incorporated into our donor programs. We need to develop these skills to ensure that we are maximizing opportunities. Here, too, these skills are acquirable. We can apply what we do with potential donors of material, while working closely with those people skilled in development.

This chapter is informed by my experience of collecting personal and organizational papers and many types of collections to build the Kansas Collection at Kenneth Spencer Research Library, University of Kansas, over a lengthy career. I've had successes and failures, worked with some characters, and met some lovely people. I estimate that I have worked with approximately 1,500 donors. Through it all I've discovered a genuineness in these connections that carries me forward. My work is enriched by their stories, and the experience gives valuable context to my work with historical collections.

Background

Archival and special collections literature on collecting has focused on selection, appraisal theory, and strategies for ensuring the inclusivity of the historical record. Recent publications also cover ethical and legal issues related to donation.[1] But very little focuses on the "softer" side of collections work. A recent publication by Aaron Purcell takes the first book-length look specifically at donor relations from an archival perspective.[2] Allied fields in fund-raising, psychology, and gerontology provide valuable sources that can expand our understanding of how to work with donors.[3]

F. Gerald Ham, in describing field work with donors, has written "The best field agents have the nose of a bloodhound, the persistence of a Fuller brush salesman, and the tact of a diplomat."[4] A librarian or an archivist must possess a number of basic characteristics to work successfully with donors. At the heart of this work is understanding that, though we are working to acquire collections, we are working with people. You are uncovering their stories and their experiences. You need to be comfortable working with a diversity of people in a diversity of settings. Any archivist or librarian who does not like working around people would have a harder time asking them for collections or money; it's that simple. But you don't have to be an extrovert to do this work. Being successful is all about how you relate to the donors, the impression you make, and the bond of trust that is formed.

Key Traits: Listening

Good field work requires good listening skills. It is important to hear what the donor is saying—not just with words, but, sometimes, what is behind those words. According to Steven Covey:

> Empathic listening gets inside another person's frame of reference. You look out through it, you see the world the way they see the world, you understand their paradigm, you understand how they feel.[5]

This kind of listening builds rapport and trust with donors.

I was once visiting an elderly lady in her home and discussing her family papers. Her father had been active in local politics and she had many scrapbooks documenting his career that spanned a lengthy period. She described the scrapbooks to me, but indicated that they were stored in the attic, and she would need help in retrieving them, so she couldn't show them to me. She thanked me but declined my offer to go up into the attic and retrieve them for her. She said she didn't want to put me to any trouble. I assured her it was no trouble; I was used to climbing stairs and going into attics was something archivists often have to do. Her body language became stiff, her face looked troubled, and she again said, no, she would get someone else to help her another time.

It was frustrating. It would have been easy to retrieve these scrapbooks for her. Then I realized that she was saying (through words and body language) that she really didn't want me in her attic. I didn't know exactly why, but could imagine that maybe she didn't want anyone seeing a space that might be messy or disorganized. Backing off, we agreed to meet at a later date.

Eventually, after getting to know me better, she did let me up in her attic, apologizing all the time for its disheveled state. I assured her that I was used to attics, basements, storage closets, and other spaces and could easily work there. Obviously she trusted me enough not to be judging of her space, and allowed me access. Working with donors is like a dance: sometimes you lead, and sometimes you follow, but always, you listen.

However good at listening we are, though, it doesn't mean we must be captive to doing only listening through the whole interaction with the donor. Many people like having an audience; your attention is flattering. They may be lonely, and excited to have someone listening to their stories. It can be difficult to move a loquacious donor through a meeting productively. It is important to listen, but it is also important to maintain control of the encounter by gently guiding the discussion back to your original proposal. You may have to do this repeatedly, and it gets easier with experience. Try establishing time limits at the beginning of a meeting in order to help move things along.

Key Traits: A Good Communicator

Along with listening also comes the need to be a good communicator. Being articulate in representing your institution, your repository, and the reason you are interested in the collection of the donor is of utmost importance. Many people have had no reason to think about what an archive or a library does, or why there would be interest in their papers or collections. In fact, many people do not know what we mean when we talk about their "papers." Countless times potential donors told me that they have "nothing like that." Sometimes they don't, but often they do; they just don't know what we are talking about. We have to find ways to explain what we mean in a compelling and succinct manner, talking conversationally, without jargon, finding the points of common interest. If you are new to this work, do some role-playing with a colleague to better understand what it might be like, and how you would present your case.

You can also expect to be challenged by the often asked question "Why would anyone be interested in looking at what I have?" The idea that something of personal interest has greater research value in the broader community is a difficult concept to convey. It helps if you have thought about this ahead of time. I usually tell donors that a lot of people have this question, and provide them with some examples of collections at my repository that have been used for research. This helps to get them thinking in a new direction, and most warm to the idea that their stories and experiences are important.

Key Traits: Patience

Patience is a critical skill to have when working with donors. A potential donor may not be ready to donate something for many weeks or many years. It can be an emotional experience to contemplate letting go of something precious. The donor needs to be ready to do so, and may not be initially. I always reassure potential donors that we do not want to "take things from them." We want to help them preserve their collections, and we want to do that only when they are ready. They are in control of the timetable. This reassures people, and helps develop the trust that is needed between the donor and the institution.

Once when working with an elderly donor who had a large and interesting collection of family papers that spanned several centuries, she showed me many interesting things at our first meeting. She was only willing to donate a handful of letters, with the promise that she would add to this. She called me to her house several times after that over many months, each time making me hopeful for the rest of the collection, and each time I was leaving with only a small number of letters. When she told me she was handwriting a transcription of every letter on index cards before giving them to me, I explained to her that this was not necessary. We could read the letters in their original form just fine. She would nod and smile, but she kept on transcribing. I realized that she was not ready to part with her letters until she had completed the transcriptions. It was her way of saying good-bye to them, and that part of her life. It was her process, and I needed to patiently respect that process. Ultimately we did acquire the entire collection, though she passed away before completing all the transcriptions. I do not think we would have acquired any of this collection if she was pressed to donate more quickly.

Key Traits: Respect

Being patient is part of treating donors with respect, which is crucial to a successful acquisition. You also respect a donor by being on time for an appointment, dressing professionally, following through on anything you agree to send them or provide to them, staying in touch with them, and genuinely being interested in hearing their story.

Key Traits: Be Prepared

Respect is also conveyed by learning about the donor before meeting with him or her. Find out what you can with any lead time you have. If you aren't able to collect much or any information in advance (such as with donors who pop in on you unexpectedly) ask questions at the initial meeting and document conversations to help you in assessing what the donor's experiences have been, and what he or she may have that would be of research interest. Through gentle questioning you can elicit much that will be helpful to you.

Donors often want to find out what you know about them by testing you through questions. "What do you know about the Kansas Emergency Relief Committee?" a potential donor once asked me. He had been the executive director when it was established in the 1930s. Since I had done some research on him in advance, I could respond positively to this question, but we quickly exhausted my knowledge. He then asked me about the Homestead Corporation Commission (HCC), a topic that was clearly near and dear to his heart, and of which I knew nothing. I responded that I was not familiar with the HCC but would enjoy learning about it. He was delighted to educate me.

It may be tempting to say you know about something when you don't. You may be afraid that by saying "no" you will reveal your lack of knowledge, and the donor will not want to work with you. It is better to admit to what you don't know. In the above example, claiming familiarity about the HCC would surely have tripped me up in further discussion, revealing my lack of familiarity. Donors appreciate honesty; always answer their questions truthfully.

Key Traits: Professional Expertise

It may seem obvious, but an important skill in donor negotiations is to be engaged, professionally, with library/archival best practices in acquiring collections, and to know your institution's policies. Knowing what you can and can't do is important to think about before getting started in this work. You will need to be conversant with a deed of gift, issues of copyright, and how donated materials will be handled and accessed. Will book collections be kept together? Will paper records be digitized? Some donors assume so, while others may be dismayed by the idea. How are sensitive materials to be handled?

The question of appraisal comes up frequently. Archivists and librarians of receiving institutions cannot provide a monetary appraisal of donated materials, nor can they give tax advice. But the donor may want to pursue an appraisal independently, and you need to be prepared to talk about what options exist.

The Society of American Archivists has developed brochures that are very helpful in working with donors of personal and family papers and organizational records. They cover basic issues of what an institution might be interested in, what the donation process looks like, and things to consider such as access to collections and copyright. They include a statement on monetary donations as well, encouraging donors to recognize the expense involved in processing and maintain collections, and to consider a monetary donation to support these activities.

A third brochure focuses on deeds of gift, outlining the elements included and the issues to be addressed through the instrument as access, transfer of intellectual copyright, and how unwanted or duplicate materials will be handled. All these brochures are available in English and in Spanish from the Society of American Archivists.[6] They are very helpful in working with donors as they provide basic information about complex issues that you can leave with the donor for perusal.

The Personal Connection

Through all the potential donor interaction and negotiation, it is important to recognize that your involvement is playing a key role in determining the outcome. A potential donor will make his or her decision to donate the collection based largely on the relationship that has developed with you. While an institution is the recipient, the personal dynamics in play facilitate the decision made.

Your race, age, and gender can impact the dynamics of a situation as well. Being a younger (or later older) female and white either facilitated or was something to overcome in the development of donor rapport. Being aware of these issues can help to alleviate any problems encountered. Also, working with another librarian or archivist can bring more diversity to the situation and can be productive. I first came to Kansas to work from Michigan. I talked faster than many people here, and it was obvious I was from somewhere else. Much of my donor base is Kansan. I would often get asked immediately where I was from. I was very aware that I was the outsider. It was necessary to show that I was very conversant with Kanas life and history. Gradually this became less of an issue. Again, be patient.

Often, donors want to know more about you personally. At times they can ask questions that border on insensitivity. I have been asked what church I attend, what political candidates I support, my views on current events, the age of my children, and, once, even more personal, if I was pregnant. Fortunately, to the latter question, I could respond "yes." Questions like these are seldom asked in an assessing way, but can lead to an uncomfortable exchange. It's best to respond, generally, with some humor (if appropriate) and steer the conversation back to them. It takes some finesse that increases with experience.

Getting to know potential donors can be fascinating. It can also take an emotional toll on you as well. A donor may be grieving the loss of a loved one, or may be quite ill. Maybe they are facing a difficult family or financial situation. They may have just been diagnosed with a terminal illness. As the person of contact, you end up knowing their stories, histories, and family context. Their passing has an impact on you too, and leaves you with the realization of the trust they have given you, in sharing their papers or collections with your institution, through you.

Donor Motivation

In thinking about how to work successfully with donors, it is helpful to be aware of what is motivating the person to donate his or her collections. Donors may be concerned with leaving a legacy. Perhaps they are downsizing and this may be painful, or, they may just want to "get rid of the stuff." Maybe their spouse is pushing them to clean out that attic or garage. They may be dealing with settling the estate of a family member, or overwhelmed with the need to clear out a family home for a quick sale. Purcell identifies several categories of donor motivation that occur frequently including the right thing to do, sense of immortality, institutional allegiance, or tax deductions, or they are required to do so because of a position they hold within an organization or government.[7] Donors' expectations of the donation process vary, with some requiring more attention than others. Understanding their interest in a donation gives you an opportunity to work more effectively with that donor, and insure a successful outcome.

Working with the Elderly

Much of our interaction with donors involves working with the elderly. Some relationships play out over time. You may know the donor well or meet the donor for the first time when they are approaching the end of their life, or you may work with family and friends after someone has died to provide for the deceased's legacy. You have a definite role to play here, and it's not one that you are necessarily trained for. Geoff Wexler writes "Archivists have a responsibility to all these people—perhaps even a sacred responsibility, to preserve the records that remain.[8] Not only do we have this responsibility but also we are often there with the person through the process of aging and dying. Linda Long writes compellingly about her experience working to acquire the papers of an artist who was dying:

> I had not realized that the archivist or manuscript librarian plays
> a major role when a donor is dying . . . The experience taught me
> that the archivist is the keeper of someone's life, as the collector
> and manager of someone's papers.[9]

She also includes an excellent set of suggestions for working with donors in
this situation. She points to the need to develop a good working relationship
with your development officer, to think in advance about wordings in wills
that are most effective for the institution, and to consider how to talk with
donors before they die, letting the donor talk about his or her feelings and
the legacy he or she is leaving.[10] Recognize that you have the potential to be
impacted personally by the death of your donor. Despite the boundaries of
professionalism, the donor is likely someone that you have been able to get
to know. You carry their stories, their collecting passions. You may interact
with and comfort their family, and you connect who they were with the future
through your work.

Asking for Money

It is always difficult to bring up the need for money to care for our collections. It can feel awkward because most of us are not accustomed to doing it.
On the one hand, you are in a position of convincing a potential donor to put
his or her collection in your repository, and you are touting what you can do
to care for such a collection. On the other hand, you need money to care for
your growing collections; every cultural heritage institution faces budgetary
pressures. As Elena Danielson has so correctly observed, "Accepting a gift is
taking on a financial obligation in perpetuity."[11] How you successfully integrate fund-raising as part of your work will determine your future success.

We may be uncomfortable with asking for money because it takes us outside our comfort zone. We know about collections, rare books, and manuscripts. But we have no experience working with someone's financial status.
Not all donors are financially able to commit funds. It may not feel "right"
to be meeting with someone and wondering if they have capacity to give,
especially when we are already asking them for their collections that may
have monetary as well as the cultural or research value.

Yet, many of the qualities that make a good field archivist or librarian
are the same qualities that make a good fund-raiser. Robert Wedgeworth
writes, "For all potential donors, the process of creating and maintaining a
relationship is at the heart of any successful fund-raising campaign."[12] The
same is true for success in acquiring collections. Tomalea Doan and Sammie
Morris also note, "Successful fund raising depends as much on the energy,
communication and interpersonal skills of those involved in fund raising
activities as it does on his or her sound knowledge of fund raising methods."[13]

So, if the important skills are the same, how can we move ourselves from
positions of discomfort to being more proactive in fund-raising activities? You
start by making a closer alliance with those that already work in development in your institutions. You need to know how fund-raising is handled in
your setting, who has the authority to do this, and insert yourself into the
process. This might be someone other than you from the library or someone
from within an endowment organization or foundation. Once you know who

the players are, you can work generally to introduce them to the world of special collections, and rely on their cooperation with you in the meeting and discussion stage when working with prospective donors.

We, special collections librarians and archivists, have a lot in common with those working in development, but we don't always recognize the commonality. We don't necessarily know what development officers do, and on the development side there is often little understanding of what special collections librarians and archivists do. According to Purcell,

> [A]rchivists have the responsibility for educating development officers and other institutional fund raisers about archives. This is an ongoing process designed to familiarize the leaders of organized development with the needs, wants, policies, mission, and gift-giving potential of archives programs.[14]

Explaining how we work with donors and bringing to light our stewardship responsibilities help to demystify our world, and lead to greater cooperation.

Having regular meetings with the development person in your organization is a good way to promote opportunities that serve everyone's needs. The more they know about who you are working with and what you are trying to accomplish, the more help they can provide. Invite development staff to exhibit openings, talks, or other special events held in special collections. Offer to bring staff over to give a specialized tour with selected materials to illustrate special collections/archives. There may be opportunities to meet with a donor together. As Doan and Morris note:

> Librarians and archivists must be able to communicate clearly to donors, sometimes without advance warning and with very limited time, what the library stands for, what it does to benefit others, and why its existence is vital to the growth, success, and well-being of its user community and institution. Being able to speak effectively spontaneously is a skill that does not come naturally to all library professionals, but can be developed.[15]

The development of these skills requires practice.

Working cooperatively with development staff moves the donor program forward for the benefit of all. Archivists/librarians can make clear their funding priorities, and provide contacts and mission-specific value that strengthens the fund-raising opportunities. Likewise, those in development may provide new leads for collections and opportunities to strengthen the library/archives, in addition to building much needed financial support.

Stages of Donor Work: Initial Contact

The stages of donor work include initial contact, a period of meeting and discussion, negotiation, transfer of collection, and ongoing stewardship. These stages may be compressed into one meeting, or take place over years. Through all these stages you must create and maintain documentation.

Initial contact with a potential donor can come in many ways: a phone call, an inquiry based on information on your institution's website, or even a conversation in a personal setting. An initial potential donor file should record at a minimum the name, address, and phone number of the donor; brief biographical information about the donor; any known previous connection with your institution; brief information you have been given about the collection; a list of all interactions, including phone calls, with dates, and content of discussion; and any follow-up needed such as sending information about your repository.

It is important to add to this file as the donation progresses and you learn more. Typically included would be expanded description of the materials in question; the condition and location of materials; name and location of family members or legal representatives who might have a role in the donation; physical issues the donor might have that would be important to know, such as being hard of hearing, or unable to sit for lengthy periods of time; and questions asked with a brief description of the discussion. The more candid you can be in these notes, the more helpful they are later on. It is not always easy to make the time to prepare this documentation, but it is essential to do so as soon as you can, following each interaction. You may think you will remember what was discussed, but when you compound the interaction with multiple contacts going on simultaneously, you will forget things.

Stages of Work: Meeting and Discussion

The meeting and discussion stage is a time to learn all you can about the donor, the collection, and issues that might need to be worked out. If you are working with collectors of books, ephemera, or works of graphic design, they most likely will want you to understand the collection they have assembled and their work (often a labor of love) to assemble it. Take copious notes, and ask questions if the information you need is not forthcoming. Always ask collectors if they have written anything about their collection, explaining its focus and history. If they have, this can be an invaluable addition to accompany the collection. If they haven't, encourage them to write something for you to use.

Stages of Work: Negotiation

The negotiating stage includes the discussion of a deed of gift, which documents the donation, and is signed by both parties. You need to clearly explain issues of transfer of physical ownership, copyright, reformatting, disposition of duplicative materials, and deaccessioning. Potential donors may have expectations about the repository and its processes that are not realistic. They may think that everything they donate will automatically be digitized, or that what they are donating will always be on display. They may assume that only certain categories of researchers will be allowed to look at the papers they are donating. You must clearly and succinctly be able to explain these issues, resolving unrealistic explanations with information that is affirming and reassuring to the donor.

Most donors want reassurance that they will have access to their papers. Some donors may want an appraisal and you will need to explain why you can't provide one. A good summary of this process is provided by Menzi Behrnd-Klodt.

> Both the archives and the donor must negotiate fairly, and in good faith, without any coercion, fraud, or misrepresentation on either side, or pressure from outside parties. Archivists have ethical and

legal responsibilities to their institutions, archives, donors, public, profession, and themselves to be good stewards, trustees, and fiduciaries to several different groups.[16]

Stages of Work: Transfer of Collection

You may be involved in the transfer of collections and you need to know beforehand how much material is involved and where it is located. It is better to be involved in the packing and transfer, if possible, to ensure that order is maintained from files or shelves and that materials are packed carefully so as to avoid damage in transit. Packing a book collection from a donor's home provides you with the opportunity to understand the arrangement used by the donor, and to reflect that in transfer to the institution.

Packing materials can be a dirty, dusty job that often takes place in less than ideal conditions. It is common to complete this work in attics, basements, storage units, and sometimes very unusual locations. Care must be taken to ensure that the work is completed in as safe an environment as possible, minimizing the risk of injury.

Stages of Work: Ongoing Stewardship

The donor relationship does not cease once a collection is acquired. Donors may be anxious to see how their materials are processed, rehoused, stored, and so on. If they have not already visited the library or archives, they may want to do so, and, indeed, it is good to foster their interest in the broader library/archival operation. It is important to share information with them, and invite them to exhibit openings, talks, or other special events. Often they may want to look at their papers or donation, or bring in family members to see their collections housed in your institution. They may have suggestions for other collections that you might want to pursue. They can be of invaluable help in reviewing finding aids, and providing explanations for items in their collections. They will want to maintain the relationship they have established with you initially. This is time-consuming, but it is vital to your work.

This is a golden opportunity for expanding goodwill toward your institution, which can lead, down the road, to further fund-raising potential. Development staff will want to be kept in the loop with donor recognition and involvement in order to grow their own stewardship responsibilities.

Conclusion

In summary, successful donor relations rely on your ability to connect with the donor in a relationship of trust. Skills such as being a good listener, communicating clearly and articulately, employing patience, exhibiting respect, information gathering, and documenting all activity are essential to a successful outcome. These traits can be developed through practice and experience. The same skills are beneficial to working with potential donors in a fund-raising setting. You must become comfortable with developing approaches for both collections and money by partnering more closely with fund-raising professionals in your organizations.

Notes

1. Several examples of titles in this area are: F. Gerald Ham, *Selecting and Appraising Archives and Manuscripts* (Chicago: Society of American Archivists, 1993); Frank Boles, *Selecting and Appraising Archives and Manuscripts* (Chicago: Society of American Archivists, 2005); Elena S. Danielson, *The Ethical Archivist* (Chicago: Society of American Archivists, 2010); Menzi L. Behrnd-Klodt, *Navigating Legal Issues in Archives* (Chicago: Society of American Archivists, 2008); Randall C. Jimerson, ed., *American Archival Studies: Readings in Theory and Practice* (Chicago: Society of American Archivists, 2000); Mary Caldera and Kathryn M. Neal, eds., *Through the Archival Looking Glass A Reader on Diversity and Inclusion* (Chicago: Society of American Archivists); Richard J. Cox, *No Innocent Deposits: Forming Archives by Rethinking Appraisal* (Lanham, MD: Scarecrow Press, 2004).

2. Aaron D. Purcell, *Donors and Archives: A Guidebook for Successful Programs* (New York: Rowman & Littlefield, 2015).

3. Several examples of titles are: David D. Van Tassel, ed., *Aging, Death and the Complexity of Being* (Philadelphia: University of Pennsylvania Press, 1979); Elisabeth Kubler-Ross, *On Death and Dying* (New York: MacMillan, 1969); Janet L. Hedrick, *Nonprofit Essentials: Effective Donor Relations* (New York: John Wiley and Sons, 2009).

4. Ham, *Selecting and Appraising Archives and Manuscripts*, 38.

5. Stephen R. Covey, *The Seven Habits of Highly Effective People* (New York: Simon & Schuster, 1989), 240.

6. *Donating Your Personal or Family Records to a Repository; Donating Your Organization's Records to a Repository*; and *A Guide to Deeds of Gift* (Chicago: Society of American Archivists, 2013).

7. Purcell, *Donors and Archives*, 11–15.

8. Geoff Wexler and Linda Long, "Lifetimes and Legacies: Mortality, Immortality, and the Needs of Aging and Dying Donors," *American Archivist* 72, no. 2 (fall/winter 2009): 478.

9. Ibid., 489.

10. Ibid., 493.

11. Danielson, *The Ethical Archivist*, 77.

12. Robert Wedgeworth, "Donor Relations as Public Relations: Toward a Philosophy of Fund-Raising," *Library Trends* 48, no. 3 (winter 2000): 535.

13. Tomalee Doan and Sammie Morris, "Middle Managers and Major Gifts: Fundraising for Academic Libraries," *The Bottom Line* 25, no. 4 (2012): 192.

14. Purcell, *Donors and Archives*, 11–15.

15. Doan and Morris, "Middle Managers and Major Gifts," 194.

16. Behrnd-Klodt, *Navigating Legal Issues in Archives*, 45–46.

Chapter 12

You and What Army? Making the Most of Student and Volunteer Labor in Contemporary Special Collection and Archives

Dana M. Miller

Introduction

It is not news to most archives that we encounter a shortage of labor in almost every size and type of repository. Also not surprising are the ubiquitous backlogs of collections and materials thoughtfully taken in, but by necessity left unprocessed, underdescribed, or otherwise inaccessible. We operate simultaneously within two opposing paradigms: a growing abundance of collections confronts a world of workforce scarcity, in which ever more limited budgets dictate that there is never time enough nor labor enough to treat everything we collect in the way we might prefer according to archival principles and nationally standardized practices. We have always more mouths to feed, and always fewer resources to go around. For decades since the exponential growth of records that occurred with the dawn of the computer age, manuscripts librarians and archivists have accepted that we often don't have the means to perform essential functions of our jobs to the fullest. In the push to do the best with what we have, difficult judgment calls, prioritization decisions for treatment, and creative solutions have become primary tools of the trade.

Assuming we are not willing to abandon our goals to provide access to materials, how do we address such wide and crucial need? Common sense reigns: if there are not enough librarians, archivists, or paraprofessionals permanently on staff in a given repository and not enough money to hire more, other avenues must be explored. One response might be to obtain soft money in the form of grants in order to hire temporary project workers, which is how many early career archivists get their start, though the benefit to the worker and the repository extends only the length of the project and there is a finite amount of grant funding to go around. Another key strategy is to create a framework whereby professionals can effectively direct the work of a small, rotating group of nonexperts in the form of students, interns, and volunteers in order to achieve adequate or even excellent results for our collections and their users.

The use of student, intern, and volunteer labor has been in existence in nonprofit and cultural institutions for decades if not longer, and special collections libraries and archives are no exception. There are a number of benefits to the strategy for both the repository and the worker. The repository has the opportunity to complete work that might not otherwise get done, to perform outreach within its community through a prolonged one-on-one interaction, to recruit future supporters and lovers of manuscripts and archives for legislative and financial support, and to see itself through the eyes of a newcomer.

For their part, students, interns, and even volunteers gain valuable work experience applicable to many fields, make contacts, and network for references, all of which can help them get a job later where that is the end goal. Some such workers in an academic archive or special collections library may even earn a modest wage or stipend as part of a student job; there is also the occasional paid internship. Finally, the research skills and exposure to primary resources that come as a side effect of archival work are a very valuable benefit to most of these potential workers, as is the chance to interact with materials of historical and cultural significance.

However, the use of such labor does not come without its challenges and even drawbacks, which should be taken into careful consideration. For one, we can reasonably expect students, interns, and volunteers to leave, so training and procedures must be carefully constructed and documented to allow for a rotating lineup while minimizing the time spent by the repository staff. Second, that they are nonexperts with no archives background ostensibly makes their work require additional quality control. Quality training, consistent supervision, and good project management by a professional are not often taught in the master's programs that graduate future archivists. Perhaps the deepest concern is that the successful use of student or intern labor will inspire management to perceive the manuscripts librarian or archives professional as replaceable, perpetrating a devaluing effect on the professional overall while exploiting the free or low-cost labor of nonexperts. However, projects may be structured and work stratified in such a way as to create an apprentice environment that highlights and emphasizes the value of the professional's perspective, input, and work contributions rather than obfuscating them.

Despite the challenges and constraints, the use of student, intern, and volunteer workers in archives and special collections offers a multitude of rewards that make it worth the effort. Archivists from all corners of the profession should embrace this reality and work together to share their programs, documentation, and training to expand into new avenues of the archival enterprise.

Historical Snapshot

Even prior to mass computerization and the attendant proliferation of records and backlogs, archivists have acknowledged the need for and use of student and volunteer labor and discussed successful implementations in the archival literature. A 1980 article by Hansen and Newman outlines a program within the Colorado State University history department in which graduate students worked with university archives collections to the benefit of both the students and the archives. Two choices were offered to prospective student workers: an eight-week practicum focused specifically on mutually chosen processing projects, or a semester-long program for those interested in an archives career, which also allowed students to act as part-time archival assistants by accessioning new collections, staffing the service desk, and helping with reference.[1]

Thirty-five years prior to this writing, their reasons for creating such a program were the same as they are today: being short of adequate personnel to process collections, wanting to give prospective archivists and historians an opportunity to practice the essential basic skills of their professions, and needing to provide access to hidden collections. Another familiar woe they mention, which so many archivists today can still relate to all too well, is the desired amount of processing not getting done by the special collections librarian due to the professional's numerous other duties that often overshadowed or completely overtook their manuscript duties, even though manuscript "care and feeding" was their primary assignment.[2]

In their 1981 piece about using these types of nonexperts to process collections in the Archives of Appalachia, authors Kesner, Karnes, Sims, and Shandor discuss an experiment in which they assigned processing work to undergraduates. Because the authors recognized that "certain aspects of collection arrangement and description are also highly repetitive," it made sense to have undergraduates act as processing assistants as well. Using student workers "freed processors for more important professional responsibilities," such as reference, outreach, and collection development.[3] The team approach delivered high-quality finding aids in a much shorter time frame.

Moving forward a decade, Floyd and Oram specifically focus on undergraduates as employees in university archives. In their survey results, 89 percent of the archives reported using undergraduate workers. The work most often assigned was mundane clerical work such as typing, filing, and paging, but 86 percent of the respondents agreed that there is a place for undergraduate workers in university archives beyond routine clerical work. Moreover, 80 percent of the archives reported using undergrads for at least minimal processing work, 50 percent used them for public services, and 50 percent used them for light preservation work. The authors go on to point out the proliferation of articles on managing student labor in libraries but the distinct lack of same regarding archives, citing the difference in the nature of the work as the primary reason, and encouraging taking greater care to find good workers and paying them more in comparison.

Archivists have also taken steps to structure their student and volunteer labor programs to make them more practical and efficient and less labor-intensive over time, defining tiers of work and creating training and documentation. They can copy, modify, and integrate new models of successful implementation of such programs that have begun to gain strength across the profession. One such example is the University of California, Los Angeles, Special Collections Center for Primary Research and Training (CFPRT). Launched in 2004, the CFPRT aims to tackle the hidden collections and backlog problem by pairing interested students with unprocessed collections relevant to their field of study in a highly esteemed and donor-funded program.

Students are enthusiastic about working with materials relevant to their personal educational goals, and they have been producing high-quality, high-value finding aids and cataloging ... In addition, by providing financial support to graduate students ... CFPRT benefits the university at large, aiding in recruiting top students and accelerating and focusing the progress of students to the completion of their degrees.[4]

The CFPRT also attracts significant donor money, usually an extremely difficult feat to generate for processing projects. The center succeeds by linking donated money to the students who work there.

From these publications and initiatives emerge a pattern of progressively increasing tolerance toward the involvement of student workers as assistants in most aspects of special collections and archives work. Volunteer is a somewhat different animal in terms of nonexpert labor. Literature on the topic runs from the 1970s to today, but Leonard offers an especially clear and cautionary discussion of the volunteer in the archives, asserting that, "using volunteer labor effectively is an effort that rewards planning."[5] Helpfully, he defines volunteers in two categories: formal apprenticeships (or internships) for students or recent graduates of archival education programs, and offers of free labor from either the former group or members of the community with interest but no specific ambition to become professional archivists. These two groups have different needs and somewhat different things to offer an archive, and their projects should be designed accordingly.

Recent surveys and reports on the profession as a whole confirm that the need for student workers and volunteers has not diminished over time; rather the associated facts suggest that the need is only too likely to persist. In their comprehensive 2010 survey of North American special collections and archives, Dooley and Luce state that, "the data show that 75% of respondents saw their 2008–09 budgets drop as a result of the recent decline in the global economy. Endowments have fallen significantly in value, and governmental budgets have been severely reduced. The inevitable belt tightening is well underway."[6] Though their data showed that staffing had remained relatively stable since 2000, many of the organizations they surveyed are private research libraries that have far more staff than most, particularly public organizations that operate as part of a larger library unit. Yet even among this population, significant decreases in functional areas such as public services were noted. At the same time user demand for access to collections grew, with 43 percent to 65 percent of responding repositories reporting their use by various categories of users going up by more than 60 percent; many repositories have decreased the size of their backlogs but 25 percent reported an increase in backlogs for bound volumes and 41 percent increase in other materials.[7] One major question to come out of the report evokes the tone of the archives profession in the 21st century: How much longer can we continue to do more with less? Leveraging student and volunteer labor is one way to take off some of that pressure, though it is not a comprehensive or permanent solution to the overall problem.

Benefits to Special Collections and Archives

Getting More Done

The most obvious benefit to using student and volunteer labor is to allow a special collections or archives staff to complete work which might not otherwise get done. This very clearly applies to basic clerical duties and a variety of arrangement and description work but can also apply well to public services staffing, preservation work, and metadata projects. It is up to the repository to determine what types of work will be assigned to students and volunteers, keeping in mind that creating and articulating the broader goals of the repository or project, program development, and management should remain unique to the sphere of the archives professional, as should any work that cannot be performed without a background or significant experience in archival work. A time-tested method for success is to use a tiered approach tasking the expert to design, guide, and review the work according to the perspective and proficiency offered by his or her knowledge, experience, and awareness of professional context, while nonexperts focus on executing that work in smaller portions. The archivist works with the student or volunteer to come up with a processing plan, trains them in basic arrangement and description according to local practice, and periodically checks in to assess the quality of the work. Even a skill such as metadata creation can be tiered this way to positive results: descriptive or evidential types of metadata such as physical description, years covered, formats, and general scope and content can be entered by nonexperts. The work of creating a controlled vocabulary, indexing for names and subjects, determining the "aboutness" of a collection or item, and review of the overall record is left the purview of the experienced manuscript librarian or archivist.

Almost all archives professionals are familiar with the pitfalls of juggling many competing responsibilities while also handling a multitude of projects. Outcomes are not as strong or successful as they could have been if more focus and time were available. Students and volunteer responsibilities should have a much narrower focus and time that can be devoted to specific tasks and projects. They are thus far more likely to complete these smaller projects in a reasonable time frame than a busy professional or manager might. The price of that labor is not insubstantial: the initial time it takes the archivist to select projects, prepare training and documentation of standards and procedures, routinely check work, and communicate with workers can be significant. Kesner et al. provide a good example of the rewards of such preparation: "Whereas a single archivist working alone processed the presidential archival collections at the rate of 4.8 linear feet of finished materials per month, the team (of student workers) approach achieves a rate of about 14.4 linear feet per month."[8]

Creating Relationships with Your Community

Using student workers and particularly volunteers creates a unique outreach opportunity for special collections or archives to nurture a prolonged one-on-one relationship with a member of its community. These more personal relationships go a long way to establishing the repository and its archivists as a place worth supporting in a myriad of ways. In a university setting, it creates positive relationships with students; a desirable environment can help attract future student workers through word of mouth. Working with community volunteers who give generously of their time is a relationship-building step that goes beyond the individual and disperses among their network. You never know how your volunteers might be connected or come to your aid in the future. "Retiree or elderly volunteers especially may be well-connected members of that community and can open channels of contact between an archive and the people it serves . . . volunteers are prized because they reinforce ties between an archive and its public."[9] Volunteers and students can become lifelong lovers and supporters of archives and manuscript repositories, helping to recruit both legislative and financial support when needed. While collection development should be steered by a full-time professional, volunteers can also assist with outreach and collection development efforts through their networks.

Gaining Perspective

While it can be uncomfortable, it is often very helpful for an archive, special collections library, or any similar organization to see itself through the eyes of a newcomer. This new perspective can reveal inconsistencies in procedure, inadequate documentation, confusing or contradictory rules, or a host of other issues that archives professionals might become blind to the more they have been exposed to them through long-term employment. Questioning is periodically necessary for archivists to ensure their policies and procedures are viable, comprehensible, and efficient.[10] Special collections and archives are specific environments. It is useful to step outside ourselves from time to time to see how our users and community might perceive our esoteric holdings and eccentric ways. This allows archivists to consider how they might improve the user experience, the most important public element of their profession.

Benefits to the Worker

Hands-on Experience

The student worker, intern, or volunteer also gains important rewards from working in an archival setting, though the exact nature of the benefit changes with the goal of the participant. Most student positions receive a very small wage or stipend as remuneration for the job, and a small number of internships are paid. For the majority of nonexpert workers, the real rewards of their labors are not financial. For students seeking future employment in the archives field, obtaining meaningful work experience is required during many master's level degree programs in the form of internships. For those who seek to better understand what the job itself entails before they embark on a career, learning by doing was better than anything else: "Nothing could match the knowledge derived from analyzing management survey questionnaires, visiting storage areas of campus offices, wrestling dirty cartons onto a pickup truck, appraising documents for retention or disposal, and processing records at the University Archives."[11]

Broader Application and Network Building

Even when student workers and volunteers do not plan to go into archival work, some aspects of archival work and the skills it imparts are applicable to a diversity of fields. The superior physical and mental organization skills and extended focus required by archival work are strengths in any industry, particularly in the sciences and lab work. The categorization and analytical thinking skills required to arrange collections and the clear, concise language skills required to describe them are widely applicable, as are the people skills that public service demands. The professional who hires student workers and volunteers should reasonably assume that they will at some point provide professional or informal references for those workers in exchange for the labor they provide us. Besides knowledge and experience, making contacts is a key to gaining employment where that is the end goal; if we treat our student workers and volunteers as professionals, we should expect to help them to not only build their knowledge but also build their professional networks in special collections, archives, and beyond.

Research Skills and Interaction with Primary Resources

In a time of online accessibility and wide distribution, the unique resources that special collections and archives have to offer remain just that. We might realistically expect that nearly everyone in a developed country might read a book or newspaper in their lifetime, but the same most certainly cannot be said for using archival materials or performing research with primary resources. A side effect of most archival work even at the nonexpert level is a degree of familiarity and comfort with primary source materials and the often esoteric tools used to discover them. When nurtured and adapted, these are extremely useful in scholarly as well as other types of other research. The historic and cultural documents in repositories have a desirability factor much like the objects and art pieces in museums; people want to see them, even touch them, and learn about them. Students and volunteers (and even professionals) are often motivated and feel connected to a repository due to the materials they get to work with, share with others through their work, and generally be around on a regular basis. This intrinsic value of awareness and contact with historically and culturally significant documents should not be undervalued.

Challenges and Opportunities

Recruiting a Suitable Army

"The number of people . . . eligible or likely to seek a volunteer position" with an archival repository is relatively small because "the profession is not well known and only a small percentage of people ever gain exposure to an archives, its collections, or its staff."[12] Special collections and archives situated within universities generally have a ready supply of student labor available, though choosing exactly which students to hire can be daunting and may only improve through trial and error. An important point to remember is the significant amount of time required to set up and manage such a program, to train and supervise the workers, to check their work products, and to maintain those relationships over time. In this light, less is always more. One professional archivist can only effectively manage three to four students and volunteers at one time before his or her own work productivity in other areas is compromised and their supervision becomes ineffective.

To attract nonexpert workers where more are truly needed, archives or special collections might recruit among current students and volunteers and thereby tap existing extended networks of those already devoted to the cause. Outreach through a number of community channels and mediums by focusing on a theme or specific historical topic or event for which volunteers and students are sought may also help. So long as they get the message, those with established interest and sufficient availability and motivation are likely to turn up. When presented with a multitude of options choosing among applicants is both a luxury and a burden; organizational skills, extraordinary attention to detail, love of history, evidence of excellent written and verbal communication skills, and ability to work with others are essential qualities to seek, along with reasonable availability and reliability.

Training, Turnover, and Return on Time Investment

A common complaint against the use of student or volunteer labor centers on the time the archivist or librarian must invest in training only to see the student or volunteer leave after a semester or year-long engagement. However, with solid planning and clear documentation, a repository can adopt a structured system that allows it to easily and simply train nonexpert workers in a variety of tasks according to professional standards and local best practices.

- Write a separate processing manual, public services instructions, or metadata input guide exclusively tuned to the tasks performed by nonexpert workers.

- Disseminate it widely throughout the organization.

- Update it regularly when procedures or tools change.

- Provide accessible examples of how you want the work performed.

- Provide, possibly, counterexamples of what not to do so they know what to aim for and what to avoid.

- Adopt a style of training that expects nonexperts to repeat instructions back to you.

- Be approachable and let them know that if they are stuck they must ask questions.

The ideal balance is for nonexperts to perform at the highest level of difficulty at which they are comfortable, but not struggling so much that it would be faster and simpler for a professional to do the work. A tiered approach in which nonexperts focus on the low-hanging (but not necessarily always boring) fruit while the professionals handle complicated trees and forests (and even jungles) is helpful toward this goal.

Scheduling as Related to Time Investment and Project Management

In gratitude and in an attempt to be flexible, we tend to allow our volunteers and student workers to have wildly irregular schedules with not enough contiguous hours in them to allow for finishing projects. Scheduling these workers can be a time-consuming, acrobatic act in itself. This creates a problem that can derail labor management and negatively affect work quality and completion rates, as "limited, irregular schedules are ill-suited for tasks needing frequent attention."[13] Thus some assertiveness is required of the professional or manager in charge of student and volunteer labor to maintain a modicum of control.

It is reasonable to assume that the archivist, as a professional, has other important things to do besides scheduling and supervising others. It follows that it is reasonable for the professional archivist to set up specific days during the week or a reasonable range of hours during which volunteers may come in to work, as opposed to allowing freedom to choose between any hours the repository is open; this should be coordinated with a supervisor being present. It is also advisable to require that shifts worked by students, interns, and volunteers have a minimum length, such as two to four hours; that they occur at a minimum regularity, such as twice weekly; and endure for a minimum time frame, such as three months, in order to get a project or goal accomplished. Setting these types of boundaries up before hiring students or taking on volunteers saves the archivist precious time, communicates to potential nonexpert workers the value of the archivist's time as well as theirs, clarifies the repository's needs and expectations, and helps prospective workers self-select depending on their level of interest and availability.

Quality Control and Effective Supervision

The likelihood that nonexperts will be unfamiliar with an archives or special collections environment and its niche aspects may further frustrate the professional's ability to draw quality work products out of volunteers and student workers. Even newly hired professionals with experience in the field need guidance and consistent feedback in order to succeed. One must establish and communicate clear expectations of all workers, train them carefully, provide written documentation and examples, and designate a supervisor who is present and approachable for questions.[14] Training and documentation are as important as carefully choosing appropriate assignments. It is often advisable to build in extra time for regular review and quality control checks until trust is built. Regular review and open, honest-yet-friendly communication are major components of good project management.

Aptitude and interest level are more difficult to determine for nonexpert workers, as opposed to professionals who by and large can be assumed to have self-selected based on one or both criteria.[15] Just as not everyone can be a chef or astronaut, not everyone is able to master all aspects of archival work, and some excel at only parts of it. When all avenues for improvement have been exhausted and a student or volunteer still cannot perform adequate work, it should be accepted without blame or guilt, and a genuine attempt made to reassign the student/volunteer elsewhere for a better fit. Finally, the archives should manage its expectations when it comes to nonexpert work products. Work should contribute to the repository's goals and work products should be helpful and functional, but perfectionism or holding these workers to the same standards as experienced professionals is not within the bounds of good sense. A good rule of thumb is if the nonexpert can perform the work, which would otherwise not get done, at 70 percent of the quality and speed at which a professional could perform it, that is adequate.

Creating a Positive Experience

Retention of student workers and volunteers lies with the archivist's ability to effectively train and supervise, and to communicate the importance of the work they will perform and how the repository and its users will benefit from the outcome. While different from the work a professional performs, nonexpert work should vary as much as feasible and offer some amount of interest capital. Tempting as it may be, "volunteers should not be shunted into activities that are or that are perceived to be unimportant and undesirable," lest their motivation and commitment be reduced in consequence.[16] For times when routine work is all that is available at a given time, it is important to speak honestly about it without being negative and to focus discussion on the exciting outcome versus the drudgery of the work, to thank them for their efforts, and be sure to offer them a more interesting project as soon as one becomes available. Having two or three varying projects lined up for student workers that require different types of thinking (for example, building archival boxes for bound materials and creating basic descriptive metadata in a database) may allow them some needed mental flexibility over the duration of a semester.

In establishing your reputation as an attractive place to work or volunteer, the element of joy and feeling appreciated cannot be overlooked. Genuine thanks and celebrating such workers and their efforts from time to time, such as treating them to coffee, arranging a potluck in their honor, or giving certificates of thanks to volunteers, will go a long way for a very small cost.

When it comes to correcting or criticizing work, a fair and gentle but firm approach focused on appropriate standards and procedures is best. "The work product of a volunteer, because it is freely and generously given, can be difficult or even painful to criticize or to correct when problems arise."[17] Nonetheless the message that improvement is needed or a different direction would be better is an important one and should be delivered clearly but without harsh judgment. Respect for those who give their time to the common cause of special collections and archives comes in many forms, one of which is honesty as you work toward a shared goal.

Concerns of Displacement of Professionals by Nonexperts

While a few work tasks might overlap, nonexperts should not be asked to perform the same jobs that professionals perform. Nonexperts do not have the background or experience in making the level of decisions expected of a professional archivist. If the routine stuff of archives is your personal bailiwick, you are probably focusing on the wrong work tasks and ignoring the forest for the trees. Professionals should be structuring work appropriately in tiers—designing frameworks, determining best practices and rules, creating master plans and documentation—all of which student workers, volunteers, and other staff can be deployed to execute in varying degrees of minutiae: "the intellectual aspects of arrangement and description remain in the hands of those trained in these procedures while the time-consuming, routine, but essential maintenance aspects of the work were accomplished by the relatively unskilled. Thus the archives realized the most economical utilization of its personnel."[18] This is exactly the desired outcome regardless of what type of work students, interns, and volunteers are performing. After all, if archivists self-define in the profession as mere file clerks, then they will be assumed to be just that. It is incumbent upon the archivist to assume the role of information professional; to think more globally and contextually about structure, access, and user experience; and to manage projects and represent our repositories with grace and intelligence.

Conclusion

Special collections and archives have long been making use of student and volunteer labor to achieve access and service goals, and the conditions that make this necessary are not only unlikely to go away but may in fact become exacerbated to create even more need. While not an ideal model under any circumstance, archivists should embrace this option as a possible solution to labor shortages. While it requires much upfront investment in training, documentation, management, and quality maintenance, it also promises long-term returns in completed projects, connection to community, and relationship-building with future archival advocates. Archivists can do themselves and their profession a favor by engaging nonexpert workers from a perspective that recognizes their positive impact, respects their contributions, and focuses on the added value they bring to the archives as complementary to existing professionals on staff.[19]

Notes

1. James E. Hansen II and John Newman, "Training History Students in Working Archives," *The History Teacher* 13, no. 2 (February 1980): 215, accessed April 28, 2015, http://www.jstor.org/stable/491922.

2. Ibid., 213.

3. Richard M. Kesner, Susan Tannewitz Karnes, Anne Sims, and Michael Shandor, "Collection Processing as a Team Effort," *American Archivist* 44, no. 4 (Fall 1981): 356, accessed April 28, 2015, http://www.jstor.org/stable/40292436.

4. Victoria Steele, "Exposing Hidden Collections: The UCLA Experience," *C&RL News* (June 2008), 316, accessed May 27, 2015, http://crln.acrl.org/content/69/6/316 .full.pdf.

5. Kevin B. Leonard, "Volunteers in Archives: Free Labor, but Not without Cost," *Journal of Library Administration* 52, no. 3–4 (2012): 313, accessed May 27, 2015, http://www.tandfonline.com/doi/pdf/10.1080/01930826.2012.684529.

6. Jackie M. Dooley and Katherine Luce, "Taking Our pulse: The OCLC Research Survey of Special Collections and Archives," *OCLC Research Report* (2010): 23, accessed May 28, 2015, http://www.oclc.org/research/publications/library/2010/2010 -11.pdf.

7. Ibid., 36, 48.

8. Kesner et al., "Collection Processing as a Team Effort," 357.

9. Leonard, "Volunteers in Archives," 316.

10. Ibid., 315.

11. Hansen and Newman, "Training History Students," 212.

12. Leonard, "Volunteers in Archives," 316.

13. Ibid., 316.

14. Kesner et al., "Collection Processing as a Team Effort," 357.

15. Hansen and Newman, "Training History Students," 217.

16. Leonard, "Volunteers in Archives," 318.

17. Ibid., 316.

18. Kesner et al., "Collection Processing as a Team Effort," 357.

19. Leonard, "Volunteers in Archives," 318.

Chapter 13

A Janus Perspective: Origins and Future of 21st-Century Preservation and Conservation in Library and Archives Special Collections

Priscilla Anderson and Whitney Baker

Introduction

In the year 2076, a history professor will enter a special collections reading room and expect to show students a letterbook bearing John Hancock's own account of the Boston Tea Party,[1] alongside a searchable scan of that text, its provenance, related collections, and the conservation record of treatments and assessments that have formed part of the entire Hancock collection's care over its 300-year life span. A hundred years earlier, 20th-century preservation practitioners suspected that a bound letterbook such as this might only be touched once by a professional conservator, and therefore often recommended highly skilled, time-consuming conservation work regardless of how the artifact was expected to be used. Early 21st-century conservation practice bridges between these two worlds by identifying a spectrum of options, ranging from preventive measures to minimally invasive repairs to complex conservation treatment, prioritizing the work to support current use. Special collections preservation efforts strive to prevent damage to already massive and ever-growing collections so they will be accessible for future use, including the documentation that records the artifacts' values, significance, history, and prior use.

Broadly speaking, special collections preservation focuses on prevention of damage to a physical artifact and its digital derivatives, and conservation focuses on repairing that damage. These undertakings are neither easy, nor inexpensive, nor quick. To understand why it is important to preserve special collections in libraries and archives both large and small, one must first understand how these collections are used and valued. Simply put, in order for people to use or benefit from any special collections, the aspect that is of value must be accessible to the users; preservation and conservation activities work toward making both current and future access possible. If seeing John Hancock's authentic signature is to inspire a group of school children to become civic leaders, then that letter should be displayed for them to admire it. If the physical condition of Hancock's letterbook informs a researcher's understanding of how such records were used over time, then that researcher should have access to the original bound volume and its conservation records that document changes over time, from either intentional repairs or unintended degradation. If another researcher wants to compare use of the word "tea" over the centuries, then that data must be able to be discovered and mined from the content of Hancock's historic account. To provide any of these values to the user, the artifact physically must be able to withstand the intended use; by preventing and repairing damage, preservation and conservation activities strive to ensure that physical stability over time.

The authors of this chapter are a collections conservator and a preservation librarian from two university libraries in the United States with substantial special collections holdings. In this chapter, we will summarize the basic principles of early 21st-century preservation and conservation of library and archives special collections, looking back to the 20th-century practices that persist, and looking forward to changes in the field that are necessitated by rapid and fundamental developments in technology, research methods, and climate change. For example, analog artifact collections are viewed differently in an increasingly digital information world. This technological and cultural shift has necessitated changes to preservation workflows, which presents challenges in training preservation and conservation professionals to manage the new workflows. Different approaches and resources are used by smaller institutions that do not have ready access to these professionals. In a broader context, both preservation and conservation of special collections in libraries and archives have a significant role to play in sustainability of both natural and cultural resources.

Role of Analog Collections

For decades, conventional wisdom has assumed the demise of the printed book in favor of digital versions,[2] much to the chagrin of library conservators who may see their livelihood threatened. In fact, the printing industry is still producing books. It will take another kind of technology to replace the portable, personal, private, silent codex. This may happen during the 21st century, but, at least for now, the public is still buying printed books, magazines, and newspapers; printing and storing paper archives and images; and collecting paper ephemera; these and other personal memorabilia will become the analog special collections of the future. In another hundred years, these collections may be valued for their unique content, their association with a notable person, or evidence of their use and importance (for example, notes in the margins, grime, and wear patterns). The content may or may not be available digitally, depending in large part on how well we establish good digital preservation habits now. The challenge for preserving today's personal collections will be addressing the needs of a greater diversity of materials with accelerated degradation and obsolescence issues.

Preservation of decaying, brittle books and implementation of a permanent paper standard for publishers were major focuses of large, research libraries in the 1980s and 1990s. While brittle paper is still a common and pressing concern among librarians who continue to care for "medium rare" paper-based collections of the 19th and early 20th centuries, this issue may be overshadowed by audiovisual and digital materials that face risk of substantial loss within a decade or two due to their more rapid deterioration as well as obsolescence of playback equipment and software.[3] The greater urgency of audiovisual materials' deterioration and obsolescence, combined with exponentially greater resources required to reformat and store the digitized audiovisual files, will rapidly necessitate an expansion of preservation resources and professional expertise. Our increasingly digital world is also an increasingly audiovisual world, and these untapped special collections may become more desirable sources as society's cultural output shifts from primarily text, including books, newspapers, blogs, and dissertations, to multimedia productions such as educational video games and visualized data presentations. In addition to the large amount of audiovisual and digital media, preservation and conservation staff will also be challenged to provide physical care for rapidly changing modern materials with increasingly sophisticated and secret manufacturing methods. Consider the challenges of determining how to preserve a family album with digital prints that fade unpredictably in the dark;[4] or the adhesive tape attaching writer Margaret Yourcenar's emendations to her typescript;[5] or the plastics, wax, and saturated ink components of artist Dieter Roth's mixed media scrapbook album, *Snow*.[6]

Despite this major shift predicted in preservation focus, there are still massive paper-based collections to be preserved and provided for research. Many larger research libraries have responded to the challenges of storing physical materials by creating off-site, often high-density, storage facilities that use a warehouse model of housing materials by size to maximize space.[7] These facilities generally maintain tight environmental controls, with lower temperature and relative humidity settings than are normally found in traditional storage environments in order to more greatly prolong the life span of collections. Campuses with space restrictions may build these facilities at a significant distance from patron service points, necessitating safe transportation of often fragile collections to a reading room. In many cases, research libraries have banded together to create "shared print repositories" in which one or a few best copies of a journal or book are kept, often in an off-site location.[8] Preservation personnel assess completeness, physical condition, potential digital surrogates, and artifactual value as part of the decision-making process. When libraries mutually agree to share collections, they evaluate how such collections will be used and accessed in the future, keeping in mind that today's general collections could be tomorrow's special collections.

Analog collections are experiencing more and different kinds of current use, stretching conservation skills and budgets: exhibition visitors expect aesthetically authentic display; digitization projects require quick turnaround and minimal stabilization to make the information accessible to the cameras; and increasing donor tours and classroom use increase repeated handling and risk of damage. Preservation and conservation approaches must respond to rapid changes in higher education, the publishing industry, and technology, while proactively protecting the increasingly valuable physical assets found in library special collections. Shifts in institutional priorities drive much of preservation's work, and challenge preservation professionals to optimize limited resources including skills, time, space, and funding.

Preservation and Conservation Principles, Training, and Professional Duties

The field of library preservation is a specialty within library science that focuses on programmatic approaches to preventing damage to collections. Training for preservation professionals may include higher-level coursework or a certificate program, but on-the-job training often provides the bulk of a preservation professional's practical training. The core principles of preservation are derived from closely related conservation principles. These principles are grounded in the conservation field's strong Code of Ethics and corollary Guidelines for Practice that underscore the rigorous training required for professional status as well as an evolving set of professional duties.[9] These core principles include: acting as an advocate for cultural property, endeavoring to prevent damage and deterioration, selecting working methods that do not adversely affect future investigation or use of the material, documenting changes that are made to the materials, and promoting awareness of conservation work through outreach to allied professionals and the general public. These core principles were developed over 30 years beginning in 1961 by the American Institute for Conservation of Historic and Artistic Works, the professional organization for museum and library conservators in the United States. Conservation professionals continue to clarify and update the content to reflect 21st-century challenges and technological developments.[10]

Studying to be a conservation professional in the late 20th century was generally accomplished through a handful of graduate-level training programs. Training was available in both library/archives and museum contexts. Since the closure of the only library science-based program in 2009,[11] a book conservation specialty has been added to several art conservation training programs. Graduates from these art conservation programs concentrating in rare book conservation may differ from the previous library science graduates. One likely outcome is the enhanced focus on material science research in the museum-based programs, which may lead to new discoveries about special collections materials.

In general, 20th-century conservators departed from the role of skilled craftspeople descended from many centuries of bookbinders to prove themselves as professionals with in-depth knowledge of materials and the science behind their deterioration, while still serving as highly skilled surgeons practicing delicate repairs. In the early 21st century, conservators must now return to the source, defending the value of the original object itself against the lure of convenient access to digital surrogates, sometimes as an interpreter of evidence and sometimes as an evaluator of research value. Many preservation librarians who once focused on care for physical collections are finding themselves also managing digitization and digital preservation workflows. Despite these changes, conservation and preservation professionals have always required an awareness of broader library activities and trends, including current terminology, technology, and priorities.

As an example of how 21st-century preservation and conservation professionals have expanded their skillsets, consider the entirely different mind-set required to do outreach. They are spending more time on these outreach efforts than ever before, posting blog, wiki, and website content;

teaching workshops; offering advice to listservs, online discussion groups, and the public; hosting fund-raising events; performing conservation treatments in front of an audience; giving tours; and liaising with other departments. Supported by a cross-disciplinary group of professional organizations, preservation professionals create and engage in the American Library Association's Preservation Week public outreach events each April, ranging from lectures, webinars, and demonstrations, to public clinics where they examine precious heirlooms and advise their owners on how to prevent damage by following handling, storage, and display guidelines.

Increased focus on outreach signals that the profession has matured, and its 21st-century practitioners are now more comfortable sharing expertise and knowledge outside the field. Preservation professionals are equally motivated by the pressing need to build the case for protecting cultural heritage in a society where increasingly disposable and digital ways of life decrease the personal connection people have with their material history and cultural heritage. Libraries can no longer rely on funding from government and private granting agencies to support conservation treatment projects; instead, they must integrate conservation with other initiatives such as digitization projects and must develop a culture of pervasive outreach to tug persistently on the heart- and purse-strings of individuals who cross paths with their work. Development directors, library deans, and granting agencies now may ask preservation librarians and conservators to provide not just number of items treated but also specific evidence of the impact of preservation activities.

It is increasingly important to build working and research relationships with respected scholars outside preservation and conservation. With many universities placing growing emphasis on collaborative research and interdisciplinary massive online open courses, the in-house conservator is well positioned to contribute depth and breadth to historical investigations that are rooted in primary sources, as the information about how those material objects were created, used, and physically cared for can provide new interpretations of the intellectual content.

Continuing and Changing Workflows

When many preservation departments were founded in the 1980s and 1990s, the role of analog collections necessitated typical workflows that were somewhat different than they are today. Run by a preservation administrator, the preservation department of the past often included a robust commercial binding operation, in which general collections serials and monographs would be sent off-site to be bound in a semi-mechanized fashion; a book repair, or "mendery" unit, in which circulating books were repaired in-house by trained staff; and special collections conservation, featuring conservators who often spent a great deal of time on treatment of items of single items of high value and restricted use. In addition, many departments managed workflows for reformatting brittle books, with microfilm or preservation photocopy and sent books off-site for mass deacidification to counteract the effects of acidic book paper. These departments were and continue to be responsible for working with facilities staff to monitor and manage temperature and humidity in storage and exhibition areas. In addition, preservation personnel have and will always spend time evaluating potential risks to collections, writing disaster plans, training staff to prepare for and respond to emergencies, and leading collections salvage efforts during emergency recovery.

In recent years, digitization and other new workflows have been added to preservation departments, and more attention and resources have been placed on caring for special and distinctive collections. As acquisitions costs skyrocket, Internet access increases and research travel budgets are slashed, special collections increasingly are focused on digitization of analog resources and providing access to them through digital delivery.[12] Because digitization often involves entire collections or discrete projects, the sheer volume of material has led to different conservation workflows. Conservation personnel are often involved in first selection of material to identify items that would be too fragile or unwieldy to scan. Conservation assessment also helps to prioritize and schedule production for large collections; conservation treatment focuses on making the content of damaged collections accessible to the cameras (in other words, unfolding brittle creases), and stabilizing fragile artifacts so they are not further damaged by handling during digitization. Conservation staff also train digitization staff in care and handling of collection material, and may be present during scanning of select items at the request of the curators. With so many items usually featured in digitization endeavors, a new focus on stabilization, rather than full treatment, of items in the queue has become the norm. Preservation then steps in to preserve the digital files for posterity, and to provide proper storage and housing for the archival master. This master may or may not experience further handling; sometimes digitally exposing intriguing content results in more requests for the original than before it was digitized. Adding digitization to existing departmental workflows has often resulted in very real effects on conservation budgets, priorities, and departmental deadlines.[13]

Exhibition of special collections materials presents different concerns for materials to be displayed. Conservators may assist curators during planning and installation, create mounts and cradles, prepare materials to be sent on loan to other institutions, and monitor environmental conditions in exhibition areas. Some conservation laboratory workflows focus primarily on treating material in preparation for exhibition, but ideally this workflow is one of many workflows matched to institutional priorities and core functions. The lines between digitization and exhibition may be blurred, as material may be displayed in physical or digital form, or both.

Concurrent with the rise of conservation efforts related to exhibition and digitization, research libraries increasingly capitalize upon, and in some cases monetize, their physical "distinctive collections." These materials are exposed repeatedly in classroom teaching, highlighting them for donors and producing curated digital collections that add value with metadata and enable close comparison of items that reside in different institutions. Without careful observance of preservation-minded handling procedures, these repeated uses can increase fragility and cause damage that may affect the value to the next generation of users.

In classroom instruction, special collections librarians and professors connect students and other researchers with physical collections, reminding them of the richness of physical information and tactile experience that is not conveyed in an increasingly digital world. This use can result in the same small selection of collection items being used semester after semester, which may stress the condition of these materials. Conservators may be asked to treat materials especially for classroom use, be involved in the setup of material prior to class, and be present during classroom sessions to aid in handling. This use places new demands on conservators' time, although they share librarians' interest in connecting more individuals with physical materials. Having conservators in the classroom leads to greater exposure to the profession and can demonstrate respect and enthusiasm for physical objects.

Another overall trend is the focus on collection-based, rather than item-based, decision making and treatment. This work may include sampled condition surveys of entire collections, and collectionwide projects to improve storage conditions, to create protective enclosures, or to provide stabilization, rather than perform full treatment, for a wide range of materials in a collection. Preventive conservation, as it is often called, allows a small staff to potentially provide at least some attention to a wide swath of collection material, but an unintended consequence may be languishing bench skills for conservators who were trained to provide more invasive, high-level treatment to individual items. Many preventive conservation tasks may be performed more cost-effectively by conservation technicians and archival processors than by graduate-trained conservators.

Many special collections with manuscript collections and archives have been influenced by the tenets of "More Product, Less Process" (MPLP), authored by archivists Mark Greene and Dennis Meissner.[14] This approach aims to make collections more accessible by reducing time to process collections, limiting descriptive information in the finding aids, and, in many cases, not replacing original folders or removing fasteners. Conservator Laura McCann deftly summarized the preservation viewpoint on MPLP,[15] including correcting Greene and Meissner's scientifically incorrect assertions about acidic paper that could have deleterious effects on collections that are housed in storage conditions without good temperature and humidity control. The increased output resulting from a high-volume approach to processing has often resulted in a greater, rather than reduced, workload for conservation. Although MPLP advocates a reduced role for preservation, as long-buried collections are rediscovered, unusual format items often appear and require preservation attention when the collections are requested for research or other use.

Preservation in Small Special Collections

While many large research institutions employ dedicated preservation and conservation professionals, in institutions without such personnel it is not uncommon for a library staff member in another area to be assigned preservation duties in addition to other work. In such cases, a preservation program may not be all encompassing but can still be effective at mitigating risk of damage within a more limited sphere of influence. The key is to make sure that staff members with these responsibilities know where to get training and information they need to make informed decisions and use limited resources effectively.

Many reliable sources of information about preservation and conservation may be found online, supporting preservation and conservation professionals' desire to convey sound advice to a wider audience. One of the first websites around of any ilk, and still in existence today, is Conservation Online.[16] This complex series of web pages feature collections care topics, full-text publications of conservation journals, and research papers. As a companion to this repository of formal content, the Conservation Distribution List[17] is open to anyone with an interest in cultural heritage conservation, with postings on conservation conundrums and new initiatives, as well as advertisements for seminars, internships, and permanent positions. These two resources alone have connected the conservation and preservation community across the globe with the immediacy and familiarity that was impossible before the Internet. The widespread distribution of the list to people outside the conservation community has led to a greater sense of openness about sharing what we know.

Connecting to Collections Care Online Community,[18] hosted by the Foundation of the American Institute for Conservation of Historic and Artistic Works and the Institute of Museum and Library Services, provides a no-charge clearinghouse of information ideal for collections care staff of small and mid-sized cultural institutions. The American Institute for Conservation also maintains a more technical and dynamic collaborative wiki[19] on collections care and conservation topics, reflecting a sense that our professional body of knowledge is evolving quickly, rather than being a static canon. Regional centers, such as the Northeast Document Conservation Center[20] and the Conservation Center for Art and Historic Artifacts,[21] as well as the National Park Service publications,[22] also provide high-quality online resources for preservation managers. In addition to these institutional resources, many conservation and preservation professionals are using social media to disseminate information. While too numerous and ever-changing to list here, a quick Internet search for "library conservation blog" yields a rich list of them.

Training in collections care and preservation topics for staff members with preservation responsibilities may be accomplished in various ways. Nondegree training programs, such as the one offered by Rutgers Preservation Management Institute, provide blended learning opportunities and professional certificates. Likewise, many libraries and archives are part of regional, nonprofit membership organizations such as Lyrasis[23] and Amigos[24] that offer preservation training modules. Other conservation professionals and organizations offer conservation and preservation training workshops both online and in-person. The Conservation Distribution List, mentioned earlier, is a good resource to learn about upcoming workshops.

Some collection material will warrant individual item or "full" treatment. When an institution does not have a conservator on staff, such items may be sent off-site for conservation treatment. Nonprofit regional conservation centers or individual conservators in private practice provide treatment services for institutions without conservation expertise onsite. The American Institute for Conservation maintains a searchable website[25] that allows querying by type of object and location, along with many other filters, to locate an appropriate conservator or preservation specialist. Several granting institutions both publicly and privately funded award grants and other funding to small institutions for both assessing collections and for implementing the recommendations made in those assessments as project or program support. The National Endowment for the Humanities and the Institute for Museum and Library Services are two of the most generous funding organizations.

Sustainability

Preservation and conservation of cultural heritage have always had an awkward semantic relationship with environmental preservation and conservation. "They" are preservationists and conservationists, and "we" are conservators and preservation administrators; the term "preservator" remains unclaimed. However, with climate change looming as a serious threat to the longevity of cultural collections and to the budgets of the institutions that house them, library/archives preservation professionals would be wise to examine closely the alignment of philosophies and terminology between the cultural and the environmental sides of the preservation coin. Increasingly, budgets will be influenced by "sustainable" efforts. A recent discussion group of library conservators recognized that greening work habits, materials, and workplaces is a not just a trend; it is a necessity.[26] Preservation professionals will spend more time and resources preparing for and then inevitably responding to the increase in climate change-induced emergencies.

A number of energy-saving measures may be positively impacted by preservation recommendations. Active management of temperature and humidity in collection storage environments results in improved preservation and energy savings.[27] Both financial considerations and reevaluation of the physics and chemistry of deterioration of library and archives materials have led to a shifting perception of collections storage "standards" away from the "70 degrees Fahrenheit/50% relative humidity" museum model of the 20th century. Coupled with institutional imperatives for reducing energy use, a new approach toward storage environment management is driving the concept of the win-win of energy savings and improving the collections preservation environment.

Careful planning, monitoring, and working with facilities and curatorial staff in a team-based approach to heating, ventilation, and air-conditioning or HVAC enhancements and operation are the fundamentals. Preservation goals for a particular type of collection should be established to emphasize keeping collections cool to slow chemical deterioration and keeping humidity moderate, neither too much nor too little. Once these preservation goals are agreed upon, energy savings may be found by employing strategies such as improving insulation and reducing air leakage, reducing the amount of outside air brought into areas with low human occupancy, minimizing the speed of fans that move air through an HVAC system during unoccupied or night-time hours, allowing conditions to drift with minimal control during transitions between the heating and cooling seasons, or allowing conditions to drift with minimal control within an accepted range rather than using tightly controlled set points.

One energy-saving strategy that may gain traction is that of separating study/work spaces from long-term storage spaces, thus enabling the air conditions of each type of activity to be customized. Library materials' longevity improves dramatically when stored at cool temperatures (40–60°F); humans prefer a more constant "room" temperature (68–72°F). Attempting to accommodate both populations in the same space results in conditions that are detrimental to one group or the other and that strains energy budgets. Additionally, humidity requirements for collections (generally 35–50 percent relative humidity) are often not addressed, likely because humans cannot feel small changes and can tolerate a much wider humidity range without complaint. This new approach to collections storage may conflict with the convenience to researchers and staff provided by immediate proximity to collections.

Collections can be quickly and irreparably damaged during emergencies involving water leaks, floods, mold and other biological contamination, smoke, and fire. Given the higher risk of severe weather due to global climate change, emergency preparedness and effective response are considered to be an important part of a sustainable society.[28] Preservation professionals help staff in libraries and archives understand and mitigate such threats to their collections. Library conservators developed many methods for salvaging water-damaged special collections following the 1966 flood of the Arno River in Florence, Italy, that greatly affected centuries-old collections of the Biblioteca Nazionale Centrale. Typical approaches include preparing written emergency response plans, stockpiling response supplies, training staff, working with facilities staff to mitigate risks, and building relationships with vendors and community first responders. Various preservation organizations have made emergency plan templates and other information freely available to the public.[29] While these types of activities were common in the 20th century, more recently a better organized network of professional collections emergency advice and assistance has developed,[30] along with, sadly, a greater breadth of experience with cultural heritage recovery following major regional disasters.[31] Preparedness for emergencies in library special collections recently has received more attention as broader approaches such as risk assessment[32] and emergency management[33] are integrated into emergency planning.

Future Directions for Preservation and Conservation

While preventing catastrophic emergencies as well as the slow-burning fires of chemical decay, the role of special collections conservation and preservation will continue to evolve as society's attitudes change toward history and the artifacts that anchor our cultural heritage. New avenues to increase access to rare and special materials have the potential to result in new workflows in conservation departments, in particular because the importance of special collections in many institutions continues to rise. As resource sharing in a digital world changes, preservation professionals will likely be required to expand their skillset to respond to new uses of original artifacts. Preservation professionals are likely to continue to focus on preventive conservation, stressing housing and stabilization projects that improve whole collections, often in place of high-end, single-item treatments that require many resources for a few items. Continued and expanded opportunities to spread the message of preservation to new allies and communities, and collaborative preservation efforts among institutions, will increase. More preservation resources will be spent on reformatting audiovisual collections. No matter what the future holds, conservators and preservation administrators will discover new ways to sustain collection materials, the buildings that house them, and the profession itself.

Notes

1. Hancock family papers, 1712–1854 (inclusive), Volume JH-6 John Hancock letterbook (business), 1762–1783, p. 423; *Mss:766 1712-1854 H234*, Baker Library Historical Collections, Harvard Business School, accessed June 15, 2015, http://pds .lib.harvard.edu/pds/view/27525053?n=423&printThumbnails=no.

2. Robert Coover, "The End of Books," *New York Times,* June 21, 1992, accessed July 15, 2015, http://www.nytimes.com/books/98/09/27/specials/coover-end.html, foretold a future in which books played a minor role. Others have since refuted or softened this position. See Leah Price, "Dead Again," *New York Times*, August 10, 2012, accessed July 15, 2015, http://www.nytimes.com/2012/08/12/books/review/the-death -of-the-book-through-the-ages.html; Lloyd Shepherd, "The Death of Books Has Been Greatly Exaggerated," *The Guardian*, August 30, 2011, accessed July 15, 2015, http://www.theguardian.com/books/2011/aug/30/death-books-exaggerated.

3. Joshua Ranger, "For God's Sake, Stop Digitizing Paper," *AVPreserve* blog post, August 25, 2014, accessed July 14, 2015, https://www.avpreserve.com/blog/for-gods -sake-stop-digitizing-paper-2/.

4. Henry Wilhelm, "A Survey of Print Permanence in the 4 × 6-Inch Consumer Digital Print Market in 2004–2007," in IS&T's International Symposium on Technologies for Digital Fulfillment, 43–47 (Springfield, VA: Society for Imaging Science and Technology, 2007), accessed July 14, 2015, http://www.wilhelm -research.com/ist/WIR_IST_2007_03_HW.pdf.

5. Theresa Smith, "Cut and Tape: Marguerite Yourcenar's Emendations to a Typescript of *L'Oeuvre au noir,*" *Book and Paper Group Annual* 30 (2011): 83.

6. Brenna Campbell, Scott Gerson, and Erika Mosier, "Conservation of Dieter Roth's *Snow,*" *Book and Paper Group Annual* 32 (2013): 16–21.

7. Lizanne Paine, "Trends in Shared Library Storage and Shared Collection Management," *Proceedings, Art Libraries Society of North America* (2008): 5, accessed August 25, 2015, http://207.250.94.40/news/conferences/2008/proceedings/ses _09-payne.pdf.

8. Association of Research Libraries, SPEC Kit 345: Shared Print Programs (2014), accessed August 25, 2015, http://publications.arl.org/Shared-Print-Programs-SPEC -Kit-345.

9. American Institute for Conservation, "Code of Ethics and Guidelines for Practice," accessed July 14, 2015, *h*ttp://www.conservation-us.org/about-us/core -documents/code-of-ethics-and-guidelines-for-practice/code-of-ethics-and-guidelines -for-practice#.VaaMUfnldcM.

10. American Institute for Conservation, "Commentaries to the *Guidelines for Practice,*" accessed July 14, 2015, http://www.conservation-us.org/about-us/core -documents/code-of-ethics-and-guidelines-for-practice/commentaries-to-the-guidelines -for-practice#.VabBOfnldcM.

11. Library of Congress, "Conservation Education: Commemorating the Library Conservation Education Programs at Columbia University (1981–1992) and the University of Texas at Austin (1992–2009)," Topics in Preservation Series, accessed July 14, 2015, http://loc.gov/preservation/outreach/tops/commem-cu_uta/index.html.

12. Corydon Ireland, "Robert Darnton Closes the Book," *Harvard Gazette*, May 11, 2015, accessed June 15, 2015, http://news.harvard.edu/gazette/story/2015/05/robert -darnton-closes-the-book/. As Darnton notes, the current system of print journal publishing remains "wildly irrational and very expensive." He believes that "in 10 years open-access journals will completely dominate things."

13. Gillian Boal, "Conservation for Digitization at the Wellcome Library," *Book and Paper Group Annual* 33 (2014): 9–16.

14. Mark A. Greene and Dennis Meissner, "More Product, Less Process: Revamping Traditional Archival Processing," *American Archivist* 68, no. 2 (2005): 208–263.

15. Laura McCann, "Preservation as Obstacle or Opportunity? Rethinking the Preservation-Access Model in the Age of MPLP," *Journal of Archival Organization* 11, no. 1–2 (2013): 23–48.

16. Foundation of the American Institute for Conservation of Historic and Artistic Works, "Conservation Online," accessed July 14, 2015, http://cool.conservation -us.org/.

17. Foundation of the American Institute for Conservation of Historic and Artistic Works, "Conservation Distribution List Archives," accessed July 14, 2015, http://cool .conservation-us.org/byform/mailing-lists/cdl/.

18. Foundation of the American Institute for Conservation, "Connecting to Collections Care Online Community," accessed July 14, 2015, http://www.connecting tocollections.org/.

19. American Institute for Conservation, *AIC Wiki*, accessed July 14, 2015, http:// www.conservation-wiki.com/wiki/Main_Page.

20. Northeast Document Conservation Center, accessed July 14, 2015, http://www.nedcc.org.

21. Conservation Center for Art and Historic Artifacts, accessed July 14, 2015, http://ccaha.org/.

22. National Park Service, "Conserve O Gram" series, accessed July 14, 2015, http://www.nps.gov/museum/publications/conserveogram/cons_toc.html..

23. Lyrasis, accessed July 14, 2015, http://www.lyrasis.org/.

24. Amigos, accessed July 14, 2015, http://www.amigos.org/.

25. American Institute for Conservation, "Find a Conservator," accessed July 14, 2015, http://www.conservation-us.org/membership/find-a-conservator.

26. Justin Johnson and Danielle Creech, eds., "Library Collections Conservation Discussion Group 2014: Options for Sustainable Practice in Conservation," *Book and Paper Group Annual* 33 (2014): 92–97.

27. Jeremy Linden, James M. Reilly, and Peter Herzog, "Field-Tested Methodology for Optimizing Climate Management," in *Climate for Collections: Standards and Uncertainties, Postprints of the Munich Climate Conference 7 to 9 November 2012*, eds. Jonathan Ashley-Smith, Andreas Burmester, and Melanie Eibl (Munich: Doerner Institute, 2013), 93–103, accessed June 18, 2015, http://www.doernerinstitut.de/downloads/Climate_for_Collections.pdf; Chris Muller, "Air Quality Standards for Preservation Environments," *Papyrus: Journal of the International Association of Museum Facility Administrators* (2010–2011): 45–50.

28. Federal Emergency Management Agency, "Planning for a Sustainable Future: The Link between Hazard Mitigation and Livability," Publication 364, accessed July 14, 2015, http://www.fema.gov/media-library-data/20130726-1454-20490-3505/fema364.pdf.

29. Northeast Document Conservation Center, "dPlan: The Online Disaster-Planning Tool for Cultural and Civic Institutions," accessed August 3, 2015, http://www.dplan.org/; Conservation Center for Art and Historic Artifacts, "Mid-Atlantic Resource Guide for Disaster Preparedness," accessed August 3, 2015, http://www.ccaha.org/uploads/media_items/mid-atlantic-resource-guide-for-disaster-preparedness.original.pdf.

30. American Institute for Conservation, "Disaster Response & Recovery: AIC-CERT," accessed July 14, 2015, http://www.conservation-us.org/publications-resources/disaster-response-recovery/aic-cert#.Vaa_7vnldcM.

31. Library of Congress, "Learning from Katrina: Conservators' First-Person Accounts of Response and Recovery; Suggestions for Best Practice," accessed July 14, 2015, www.loc.gov/preservation/emergprep/katrinarespond.html; American Institute for Conservation, "FAIC response to Hurricane Sandy," accessed July 14, 2015, http://www.conservation-us.org/docs/default-source/reports/cultural-recovery-summary_for-web.pdf?sfvrsn=2.

32. Robert Waller, "A Risk Model for Collection Preservation," in *Preprints of the 13th Triennial Meeting, Rio de Janeiro, v. 1* (Paris: ICOM Committee for Preservation, 2002), 102–107, accessed July 14, 2015, http://www.museum-sos.org/docs/WallerICOMCC2002.pdf.

33. Library of Congress, "Emergency Preparedness, Response and Recovery," accessed July 14, 2015, http://www.loc.gov/preservation/emergprep/.

Chapter 14

Top Ten Questions and Answers about Digital Preservation for Special Collections and Archives

Lynne M. Thomas and Jaime L. Schumacher

What Is It?

Digital preservation is, quite simply, the long-term care and maintenance of digital materials (no matter how they were created), with an eye to future access. It is not digitization, although any digitization plan or digital project should also have a preservation component (why put resources into creating a big digital cache without planning to keep it long-term?).

Is This Really *Our* Problem?

In 2009, Whittaker and Thomas argued that "as professionals trained to consider the truly long-term care and storage of materials, our community *must* become part of the digital preservation conversation."[1] The artifacts and documents that we are creating and collecting right now are increasingly born digital: digital photographs, e-mail, and documents of all kinds. If we don't find ways to deal with archival materials that takes these creation formats into account, we are not doing our jobs. Literary manuscripts, governmental records, personal papers, and organizational records like newsletters and meeting minutes are likely to have been created digitally before being printed (if, indeed, they were ever printed as opposed to being distributed via e-mail or over the web). In many cases, the digital file is the original artifact. The fonds we are professionally obligated to respect often now exist in the context of a hard drive. Ignoring long-term preservation of digital materials (whether they are born digital or digitized) guarantees that a large part of our contemporary cultural heritage will disappear.

Can't We Just Hire Someone Who Knows Tech and Make Them Do It?

Digital preservation, even when done inexpensively, must be programmatic: a core activity of library/archival life, not something we do as a side project. Ultimately, it is a facet of acquiring and preserving a collection of papers. How many people does that process currently take in your organization? Digital preservation that even minimally meets sustainable standards requires a team of people with diverse skills from across the library or archive, from curatorial acquisitions work to metadata to networking to administrative support, from the traditional to the cutting edge, from technical to advocacy. Assigning a single staffer to solve the problem will fail both your institution and the staffer in question.

Am I Ready to Begin a Digital Preservation Program?

Yes. Many of the skills that cultural heritage professionals already use day-to-day are core to digital preservation, too: selection, metadata creation, advocacy, budgeting, planning, and policy development among them. There are already robust standards, practices, tools and services, and a huge community of practice already in place, at all levels of institutional resources. You won't have to reinvent the wheel. We may, however, need to reevaluate how we approach technical obstacles in our libraries and archives.

Digital preservation options for underresourced institutions in particular may seem impossible on first glance. In 2011, Northern Illinois University, in partnership with Western Illinois University, Illinois State University, Chicago State University, and Illinois Wesleyan University, received a National Leadership Grant from the Institute of Museum and Library Services based on the argument that the Principal Investigators' institutions (and their state consortium) weren't in a position to help address digital preservation challenges based upon current resources.[2] Our white paper "From Theory to Action," the result of that grant,[3] was published in 2011.[4] It includes case studies for our individual campuses, along with our hands-on testing of several digital preservation tools and services. We found SWOT analysis (Strengths, Weaknesses, Opportunities, Threats/Challenges) very helpful to our process, laying out our technical, money, and organizational options, discussing our short- and long-term goals. This helped us to narrow down our options further based upon what was right for us.

The good news is, no matter what your current resources, some level of digital preservation work is possible. You may already be completing some digital preservation activities at the most basic of levels.[5] The next step is applying them to a bigger picture and developing an overall plan that meets your institution's needs.

Why Now?

The greatest difference, arguably, between the preservation of digital materials and the preservation of traditional special collection materials is one of time. The speed at which digital materials must undergo processing and archiving and the subsequent frequency with which they must be managed are significantly higher than their paper counterparts.[6] An acquisition of paper manuscripts is not at a high risk of physical loss if not processed and shelved within, say, seven years (assuming a climate controlled storage space). Once processed and shelved, these materials can likely survive intact without further active management for decades—this is the beauty of "benign neglect."

There's another wrinkle, too, in terms of how much time we have, and the rate at which tools and services change or become obsolete. If you have ever experienced the selection process for, say, a library management system/online catalog, a rather typical library approach will sound deeply familiar: extensive research, followed by calls for proposals, endless meetings, and a lot of money spent. The result is a series of practices, policies, and tools that we rely upon for a decade or more.

Digital preservation tools and services change far too quickly for that model to be viable.

We need instead to plan for three- to five-year technology cycles, with choices that allow us graceful entry and exits from the tools we are using at any given time. This is especially important in organizations that have budgeting issues, whether cyclical or systemic. What is affordable and sustainable now may not be so in three to five years. The goal is to make sure that at the end of a given period, there are ways to get your data back and options for what to do next.

Sustainable digital preservation programs incorporate an iterative process. The speed with which tools and services are created, tested, adopted, and superseded means that we can't just make a single, "big" choice and assume we are all sorted out for the next decade with minor maintenance. You will set up your policies and practices and find that they don't actually work, or change your mind about your tool selection. *That's okay.* Trial and error are the order of the day. In most cases, one system/solution does not fit all, organizationally or technically.

All of These Standards Look Complicated and Expensive. Should I Be Worried about Becoming a Trusted Digital Repository or Obtaining TRAC?

If you are just learning about digital preservation for the first time, there are lots of options to bring yourself up to speed.[7] You will need to understand the basic vocabulary and processes of digital preservation but not necessarily all of the nuts and bolts at an examining-code level. The advantage of not being on the bleeding edge is that the vast majority of the digital preservation tools and services any given organization will consider have already incorporated relevant standards (such as Open Archival Information Systems) into their development. TRAC (Trustworthy Repositories Audit and Certification) and TDR are laudable and important goals but may not be right for every organization. They require significant staffing and resource levels which may be out of reach of smaller or less-well-resourced organizations. Digital preservation is an iterative process; it's not just making a single choice and then sitting back, but making a series of ongoing choices as the next set of options becomes available, based upon previous choices.

The available systems designed to incorporate large numbers of functions may assume a level of preparation of files that your organization may not have completed. Many institutions will need to perform a level of "triage" on their digital collections to prepare them for ingest into more comprehensive systems. Some tools and services may assume that you have a full PREMIS (Preservation Metadata: Implementation Strategies) or MODS (Metadata Object Description Schema) record ready to go at the point of ingest. Most tools and services assume that files have already been removed from temporary carriers such as CDs or flash drives. File formats may need to be standardized, metadata may need to be generated, and an inventory of the amount of extant material will be necessary to determine storage needs and collection growth. All of these are activities that can be taken on before a specific solution is selected, during the policy planning and budgeting process.[8]

How Do I Know What Tools and Services Are Best?

You have numerous options, with new developments almost daily. You will need to think in terms of your organization's goals and needs. Think of it as building a tool belt. It is unlikely that a single tool or service will solve all of your problems, but you may be able to find a limited group of tools that do most of the job at hand.

Here are some things to consider:

- Do you need a comprehensive system for managing your digital files, tools that only perform a couple of functions, or just secure, inexpensive storage that isn't solely on your local server?

- What file formats are your priorities? PDFs? Image files? E-mail?

- Do you plan to host software at your institution, or do you need a hosted elsewhere solution?

- Do you have sufficient support to maintain open source software, or would a vendor-based solution (either for-profit or nonprofit) work better for your organization?

- Which digital preservation tools may work the best with the systems you already have in place? Your selections will be based in part on which systems for creating metadata and/or access you are already using (e.g. ARCHON, ArchivesSpace, DSpace, Fedora, and ContentDM).

- Do your goals include emulation and migration, or merely saving materials at the bit level?

- Would a consortial or group solution be more appropriate for your setting? If so, does the solution on offer meet most of your needs?

To research and compare-and-contrast individual tools, consider the Community Owned Preservation Tool Registry.[9] The Digital POWRR white paper[10] includes our discussions of the software and services that we tested in-depth, along with our proposed individual institutional choices, which were all completely different from one another.

How Do I Choose What to Save?

Many an archivist will be faced with the donor who wants to know why you don't wish to accept all 80,000 photographs in the donor's Flickr or

Instagram account, or on the 2 TB hard drive on offer. Selection/assessment and prioritization are even more important skills in digital preservation, when the assumption is that cheap digital storage means "just saving every-thing." Selection for posterity is (in part) what cultural heritage workers *do*. There is nothing stopping us from treating different types of digital materials differently from one another, in the same way that libraries and archives often have different levels of access or preservation choices (or lack thereof) for different kinds of analog materials.[11] Please see Chapter 8, "Digital Acquisitions and Appraisal," by Sarah Barsness and Anjanette Schussler in this volume for additional details on this process.

Digital preservation is more than just keeping bits safe: provenance and contextualization are important, and what we do best! Creating and main-taining context is another part of our professional practice easily applied to digital materials. Once processed and archived, digital materials require ongoing, active care so as to ensure that file formats do not become obsolete and the setting in which they are archived remains viable.

How Do I Find the Resources to Do This?

The short answer is advocacy, planning, and budgeting. One of the key components of a robust digital preservation program is administrative buy-in, particularly at a campus/organizational affiliation level. You are working toward solving an organizational problem, not just a library-specific problem. Consistent, long-term communication across organizational levels is best done with a team of people. This is a marathon, not a sprint. Developing a new program in any organization requires laying groundwork, lots of commu-nication, long-term planning and budgeting, and leveraging what is already in place in your organization wherever possible.

The Digital POWRR project developed a series of one-page handouts to aid in this process, aimed at communicating with different organizational roles, particularly outside of the library.[12] One of the most important lessons we learned from our process is that of quantifying risks.

What Is the Cost of Doing Nothing?

The answer to this question, especially with specific examples, is what will prompt momentum out of organizational inertia. Potential stakeholders may not yet know that digital preservation affects their ability to do their jobs. Explaining to your alumni association or development office that if noth-ing is done, there will be no photographs 25 years from now of, say, your foot-ball team's first trip to a major college bowl game is likelier to get their attention. State institutions may be affected by university records disappear-ing through lack of long-term preservation that could cause legal or compli-ance issues. Initiating these conversations and pointing out that the library or archive has expertise to help other units solve problems that they didn't realize that they had may drive your proposed solutions forward.

What are you waiting for?

Notes

1. Beth M. Whittaker and Lynne M. Thomas, *Special Collections 2.0* (Santa Barbara: Libraries Unlimited, 2009), 100. Their chapter "The Elephant in the Room"

opens with a quote from Paul Conway's 1996 "Preservation in the Digital World," Council on Library and Information Resources, Washington, D.C., March 1996, accessed November 19, 2015, http://www.clir.org/pubs/reports/conway2/index.html.

2. Over the course of the period of the study, the Open Access to Research Articles Act passed in Illinois. This law requires that research created at state-supported institutions be made publicly available and *preserved long term*. Our campuses now also have a legal mandate to somehow create digital preservation programs. We're still working on it due to it being an unfunded mandate. The act can be found at http://www.ilga.gov/legislation/publicacts/fulltext.asp?Name=098-0295, accessed November 19, 2015.

3. Grant number IMLS award LG-05-11-0156-11.

4. "From Theory to Action: Good Enough Digital Preservation for Under-Resourced Cultural Heritage Institutions," accessed January 6, 2016, http://commons.lib.niu .edu/handle/10843/13610.

5. See the National Digital Stewardship Alliance levels of preservation, which is an easy assessment rubric: http://www.digitalpreservation.gov/ndsa/activities/levels .html, accessed December 4, 2015.

6. Audiovisual preservation is a whole other discussion. A good starting point is the Library of Congress's page on the topic: http://www.loc.gov/preservation/care/record .html, accessed November 19, 2015.

7. The Digital POWRR site has a Digital Preservation 101 page with a collection of links, for example; http://digitalpowrr.niu.edu/digital-preservation-101/.

8. We particularly recommend Ricky Erway's "You've Got to Walk before You Can Run"; http://www.oclc.org/content/dam/research/publications/library/2012/2012-06 .pdf.

9. Community Owned digital Preservation Tool Registry, accessed January 6, 2016, http://coptr.digipres.org/Main_Page.

10. Jaime Schumacher et al., "From Theory to Action: Good Enough Digital Preservation for Under-Resourced Cultural Heritage Institutions," August 2014, Institute of Museum and Library Services, accessed January 6, 2016, http:// commons.lib.niu.edu/handle/10843/13610.

11. The University of Utah has created a handy flowchart that illustrates this point: http://digitalpowrr.niu.edu/wp-content/uploads/2014/04/UnivUtah_DigPresDecFlowchart .pdf, accessed November 19, 2015.

12. These can be found at http://powrr-wiki.lib.niu.edu/index.php/One_Pagers _tailored_to_educate_different_professionals, accessed December 10, 2015.

Chapter 15
Discovery of Special Collections Resources at Web Scale: Opportunities and Challenges for Metadata Librarians*

Christine DeZelar-Tiedman

Introduction

Library catalogs have undergone a rapid evolution in recent years. Change in cataloging rules and practice moves at a slower pace. With a rich tradition of detailed description and attention to unique and copy-specific characteristics of library materials, special collections catalogers have been challenged to find ways to make their materials findable in today's environment of web scale discovery and mobile device–friendly interfaces. This chapter discusses problems encountered in making special collections materials more discoverable within the context of a local discovery interface, and offers some possible solutions.

A Brief and Simplified History of Online Library Catalogs

The state of the online library catalog has been one of constant change. The developments outlined here, while represented as broad phases, are not so much distinct innovations, but rather a series of overlapping events.

---

*Portions of this chapter, in a different form, were included in the author's presentation at the 2015 ExLibris Users of North America Conference in Minneapolis, Minnesota, on May 7, 2015.

Card catalogs were the norm for much of the 20th century, and early computerized catalogs, often called online public access catalogs, essentially tried to mimic the experience of browsing a card catalog. Library users would typically perform a search for an author, title, or subject by entering a phrase, which would retrieve an alphabetized list of results. While some online catalogs presented the user with a full view of the record in the International Standard Bibliographic Description format, as it would have appeared on a catalog card, others featured a labeled display, with key elements such as author, title, and series identified by offset labels, usually to the left of the descriptive data. As the sophistication of online databases grew, a greater variety of search options became available. Users could create more complex and targeted searches using Boolean operators such as *and*, *or*, and *not*. All of these innovations were an outcome of cooperative cataloging, as librarians recognized that individually cataloging the same thing at multiple libraries was not a good use of resources. The Library of Congress's catalog card program, and later, cooperative library databases such as OCLC, were developed to allow libraries to share the task of cataloging materials held at multiple institutions.

Catalogers have long held a tension between efficiency in copy cataloging and the need or desire to provide enhanced or local customization to catalog records. The need for local enhancement or variation is especially pronounced in special collections cataloging, where materials are often collected precisely for their unique and item-specific features. Bindings, inscriptions, provenance, and other characteristics may be the very things that add research value to the materials, so it is important for special collections librarians, and their users, to record and make this type of information available in the library catalog. Archival description involves providing context about the creation of a collection or set of records, typically including biographical or historical notes along with a description of contents at varying levels of detail. Specialized cataloging standards and thesauri have been developed by the special collections and archives cataloging communities in order to properly describe and provide access to these types of characteristics.

Partly in response to the needs of specialized and research-centered libraries, the Research Libraries Group (RLG) developed a cataloging database, the Research Libraries Information Network (RLIN), which allowed libraries to create and maintain an institution-specific version of a record, which could include copy-specific details. These records were part of a "cluster" of records describing the same manifestation of a resource, but all records were searchable and usable by all members of the network.

In 2006, OCLC and RLG merged. RLIN members were given the option to retain their institution-specific records (IRs), which would be attached to the OCLC master records once the two databases were merged. In March 2015, it was announced that OCLC would be discontinuing the availability of IRs. Institutions would be able to retain their local data in the form of a local bibliographic data record. This solution is seen as inadequate by many in the special collections cataloging community, as the local data will not be searchable or viewable outside the local institution. As it appears unlikely at this writing that OCLC will reconsider its decision, special collections catalogers are beginning to explore alternatives.[1]

The most rapid transformational change to online catalogs has happened in the last 20 years with the advent of the Internet. As more and more library users became accustomed to searching for information online and retrieving broad and deep result sets, catalogs began to evolve again to provide a user experience more similar to searching Amazon or Google. Most provided a single search box in which a user was asked to type keywords. Rather than an alphabetized list of results, users received a set of matching records in a ranked order based on perceived relevance to the search terms. Web 2.0 features, such as the ability to provide ratings, reviews, and tags or individualized labels that could be saved to a user's account, were often available, as well as a more visually appealing presentation, including images of book covers. Rather than crafting a careful and precise search, users were expected to rely on facets, typically consisting of elements such as formats, date ranges, subjects, and authors, with which to limit or narrow an initial result set.

Early implementation of so-called Web 2.0 catalogs received a mixed response. Many users, especially those who were web-savvy and doing general searches, found them much more user-friendly than traditional catalogs. Others, including experienced researchers and many library staff, found them inefficient and preferred traditional methods of crafting precise Boolean searches.[2] Most Web 2.0 systems do provide advanced search options, allowing the user to search particular data fields, limit searches by format or collection, or combine search terms with Boolean operators. However, these options are generally not prominently displayed, requiring clicking through to another screen, and therefore not heavily used. Many libraries using Web 2.0 catalogs have maintained a parallel "classic catalog," which provides the more traditional presentation of information and left-anchored browse searching. However, this model is not sustainable for reasons that will be discussed later in this chapter.

In addition, many libraries maintained parallel databases containing different types of assets, including digital images, archival finding aids, and institutional repositories, containing electronic theses and dissertations and other historical and research-oriented documents. Including metadata for these resources in the main catalog required duplicative work, an inefficiency many libraries could not justify or afford.

One limitation of Web 2.0 systems was the false expectation they created that users will find "everything" in a library by searching there. If a university student is looking for a particular journal article, typing the title and author of a citation into the catalog would not result in discovery of the desired target. The student would need to go outside the catalog to search a journal aggregator such as EBSCO's Academic Search Premier. Similarly, unless records for archival collections were included in the main catalog, a researcher would need to know to search the separate finding aid database to learn about their existence in the library's collection. Experiments with "metasearch" or tools that would simultaneously search multiple databases, including the catalog, were largely unsuccessful due to incompatibility of search parameters and slow response time.[3]

This leads us to the latest generation of library catalogs: the web scale discovery system. These systems integrate content from the library's local repository with licensed content such as online journal articles. While retaining many of the visual and functional features of Web 2.0 systems, they step away from being merely a representation of the library's holdings, and include other material to which the library has access. Some of these systems can also be configured to allow simultaneous search of library assets held in databases other than the catalog, such as archival finding aids, digital materials, and institutional repository holdings. The response time problem experienced through metasearch is solved by having metadata for all of the resources indexed centrally.

A number of user studies in recent years have indicated that most library users begin their research outside the library catalog, doing general searches in places like Google and Wikipedia.[4] A local library catalog is more often used by researchers performing a known-item search[5]: in other words, they already have at least a general idea of what they are looking for, and they are using the catalog to find out if the library owns it or has access to it. The need of special collections users to find specific items within the catalog serves as justification for providing local enhancements to metadata, and enabling end-user interfaces to search and display these features. In addition, incorporating metadata from other repositories makes the search process more seamless for users, but effective integration of multiple metadata schemes into a single index requires careful planning.

Why Web Scale Discovery Can Make Special Collections Resources Hard to Find

While the benefits of web scale discovery are many, this system can pose problems for locating and identifying special collections resources. Due to the sheer volume of results, it can be difficult to drill down to a level that presents and displays the precise details important to users of special collections materials. Materials from other repositories are often described at different levels of hierarchy and complexity than traditional catalog records, and context can be lost when these metadata records are brought into the catalog. For example, records for series or items within an archival collection can be confusing unless they clearly indicate the relationship to the parent record, and records for digital assets often lack enough detail identifying their character and format for researchers to be able to assess the potential usefulness for their information needs.

FRBRization and Combining of Result Sets

The Functional Requirements of Bibliographic Records (FRBR)[6] model describes an ideal structure of descriptive cataloging. Central to the model is the concept of work, expression, manifestation, and item (WEMI). For example, *Tommy and Grizel* by J. M. Barrie is a work. A particular version of the text is an expression. A specific edition is a manifestation, and a copy of that manifestation held by a library is an item (see Figure 15.1).

As a conceptual model, FRBR has been discussed and debated widely in the library cataloging community, and its complexities will not be delved into here. What's important for our discussion is that many Web 2.0 and web scale discovery systems employ a form of "FRBRization" by combining bibliographic records behind the scenes in order to simplify the user experience. In theory, most users are not interested in a specific manifestation or copy of an expression but just want *a* copy. This adage, however, is frequently

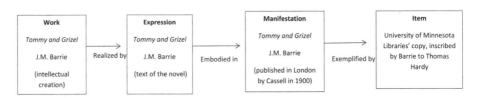

Figure 15.1   Example of WEMI structure.

untrue when it comes to users of special collections, who often want to examine a specific edition or copy. Depending on the software, a catalog may or may not allow the user to investigate further the underlying records that have been combined for the initial display, and the very details they are most interested in may be hidden from view.

Early printed resources—identified here as materials produced roughly prior to 1830—can often have minor variations that are important to scholars, but are not apparent enough to avoid de-duplication by machine algorithms. In addition, many discovery systems, assuming that the majority of users prefer access to an electronic copy of a resource if one is available, favor the presentation of online resources, sometimes even masking the availability of a physical copy. If a library has purchased or licensed online collections such as Early English Books Online (EEBO) or Eighteenth Century Collections Online (ECCO), users may not realize when the library holds a physical copy of any of the titles, because the electronic version is presented first. A user may need to click down several levels in the catalog interface before information on the print holding is presented. This does not negate the value of having access to an electronic surrogate, especially if the library does not hold a print copy, or the researcher is distant from the library and the electronic version meets his or her needs. But the physical details may be the areas of greatest interest to the researcher, requiring examination of the physical piece, and a digitized copy is not always an adequate substitute.

Lost in the Flood

At times the sheer number of search results, including licensed resources and journal articles, can make it difficult to pinpoint special collections resources of interest. By their nature, special collections are often narrowly focused on works by or about a particular author or subject. Collections may strive to be comprehensive, for example, including every known edition of a particular work. The Sherlock Holmes Collections at the University of Minnesota Libraries is a case in point. A search for the title *Hound of the Baskervilles* in the libraries' catalog, MNCAT, initially brings up a result set of over 2,000 hits. Limiting to the libraries catalog (which eliminates licensed resources) brings the number to 206 results, but the first result in the list is a combined display of 190 versions. Users are able to drill down to explore the different versions, or use facets such as material type, author, publication date, and subject to further refine the results, but given that the search is for a specific literary work, these refinements have limited utility, as the majority are printed books in English by Arthur Conan Doyle.

Simplified Displays

Another common feature of today's discovery systems is simplification of displays. Due to the rise in use of mobile devices, many library management systems employ responsive web design, providing the user a seamless experience whether a desktop computer, a tablet, or a cell phone is being used for access. These streamlined interfaces are less tolerant than traditional online catalogs of large amounts of text and complex displays, and therefore it may be more difficult for a user to view a full representation of a bibliographic record in order to verify whether it is the resource he or she wants or needs to consult. The rare materials tradition of composing detailed notes to accompany bibliographic records is at odds with a desire to display a limited amount of information on a small screen. Many online catalog systems only display notes and access points selectively, and those that are displayed are not presented in a particularly appealing or readable manner. Records for archival materials may contain a large number of access points as well as notes detailing historical and biographical information, and the scope and content of the collection. Many discovery systems omit descriptive labels for different kinds of notes, and display subject headings in a paragraph format rather than as a list.

Loss of context

When metadata from digital repositories and other types of databases is incorporated into the library catalog, meaning and usefulness can be lost. Digital repositories often use more simplified schema such as Dublin Core to describe resources, and employ students or temporary staff to enter data, some of whom have little or no previous cataloging experience. Within the context of the database, generic descriptive titles, for example, "Woman at Sewing Machine" and noncontrolled keyword subject terms may be adequate, but when these data are indexed along with all other library resources, some refinement may be needed. In cases like these, the metadata record should clearly indicate that the resource is a digital image, and decisions must be made as to how subject terms are controlled and indexed, so that they don't conflict with controlled vocabulary terms and cause confusion.

Description of archival materials can happen at many hierarchical levels. Most typically, collections are described as a whole, but depending on use and perceived research value, some repositories may also create descriptive records at series, folder, or item level. Catalog records must clearly indicate the relationship of the part to the whole.

Local Catalog Solutions

Numerous options are available at a local level to help make special collections materials more discoverable when users are searching their institution's catalog. Many institutions have maintained, as an alternative to Web 2.0 catalogs, a shadow "classic catalog" to provide a more traditional cataloging interface, with left-anchored browse searching and full record display. These types of interfaces are often preferred by faculty, experienced researchers, and library staff. However, the sustainability of this parallel model is uncertain going forward. With limited resources, it may be difficult to justify to administrators the cost–benefit ratio of maintaining two systems. As library technology evolves, vendors may be de-emphasizing traditional catalogs in favor of their newer products. In addition, many institutions are moving toward hosted or SaaS (software as a service) solutions for their library catalogs. Choosing cloud services can reduce costs for the library in that there is no longer a need to maintain local server space, and fewer staff resources are necessary for local database configuration. With these trends in mind, there are still methodologies available for customization of local records and displays in order to bring out their special-collections aspects and make them more discoverable for users.

Local Notes

One way of providing access to copy-specific details of special collections materials is through the use of local notes. The sheer number of options within the MARC format for adding local notes allows for flexibility, but can also lead to inconsistency of practice over time, and therefore difficulty when it comes to data migration. Catalogers should carefully weigh the options according to the context of their organizational structure and discovery environment, and the nature of the data they are trying to convey, and document decisions and the reasons for them.

590 Fields

Many libraries use the MARC 590 field for local notes. The nature of cataloging notes is that they lack a set structure, so they can be composed in any way that the institution finds useful to convey the needed information. As with any local field in the bibliographic record, local notes can have a drawback in multicampus or consortial library environments where bibliographic records are shared among multiple library locations and/or institutions. If multiple holdings are attached to the same record, the note should make clear to which copy it refers.

Other 5XX Fields

A number of additional note fields exist that can be useful for describing archival and special collections resources. Some (though not all) of these fields allow the addition of a subfield 5, which contains an institutional code, indicating that the note refers to a specific copy associated with a particular location. This practice is recommended for environments where records are shared among different libraries. However, it doesn't solve the problem of copies held in different collections within a single institution.

Examples of these additional note fields are:

- 535—Funding Information Note ($5 not allowed)
- 541—Immediate Source of Acquisition Note
- 545—Biographical or Historical Data ($5 not allowed)
- 561—Ownership and Custodial History
- 563—Binding Information

Notes in the Holdings or Item Record

Many special collections libraries exist within larger institutions or consortia where bibliographic records at different locations are shared within the database. Institutional or consortial policies may forbid or discourage the inclusion of copy-specific information on shared bibliographic records. In this type of environment, item-level details can be included in holdings or item records. If a collection holds multiple copies of an item, notes in the holdings record rather than the bibliographic record can make it clearer for users and library staff alike which note refers to which copy.

The 852 (Location) field in the holdings record defines subfield z as a public note, meaning it can be configured to display in a library's discovery system. Another option is the 866 field, subfield z. An advantage to the 866 field is that it allows for notes that are specific to a particular volume or issue of a multipart resource to be associated with that particular volume.

Holdings notes may not automatically be searchable or displayable in a library's discovery system. Before implementing any changes to metadata policy, it's important to make sure that the information will appear in the public catalog as expected and that it is included in indexes so that it can be searched. Catalogers should work with systems staff as much as possible to ensure the metadata they create is being used to its fullest potential.

Some librarians choose to include item-specific details in inventory records, commonly called item records. One disadvantage to this approach is that, unlike bibliographic and holdings records, there is no recognized standard for item data, and therefore data included there are more likely to be lost when migrating from one system to another. In addition, data in item records are unlikely to be searchable in user interfaces, although they may display to users.

Cataloging notes in general can be a good way to provide a narrative, human-readable description of the provenance, significance, and physical characteristics of special collections resources. However, in the context of a web scale discovery system, notes are often de-emphasized, obscured, or presented in a manner difficult for users to read or access. They are often ignored or disregarded when machine processes determine whether to combine or de-duplicate records. Typically the only way to discover them is through keyword searching. While not possible or appropriate for all situations, controlled vocabulary access fields in many cases provide for better access within the current and future discovery environments.

Access Fields

Use of controlled vocabularies and access points can help libraries provide consistent terminology for particular persons, organizations, concepts, and entities. National and international standards bodies have developed methodologies for establishing terms and forms of names, including cross-references to and from nonpreferred terms and related entities. In a web scale discovery environment, controlled access fields are more likely to be displayed prominently and readably than are free-text notes. The presence of a controlled field in a critical mass of records can also enable faceted browse searching of the term in a system that provides this functionality.

Authorized Access Points

The 700 field in the MARC record provides an access point for individuals associated with a resource. The relationship between the person and the resource being described can be defined at any of the FRBR levels: work, expression, manifestation, or item. In nonspecial collections cataloging, most entities named in 700 fields are at the expression or manifestation level, such as a coauthor, editor, or illustrator. For special collections materials, there are a number of item-level associations that a cataloger may want to describe. These include donors, former owners, inscribers, printers, and binders, among other things.

The MARC Code List for Relators[7] provides terms that can be used in a subfield *e* of a 700 field in order to assert the relationship of the individual to the resource being described. The Bibliographic Standards Committee of the Rare Books and Manuscripts Section (RBMS) of the Association for College and Research Libraries routinely reviews and recommends terms relevant to rare materials to be added to or revised for this list. Resource Description and Access (RDA), the current content standard for bibliographic description, provides a more limited list of relationship designators to be used in access fields for records. RDA defines terms based on the WEMI levels, and some of these limitations are problematic for special collections catalogers. However, there is a process in place for submission of additional terms to the Joint Steering Committee, the administrative body which oversees RDA development.

Access fields can also be used to identify a particular collection within a larger repository. These are often named collections of important donors. Some libraries define these collections as corporate entities and use a 710 Corporate Name MARC field. If a repository is a member of the Name Authority Cooperative program, they may choose to establish these collection names in the National Authority File, providing a greater level of consistency and control of how the name is represented in databases. Other librarians may choose to include these named collections in a 730 (Related title) field. Whenever 7XX fields are used to identify copy-level or local associations, the subfield 5 should always be used to indicate the institution to which the information refers. It should be emphasized that these types of access point should be added in the local catalog only, and not to master records in union databases such as OCLC WorldCat.

In addition to what's been mentioned above, use of controlled access points can provide improved options for index and display of the data. While data in note fields are typically only discoverable through keyword search, metadata from name and title access fields can be included in more targeted indexes within the library's catalog, such as author or title indexes.

The drawbacks to taking this approach in consortial settings are similar to those for local notes as described above. In addition, there can be some unintended consequences when mingling manifestation-level data with item-level data in the same index. For example, when performing a search for *James Wright* in MNCAT, because relationship designator terms are ignored when displaying facets, materials by James Wright are intermingled with a large number of items from Wright's personal book collection, which is held in the University of Minnesota's special collections.

As an alternative to the above approach, some librarians use 79X fields, which are locally defined access fields. Depending on the system, using separate fields to indicate local and copy specific associations might make indexing more straightforward and avoid intermingling of manifestation-level and item-level data in the same MARC field. For example, systems staff may be able to configure an alternative label for 79X fields. While 700 and 710 fields are typically labeled "Author" or "Creator" in online catalogs, a library may wish to use labels such as "Associated name" or "Local collection" in conjunction with the display of 79X fields. There are pros and cons of intermingling or segregating data in all types of 7XX fields in both index and display; individual libraries will need to determine for themselves the best options based on local needs and technological capabilities. At the University of Minnesota Libraries, a separate index was created for data in 7XX fields that is location- and copy-specific. Called the "Associated name" index, it appears as an advanced search option in the catalog, and includes any 7XX field that includes both a subfield *e* (relationship designator) and subfield 5 (institution code). These fields are also included in the general keyword and name indexes, but it is possible to narrow the search by using the more specialized index.

Form and Genre Terms

The RBMS Controlled Vocabularies[8] are developed and maintained by the Controlled Vocabularies Editorial Group of RBMS. These vocabularies provide terminology for physical characteristics of rare books and other special collections materials, including binding, paper, printing and publishing, provenance, and type evidence, as well as a thesaurus of genre terms. A number of other vocabularies exist to describe physical forms and types of intellectual content. Another thesaurus frequently used in special collections and archives cataloging is the Art and Architecture Thesaurus[9] maintained by the Getty Research Institute. The Library of Congress continues to develop its own list of genre and form terms.[10]

Long an afterthought or viewed as a subset of subject terminology, genre and form terms are increasingly seen as an additional form of access warranting indexing separate from subject headings. Along with the use of relationship designators, the use of genre and form terms is another area where the special collections cataloging community has been ahead of the game compared to general cataloging practice. With the increased emphasis on linked data and relationships between resources and their associated characteristics, controlled vocabularies are one way to enable more reliable linking outside the local catalog environment.

Within the catalog, controlled headings are another way to describe the features of resources of interest to users of special collections materials, whether types of bindings or printing processes, or examples of particular types of documents. Depending on local needs and system characteristics, library catalogs can be configured to provide a separate index for form and genre terms. Form and genre terms are also frequently available as navigable facets in the catalog interface. As would be the case with any type of data, it should be noted that the placement of the genre/form facet on the display may impact its usage: if it's too far down on the page, requiring scrolling, it's possible that many users will miss it entirely.

Table 15.1 summarizes the techniques described above, including pros and cons of each approach.

Catalog Expansions and Enhancements

While this chapter has focused on metadata enhancements to catalog records in order to make special collections resources more accessible, there are additional enhancements that can be made to online catalogs to help discovery. Unlike the options discussed above, these types of enhancements require broader technical expertise and, because of the resources needed to implement them, would typically involve greater consultation and buy-in at the institutional level.

Including Additional Resource Types in Discovery

A major selling point of web scale discovery systems is the ability to search across a broader array of resource types, including resources held in repositories other than the catalog. Many libraries have separate databases for management of resources such as archival finding aids, digital materials (born-digital or digitized versions of physical resources) and institutional repositories. Many current discovery systems allow the harvesting of metadata from these stand-alone systems into the primary discovery interface, providing a centralized location to search all of the library's intellectual assets. While complications can arise from the intermingling of a variety of metadata standards, it is usually possible to link from the catalog back to the native database, which may contain more context or fuller information.

Table 15. 1   Advantages and Disadvantages to Various Methods of Providing Local Data in Catalog Records

Option	MARC Field	Advantages	Disadvantages
Local notes	590	• Field is designed for local information	• Misleading when multiple copies are held
Other bibliographic notes	5XX	• Able to use notes defined for specific types of information	• Misleading when multiple copies are held • Not all 5XX fields allow for $5 identifying institution
Personal, corporate, title access fields	700, 710, 730	• Able to take advantage of authority control • Provides enhanced indexing options	• Misleading when multiple copies are held • Mingles manifestation-level and item-level data in indexes
Local heading fields	79X	• Able to define for local needs • Indexes separately from standard MARC 7XX fields	• Misleading when multiple copies are held • Adds layer of complexity to indexing configuration
Form and genre terms	655	• Provides access to physical character-istics using controlled vocabulary • Provides data for multiple indexing options	• Misleading when multiple copies are held • Difficult to implement retrospectively on existing records
Holdings notes	852, 866	• Able to associate with a single copy (852, 866) or volume (866) • Provides space for free-form notes with-out taking up space in bibliographic record	• Limited options for indexing • Less visible to users without multiple clicks (depending on local system)
Notes in item record	N/A	• Able to associate with a single copy or volume	• Lack of standardization • Limitations on ability to search, display, or migrate

For example, it is not uncommon to provide records with summary-level information about archival collections within the catalog, which link back to the encoded archival description (EAD) record in the finding aid database, including the full inventory with box and folder lists. Many discovery systems allow for the display of thumbnail images, particularly useful for digital materials. Clicking on the thumbnail, or another accompanying link, can direct the user to the full digitized image.

User Interface Enhancements

Depending on how many resources an institution is willing and able to invest, there are a number of options for customizing a discovery system's user interface. Any customization should be undertaken only when there is evidence that changes will have a positive impact on the user experience, and usability testing should be employed before any major interface changes are implemented. Methods to gather data on user desires and needs include surveys, focus groups, and routine gathering of comments and complaints made by users to public services staff. It is also important to point out that any local "hacks" to a commercial discovery system may lose functionality when software upgrades occur. Any local changes to system codes must be diligently documented, and an iterative upgrade cycle may be another deterrent to implementing too many local customizations.

A number of open source options are available to libraries wanting more customization and control of their discovery environment. One popular solution is Blacklight, developed at the University of Virginia. It has been particularly popular with libraries with substantial holdings in special collections, in part because it was designed to allow for the creation of customized interfaces for specific populations.[11]

APIs (application program interfaces) are an increasingly common method of providing customizations and enhancements to discovery interfaces. Because they require less programming investment than implementation of an open-source catalog, many institutions are using APIs to make smaller local modifications to commercially available discovery systems. For example, a library may use an API to embed a search query within the catalog interface to an external database such as a digital repository.

In advocating for interface changes that improve the experience for their users, special collections departments can be at a disadvantage, as they are often part of a larger institutional structure. The needs of special collections researchers may be at odds with the needs of other users, and the size of the collections or user base may not comprise a large enough percentage of overall users to justify wholesale changes. Special collections librarians are best able to achieve success in having their concerns addressed by regularly documenting access problems, including specific examples of records or searches that are unsuccessful and functions and features of the system that don't work correctly or make special collections materials difficult to find. When asked for feedback they should always provide it (both positive and negative), and unsolicited comments should be forwarded when serious problems arise. It can often be helpful for public services librarians to work together with catalogers to develop recommendations. First-hand knowledge of user needs and an understanding of the data and functionality behind the scenes are both necessary to fully understand the scope of the problem and the possible solutions.

Discovery Outside the Local Catalog

This chapter has focused on enhancements to local catalog records, and the corresponding search and display of those records, in order to improve discovery of special collections resources. But the local catalog is only one part of the information universe. It's becoming increasingly critical for library resources to be integrated with the web at large. Emerging forms of data organization, such as linked open data, show great promise and potential for making our unique and special local resources known to the world.

Allison Jai O'Dell's chapter in this volume will explore these exciting developments.

Notes

1. Francis Lapka et al., "Discontinuation of OCLC's Institutional Records Program," April 7–12, 2015; Erin Blake et al., "CERL as an Alternative for OCLC?" April 14–15, 2015; DCRM-L electronic mailing list discussions, https://listserver.lib.byu.edu/pipermail/dcrm-l/2015-April/subject.html.

2. Primo Management Group, Chiat Naun Chew, Jan Fransen, Susan Gangl, Lois Hendrickson, Heather Hessel, Kristen Mastel, R. Arvid Nelsen, Connie Hendrick, and Jeff Peterson, MNCAT Plus and MNCAT Classic Survey: Results and Analysis, 2010, retrieved from the University of Minnesota Digital Conservancy, http://purl.umn.edu/92473.

3. Margaret Brown-Sica, Jeffrey Beall, and Nina McHale, "Next-Generation Library Catalogs and the Problem of Slow Response Time," *Information Technology and Libraries* 29, no. 4 (2010): 214–223.

4. Lorcan Dempsey, "Discovery Happens Elsewhere," *Lorcan Dempsey's Weblog*, September 16, 2007, http://orweblog.oclc.org/archives/001430.html.

5. Christine Stohn, "How Do Users Search and Discover?" ExLibris Corporation (2015), http://www.exlibrisgroup.com/files/Products/Primo/HowDoUsersSearchandDiscover.pdf.

6. Functional requirements for Bibliographic Records, International Federation of Library Associations and Institutions, December 26, 2007, revision, http://archive.ifla.org/VII/s13/frbr/frbr_current_toc.htm.

7. http://www.loc.gov/marc/relators/relaterm.html.

8. http://www.rbms.info/vocabularies/.

9. http://www.getty.edu/research/tools/vocabularies/aat/.

10. http://id.loc.gov/authorities/genreForms.html.

11. Elizabeth Sadler, "Project Blacklight: A Next Generation Library Catalog at a First Generation University," *Library Hi Tech* 27 (2009): 57–67.

Chapter 16

Special Files on the Semantic Web: Using Linked Data to Revitalize Special Collections Catalogs

Allison Jai O'Dell

Introduction

This chapter explains Linked Data, and its utility to special collections catalogs, by using the analogy of a card catalog with special files. This analogy helps us to understand that Linked Data is built through authority control, and serves the identifying and collocating objectives of Cutter's "Rules for a Printed Dictionary Catalog."[1] This analogy also helps us to understand the power of Linked Data—that it enables new potential, such as impromptu data merger and the ability to create knowledge through inferences. The goal of this chapter is to familiarize the reader with the Linked Data principles and related technologies, while unearthing commonalities with library practice and inspiring applications for Linked Data in special collections catalogs.

Imagine a researcher who is interested in the work of the Sangorski & Sutcliffe bindery. This researcher wants to find many resources, such as examples of Sangorski & Sutcliffe bindings; examples of similar designs from the period; publications about the bindery, Francis Sangorski, and George Sutcliffe; publications about early 20th-century design; the archives of the bindery; and records in other archives related to the bindery and its founders. This researcher wants to answer many questions, such as: Where did Francis Sangorski and George Sutcliffe get their inspiration? Who were they working with and for? What designs did they produce? What techniques and materials did they employ? What equipment did they use?

Special collections have the resources, and the data, to support this research. But can our researcher find them? Will the researcher know where to look? And if so, will his or her work be efficient or complicated? Will our researcher have to run many queries of many catalogs to bring together all information related to Sangorski & Sutcliffe? Or can he or she find this information in a networked way? Can he or she find it through a web search engine? Knowing the limitations of our current catalog environment, our answers to these questions may be pessimistic. Finding all resources related to Sangorski & Sutcliffe is set to be an arduous task.

But what if related data were linked together? What if our researcher could locate resources on Sangorski & Sutcliffe from a single point of entry? This is the idea behind the design of a card catalog. If you take the concept of the card catalog, and apply it on a global scale, you find the idea behind Linked Data: to structure data so that relationships are exposed, links are created, and information can be explored as a network. Linked Data uses web technologies to make this happen, but the principles are rooted in traditional library practice surrounding the card catalog.

Card Catalogs and Controlled Vocabularies

Library catalogs have, historically, been designed to help people find two things: What they are looking for (the identifying objective, associated with searching behavior) and related things (the collocating objective, associated with browsing behavior). How does this work? In the card catalog, alphabetical filing helped patrons find what they were looking for, while standardized references helped patrons browse for related things. Special collections often maintained "special files" in the card catalog, which might focus on binders, printers, donors, physical features, and more.[2] Special files helped patrons search and browse for specialized topics.

To support card and online catalog functionality, libraries use controlled vocabularies. Controlled vocabularies specify how index entries should be phrased to ensure matches. Controlled vocabularies allow disparate data entry to occur at multiple institutions over time, while catalog indexes remain functional. That is, controlled vocabularies allow impromptu data merger. The Rare Books and Manuscripts Section (RBMS) of the Association of College & Research Libraries publishes the *Controlled Vocabularies for Use in Rare Book and Special Collections Cataloging*. The "Controlled Vocabularies" reflect the data that were typically found in special files, and are a means to control index entries relevant to special collections.[3] The *Controlled Vocabularies* are available online,[4] and are currently being published as Linked Data.[5]

This chapter assumes reader familiarity with library principles of information organization, card catalogs, and controlled vocabularies. Readers lacking this background are encouraged to consult Taylor and Joudrey's *The Organization of Information.*[6]

Linked Data

What is Linked Data, and what is it for? Linked Data, just like library catalogs, is designed to help people find the information that they seek, and browse for related things. Linked Data achieves this with the same essential mechanism as a card catalog—by matching data and by relying on controlled vocabularies. These matches create links between disparate data sets, ultimately building an interconnected network of information. When information is linked to more information, Linked Data creates context, meaning, and knowledge.

How does Linked Data work? Let us review the four Linked Data Principles:[7]

1. "Use Uniform Resource Identifiers (URIs) as names for things."

URIs are codes that uniquely identify (that is, name and help locate) resources. You are familiar with this concept through other identifiers, such as social security numbers, barcodes, and database keys. A personal name may not be unique for identification purposes, but a social security number is. A book title may not be unique for identification purposes, but a barcode or database key—such as an OCLC number—is.

URIs can be of two types: Uniform Resource Names (URNs), which uniquely name a resource, and Uniform Resource Locators (URLs), which help locate a resource (as in a web address). URIs may serve either or both of these functions. The duality of naming and locating via URIs is important to how Linked Data works.

2. "Use HTTP URIs so that people can look up those names."

The hypertext transfer protocol (HTTP) is the standard by which data are communicated on the World Wide Web. Using HTTP, URIs make an identifier scheme accessible and communicable on the web, and this is where the dual function of naming and locating becomes important. An HTTP URI such as: http://www.example.org/vocab#Allison_ODell can be used as a unique character string to identify Allison O'Dell, and also, as a web address for locating information about Allison O'Dell.

3. "When someone looks up a URI, provide useful information, using the standards (RDF, SPARQL)."

Because HTTP URIs are on the web, they take advantage of web technologies: One can point a browser at an HTTP URI and read the information that is there. One can run a query against the data, and obtain the information that is there. Thus, the Linked Data principles suggest HTTP URIs as a mechanism not only for authority control (to uniquely name and locate things), but also to provide useful information.

4. "Include links to other URIs, so that they can discover more things."

Linked Data is about links. Links between URIs express relationships between things, and direct users to related things. This is done just as in a card catalog. In a card catalog, a subject heading on a title card expresses a relationship between that work and the subject, and also points the patron to more works on the subject. In a Linked Data URI, a link establishes a relationship to another thing and points the patron to more information about it, and more resources associated with it.

If you understand the purpose of authority control in a library catalog, you already understand the Linked Data principles. Authority control allows us to name resources uniquely and consistently, which in turn allows us to locate and associate them. Whether through library thesauri or HTTP URIs, authority control allows us to build relationships and enable further discovery of information. Now, let us explore Linked Data in further detail.

Resource Description Framework and Graph Modeling for Data

The Resource Description Framework (RDF) is the standard model for creating Linked Data—basically, RDF is the model used to execute the Linked Data principles. The RDF model expresses data very simply, by naming two things and the relationship between them, a structure known as a "triple," because it is a three-part statement. You can think of a triple as the simplest form of a sentence—with a subject, predicate, and object. The subject and object are nouns, and the predicate states the action that the subject takes on the object. The simplicity of the triple structure enables impromptu merger data and the ability to make inferences. Let us look at an example set of triples:

"Francis Sangorski" "employed by" "Sangorski & Sutcliffe."

"Sangorski & Sutcliffe" "located at" "London, England."

"George Sutcliffe" "works with" "Francis Sangorski."

These three triples may come from three different sources, for instance, three different catalog records. But, they can be combined together, because the triple structure is so simple. Each part represents a single semantic concept, and we can combine the data where we find semantic matches. If we combine these three triples, we learn that Francis Sangorski works in London, England, and that George Sutcliffe works at Sangorski & Sutcliffe. We are assured that "Francis Sangorski" in the first triple is the same as "Francis Sangorski" in the third triple if they are both identified by the same URI, as in the example triples:

<http://viaf.org/viaf/290711493> "works at" "Sangorski & Sutcliffe."

"George Sutcliffe" "works with" <http://viaf.org/viaf/290711493>.

When HTTP URIs identify the parts of our triples (rather than simple character strings), we are assured of true matches. Through the globally unique nature of HTTP URIs, we can take different triple statements from different sources and connect them (allowing data merger), and also learn things based on our newly linked data (making inferences). In sum, the RDF model uses the simplicity of the triple structure and the identification capacity of URIs to link data together, creating possibilities for data merger and inferencing.

RDF is based on graph theory from mathematics, and visualizing RDF data as a graph helps to understand its structure and purpose (see Figure 16.1). In this visualization, the circles are nodes, which are the subjects and objects of our triple statements, the nouns. The arrows are edges which are the predicates of our triple statements, the verbs. We connect the nouns together by stating the predicate relationships between them by drawing arrows between the circles. We know how to draw these arrows because each node and edge is identified by a URI, and the URIs tell us about the scope and semantic meaning of concepts.

Applying the graph model to data gives us new options for storing and using data. Triplestores are databases specifically designed to store and retrieve triples. Just like a relational database, triplestores use relationships for data maintenance and merger capability, only those relationships are stated between nodes, rather than between tables. Triplestores circumvent

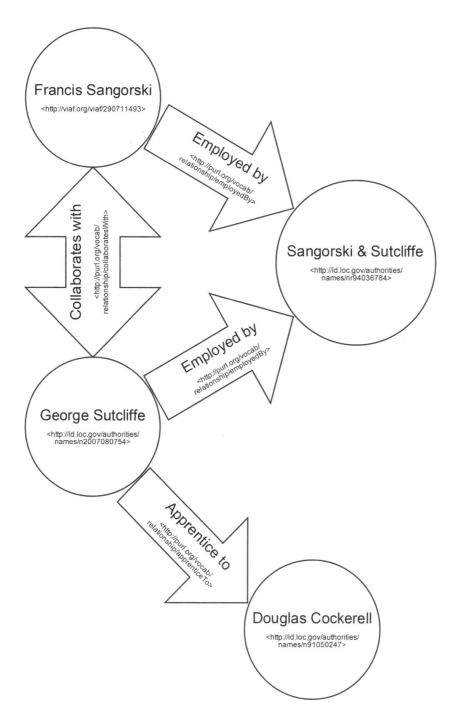

Figure 16.1 Example graph showing relationships among bibliographic data.

the confines of tables, giving us far more flexibility in defining properties and in appending new data to existing data. The graph model also gives us new ways of querying our data, that is asking questions of and making updates to our data. SPARQL is a query language specifically designed to retrieve and take actions on data stored in triples. Because triples establish relationships between individual nodes, SPARQL queries can be phrased akin to open-ended research questions, without specifying which tables and columns to query.[8]

If you understand the card catalog, you already understand RDF and its potential. On the back end, controlled data points allow new data to be merged with existing data. Whether filing catalog cards or integrating data into a graph, data merger is simply a matter of matching entries based on a controlled vocabulary. Impromptu data merger is important for special collections, which constantly intakes new catalog data from multiple sources. But the potential goes beyond cooperative cataloging. Opportunities for merging contextual information with bibliographic description, or enabling social engagement features (such as tagging and reviews), expose themselves in a Linked Data environment.

On the front end, relationships help patrons discover more information. Whether following references between catalog files or clicking links on the web, relationships create a network of information that supports discovery. Data relationships are important for special collections that support research through the robustness of their catalog metadata. But the potential goes beyond in-house resource discovery. Opportunities for connecting catalogs across institutions, connecting catalog data to context, or drawing inferences to fill in knowledge gaps expose themselves in a Linked Data environment.

Special Files on the Semantic Web

Special collections are poised to publish and use Linked Data. We have a wealth of controlled vocabularies that can be repurposed as Linked Data and delivered on the Semantic Web. And traditionally, we have data and discovery models built around links between nodes. Let us first explore publishing our catalog data as Linked Data. In the next section, we will explore applications for Linked Data in special collections discovery experiences.

The World Wide Web Consortium offers "Best Practices for Publishing Linked Data."[9] These include guidelines for project planning, execution, licensing, and marketing. They are written to be accessible, and may be consulted for further guidance. In particular, note the recommendation for selecting a data set to publish as Linked Data: "select data that is uniquely collected or created by your organization. Ideally, this information when combined with other open data provides greater value."[10] The data in the RBMS "Controlled Vocabularies" and special collections name authority records make ideal candidates for publication as Linked Data. To put what was once in special files on the Semantic Web, we need to publish our controlled vocabularies and authority records in Linked Data formats and to build links between resources.

We can publish controlled vocabularies and authority records as Linked Data by converting their encoding to Linked Data formats. Two widely used formats are the Simple Knowledge Organization System (SKOS) and Friend of a Friend (FOAF). SKOS is designed to represent taxonomies and thesauri, and is an appropriate format for subject and genre vocabularies.[11]

FOAF is designed to represent persons and their social networks, and is an appropriate format for personal and organizational name vocabularies.[12]

The RBMS' Controlled Vocabularies are being published as Linked Data in the SKOS format. Let us look at a sample from the concept description for "Gold tooled bindings":

```
<skos:concept>
    <skos:prefLabel>Gold tooled bindings</skos:prefLabel>
    <skos:altLabel>Gold stamped bindings</skos:altLabel>
    <skos:related>Blind tooled bindings</skos:related>
    <skos:related>Platinum tooled bindings</skos:related>
    <skos:related>Silver tooled bindings</skos:related>
    <skos:broader>Stamped or tooled bindings</skos:broader>
    <skos:scopeNote>Use for decorations made from the bonding of
    gold leaf to leather by means of heat stamps.</skos:scopeNote>
</skos:concept>
```

This description includes principles from thesaurus design such as preferred and alternate labels, broader, narrower, and related semantic relations, and documentary notes regarding the thesaurus entries themselves, such as their scope and history. If you are familiar with building library thesauri, SKOS will be familiar and easy to use.

But SKOS does more than re-encode library thesauri; SKOS turns library thesauri into Linked Data. In the sample above, we see some links within the thesaurus such as gold tooled bindings being related to silver tooled bindings. We can also link to external resources, such as other thesauri and library catalogs. Let us look at some samples:

```
<skos:concept>
    <skos:prefLabel>Gold tooled bindings</skos:prefLabel>
    <skos:sameAs
    rdf:resource="http://vocab.getty.edu/aat/300256003">
    Gold tooling</skos:sameAs>
</skos:concept>
```

In the above statement, we are saying that "Gold tooled bindings" in the RBMS Controlled Vocabularies is the same semantic concept as "Gold tooling" in the *Art and Architecture Thesaurus*. We have included a link to the URI for "Gold tooling" to specifically identify this concept. Mapping properties, such as skos:sameAs, allow library data to be interoperable and mergeable, even when different libraries use different thesauri. By establishing points of commonality and connectivity between our thesauri, we can start to approach *all* thesauri as one big, linked taxonomy. This allows even more searching, browsing, and data merger capability.

```
<skos:concept>
    <skos:prefLabel>Gold tooled bindings</skos:prefLabel>
    <skos:isSubjectOf rdf:resource="http://worldcat.org/oclc/9359539">
    The binding of books: an essay in the history of gold-
    tooled bindings</skos:isSubjectOf>
</skos:concept>
```

In the above statement, we are saying that "Gold tooled bindings" is a subject of the book, *The Binding of Books: An Essay in the History of Gold-Tooled Bindings*. Using the reciprocal property, skos:subject, in a catalog resource about *The Binding of Books*, creates a two-way link between the thesaurus and the catalog; that is, it creates a two-way path for browsing and discovery, achieving the collocating objective of the library catalog. SKOS helps us to define these and more links, building a full network of information related to library thesauri.

Special collections that maintain authority records about persons, families, and corporate bodies can publish these in a format such as FOAF. Let us look at a sample from a person description for "Francis Sangorski":

```
<foaf:name>Francis Sangorski</foaf:name>
    <rdfs:seeAlso
    rdf:resource="http://viaf.org/viaf/290711493/#skos:Concept"/>
    <foaf:interest
    rdf:resource="http://id.loc.gov/authorities/sh85015705">
    Bookbinding</foaf:interest>
    <foaf:based_near>London, England</foaf:based_near>
    <foaf:knows>George Sutcliffe</foaf:knows>
<foaf:knows rdf:resource="http://id.loc.gov/authorities/names/
n91050247#concept">Douglas Cockerell</foaf:knows>
```

In this FOAF description, we see that Francis Sangorski was interested in bookbinding, that he was based near London and knew George Sutcliffe and Douglas Cockerell, and that more information about him can be gained at the URI in the Virtual International Authority File (VIAF). By relating persons to their localities, their employers and other organizational affiliations, their collaborators, their interests, and more, FOAF descriptions represent social networks, and become valuable data for discovering and understanding historical connections.

Once we have published special files in Linked Data formats, the next step is to build links between resources. We can build links in two places: in our controlled vocabularies and in our catalogs. In our controlled vocabularies, we can create links between concepts, to other controlled vocabularies, and to other web resources. In our catalogs, we can create links to controlled vocabularies by adding URIs when indexing subjects, genres, names, and so on. The MARC formats include subfields for adding URIs to subject, genre, name, and citation data. BIBFRAME is designed for Linked Data, and natively uses URIs to identify things. Whether working in MARC or BIBFRAME, using URIs builds an interconnected web of data around authority control much like a card catalog, but on the World Wide Web, and globally accessible.

Applications: Better Tools, Better Discovery

Above, we have explored Linked Data and how to build it. We have learned that special collections, with our specialized foci and legacy of special files and thesauri, are uniquely poised to publish and use Linked Data. So, what can we build with Linked Data? Librarians *and* researchers rejoice; we can build better cataloging tools *and* better discovery tools.

As for cataloging tools, Linked Data can streamline authority work and indexing for library catalogs. Currently, this activity is besieged by bad data and unknown data. Catalogers are familiar with problems such as typos, minimal authority records, and uncontrolled headings that slow the work process and hinder catalog functionality. With URIs, the need to match exact character strings for collocation disappears. A display can read "Francis Sangorski" or "Sangorski, Francis Longinus, 1875–1912" so long as the URI for this person is consistent, all of these data can be linked and collocated. With technologies for querying Linked Data sets, such as SPARQL endpoints and Application Programming Interfaces, we can build URI lookup into cataloging tools. No longer need the cataloger laboriously, and separately, search several controlled vocabularies to find index entries.

Linked Data can revolutionize cooperative cataloging efforts. For cooperative cataloging to work, data must be interoperable and consistent. Currently, this is achieved with detailed guidelines for data entry (e.g., CONSER, BIBCO, and NACO standards), schemas for data elements (e.g., MARC and DublinCore), and common data entry platforms (e.g., OCLC Connexion). Owing to its complexity and necessary capital investment, our cooperative cataloging system is limited in participation to highly trained librarians and well-situated libraries. Our system and data structure do not readily accommodate outside contributions. But Linked Data can. Linked Data is specifically designed for impromptu data merger with the simple triple structure negating the need for complex schemas and URIs negating the need for complex mapping between values. Linked Data can open up metadata sourcing to parties such as researchers, archivists, and Wikipedians who are outside the library domain. This impact is humongous for special collections, where our materials and research use cases are highly specialized. The ability to incorporate more data and make inferences will revolutionize how we build special collections catalogs.

As for discovery tools, Linked Data helps us achieve the identification and collocation objectives of the traditional library catalog, but on a global scale using web technologies. In a card catalog, our example researcher might use special files for binders, bindings, physical features, or stylistic genres to locate specific names and concepts, and browse through the network of resources related to Sangorski & Sutcliffe. But our researcher would undertake this work one library at a time. On the Semantic Web, the idea of special files can be transformed into topical portals for searching and browsing. With links between library authority resources, catalogs, and other web resources, special collections research on the Semantic Web becomes a hyperconnected experience, with the catalog as just one stop along the journey. Our researcher can explore binders, bindings, physical features, and stylistic genres across collections and across the World Wide Web.

Linked Data expands the possible objectives of the library catalog by structuring metadata for use as data and by making data remixable for knowledge-building. The ability to easily combine data, and to make inferences, provides a solution to many research questions. Our example researcher wants to find out what techniques, materials, and equipment Sangorski & Sutcliffe used, as well as who the founders emulated and associated with. The data to answer these questions are available in special collections catalogs. Linked Data formats and graph modeling allow it to be manipulated and remixed, providing answers. If we know that certain tools were in a certain studio and that a binder worked at that studio, we can infer that the binder had access to those tools. If we know that a certain person studied with another person, we can infer that they shared techniques and designs. Linked Data lets the researcher draw out those connections from the catalog metadata itself.

The value of inferencing ability is enormous when we consider how vast and how varied are the data contained in special collections catalogs. Owing to the nature of bibliographic description, our catalogs contain data about cultural movements and design trends; printers, publishers, binders, illustrators, authors, and other makers; studios, spaces, and localities; equipment and technologies; typefaces and manuscript hands; provenance, annotations, and reader engagement; and much more. Converting this information to Linked Data makes it possible to combine and contextualize it, transitioning it out of the catalog record, and onto the Semantic Web.

Conclusion

Imagine what discoveries you could make by linking the data in your library's catalog! Now imagine what discoveries you could make by linking that data to other catalogs, and other web resources!

Linked Data enables web-scale and web-accessible discovery of information. This is done by taking principles from the card catalog, using controlled vocabularies to enable identification and collocation, and applying them on the web, using web technologies. With our special files in Linked Data formats, we can, essentially, build globally unified special files. We can use our catalog data in conjunction with other data. We can enable web searches and browsing across collections and across platforms.

In this chapter, we saw how special files provide an analogy to understand the function and utility of Linked Data in special collections catalogs. Keeping the idea of special files in mind, we begin to imagine the power of Linked Data to revitalize special collections catalogs. First, Linked Data achieves the identification and collocation goals of the library catalog but on and across the web. Second, Linked Data enables impromptu data merger and inferencing. Perhaps the true power of Linked Data to revitalize special collections catalogs lay in the ability to mix and remix data, combining special collections catalogs with other data sets, building unforeseen connections, and answering research questions right from one's desktop.

Overall, putting special files and special collections catalogs on the Semantic Web repurposes and reinvigorates the wealth of our data. Linked Data and RDF modeling revitalize the special collections catalog as an extensible, connectable, integrated, and discoverable web-based product.

Notes

1. Charles Ammi Cutter, *Public Libraries in the United States of America: Their History, Condition, and Management* (Washington, D.C.: Government Printing Office, 1876).

2. Deborah J. Leslie, " 'Provenance Evidence' and 'Printing and Publishing Evidence': Use and Revision of the RBMS Thesauri," *Papers of the Bibliographical Society of America* 91, no. 4 (1997): 517–523; Susan A. Adkins, "Automated Cataloging of Rare Books," *Collection Management* 16, no. 1 (1992): 89–102.

3. Leslie, " 'Provenance Evidence' and 'Printing and Publishing Evidence.' "

4. RBMS, "Controlled Vocabularies for Use in Rare Book and Special Collections Cataloging," http://www.rbms.info/vocabularies/.

5. Jane Carpenter, Ryan Hildebrand, and Amy Brown, "Draft minutes of the RBMS Controlled Vocabularies Editorial Group Meeting, Annual 2015," *ALAConnect*, http://connect.ala.org/node/243011.

6. Arlene G. Taylor and Daniel N. Joudrey, *The Organization of Information* (Santa Monica: Libraries Unlimited, 2008).

7. Tim Berners-Lee, "Linked Data," first published 2006, http://www.w3.org/DesignIssues/LinkedData.html.

8. Irene Polikoff, "Comparing SPARQL with SQL," *The Semantic Ecosystems Journal* (May 5, 2014), http://www.topquadrant.com/2014/05/05/comparing-sparql-with-sql/.

9. W3C, "Best Practices for Publishing Linked Data" (2014), http://www.w3.org/TR/ld-bp/.

10. Ibid., part 2.

11. W3C, "SKOS Simple Knowledge Organization System—Home Page" (2012), http://www.w3.org/2004/02/skos/.

12. Dan Brickley and Libby Miller, "FOAF" (2015), http://www.foaf-project.org/.

Chapter 17
Old Challenges, New Solutions: Leveraging Organizational Change to Construct a New Future

Jennifer O'Brien Roper and Ivey Glendon

The landscape of higher education in the United States has been shifting over the last decade. Online education has eroded the assumption that student must physically locate close to instructor, while globalization, the service economy, and employment options leave potential students with a variety of expectations of their college experience. In 2013 the University of Virginia ("U.Va.") adopted a new strategic plan, known as the Cornerstone Plan, designed to chart a course for a university on the brink of entering its third century of existence. The five "pillars" in the Cornerstone Plan are as follows:

- Enrich and strengthen U.Va.'s distinctive residential culture.

- Advance knowledge and serve the public through scholarship, arts and innovation.

- Provide educational experiences that deliver new levels of student engagement.

- Assemble and support a distinguishing faculty.

- Steward resources to promote excellence and affordable access.

The verbs in the Cornerstone Plan are strong and active, intended to stimulate engagement and energy within the university community. As a whole, the document identifies and reinforces what the institution does well and calls for growth in new areas. In response to the Cornerstone Plan, the University Library (also referred to as "the Library") administration began a process to enmesh the organization within this articulated vision. The summer of 2014 was devoted to intense conversation among staff (approx. 200 individuals), resulting in a complete reorganization. In order to create opportunity for growth by reducing duplication of effort and increasing communication of innovations, the reorganization was designed to directly connect staff involved with similar functional tasks rather than connecting by physical location or subjects and collections served. The goal is to allow for enrichment and strengthening of staff expertise and communication while creating space to advance the Library into new services featuring greater engagement with scholars in their field of play.

The reimagining of services reorganization of staff only affects the organization known as the University Library, although there are other libraries within U.Va: the Claude Moore Health Sciences serves the medical school and hospital, the Arthur J. Morris Law Library serves the law school, Camp Library serves the business school, and the University Library serves all other schools, departments, and units. While the four libraries do share an integrated library system and other technical infrastructure, they are four distinct administrative units with separate staffing, and independent budget sources and overlapping services. Except for the Camp Library, each library contains a special collections unit with rare book and manuscript holdings.

University Library's Albert and Shirley Small Special Collections has until recently been organized in a traditional manner, with dedicated processing, reference, curatorial, and administrative staff who report to a director (Figure 17.1). The functions of these staff mirrored staff elsewhere within the organization, with the distinguishing characteristic being a singular focus on rare and unique materials. Based on the goal of uniting staff performing similar functions, the University Library reorganization led to special collections staff reporting centrally with their cataloging, metadata, selection, reference, and administrative colleagues as demonstrated in the shadowed departments in Figure 17.2.

As a department that had previously been a fully functioning microcosm of other library services, special collections feels the instability and potential of this shifting ground perhaps more intensely than other units. With colleagues newly engaging in the work and workflows of special collections, it is challenging to not feel defensive in the face of inquiries into past policies and practices, and it takes strength to step back and sincerely ponder the reasons and necessity for tasks being done differently in a special collections environment. At the same time, there is invigoration found in the interest and investment. While everyone involved is not driven by a passion for the materials, all can unite their varied interests to steward and provide services around the collections.

Just as the University and the Library are discovering new areas for scholarship and service, special collections also needs to broaden its mission beyond the traditional. At U.Va., special collections has historically focused on stewardship for rare and unique materials. This focus is critical and remains central; however, a new, complementary focus has also been identified: serendipitous discovery within a larger universe. Rare book cataloging and manuscript arrangement and description have always been focused on discovery, albeit often in service of users who knew about or were guided to special collections. With discovery interfaces becoming more robust and able to seamlessly provide results across metadata standards and repositories, continued and growing collaboration across institutions, and the possibilities presented by the emerging field of linked data, it is vital that the organization and description of rare and unique materials adhere to national/international standards and restrict local traditions in materials description.

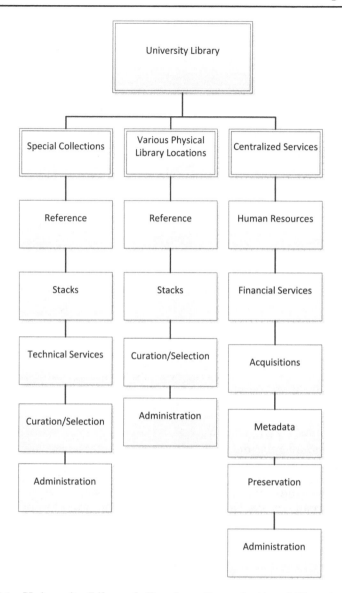

Figure 17.1   University Library's Previous Organizational Structure.

This broadened focus requires additional expertise, such as with metadata and technology, further supporting the University Library's need for an organizational structure that provides diverse expertise to special collections within a relatively static personnel budget.

Technical services staff were the first to integrate into the new teams resulting from reorganization, in part as a result of a history of necessary collaboration due to shared metadata storage and discovery systems. Special collections staff were assigned to the teams with whom they shared functional responsibilities, regardless of collection or physical location, although experimentation began before reporting lines and hierarchical structure were established. Due to knowledge and skill gaps created by retirements

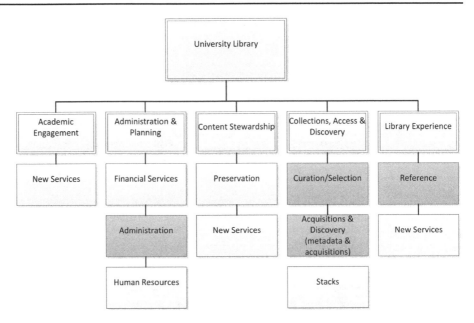

Figure 17.2   University Library's 2015 Organizational Structure.

and other departures, as well as the evolving technology infrastructure available in special collections work, there was a need for more staff working with these materials as well as an array of skills and expertise not evident among existing personnel.

Three newly formed metadata units, each with its own broad but distinct mission, include staff in the area of Resource Acquisition and Description (RAD), Metadata Creation and Organization (MCO), and Metadata Analysis and Design (MAD). RAD focuses its efforts on acquiring materials, regardless of format, and connecting resources to metadata where metadata already exists. Conversely, MCO engages in content organization and creates metadata where metadata from another source cannot be found. MAD supports both the RAD and MCO units by developing policies and guidelines for metadata standards across repositories to facilitate discovery, assesses workflows and tools for efficiency, and shares expertise in metadata standards and tools throughout the Library and the U. Va.

Lacking a budget for hiring an infinite number of staff, directors and managers identified skills and resources already available within the Library in order to focus hiring requests for skills and expertise relating to unique and rare materials that were not evident in the organization as a whole. For instance, an experienced cataloging manager worked with a rare book cataloger to determine training and guidelines in order to assign staff with experience in MARC cataloging to work with materials that do not require deep rare materials expertise. Staff with expertise in metadata analysis and design and software development collaborated with processing archivists to review finding aid guidelines and implement an archival management system.

On the other hand, the need for a full-time archivist to lead the arrangement and description for manuscripts and archives was identified as a need that could not be filled through collaboration. These early experiments greatly informed the reorganization that came together in parallel and revealed gaps in need of immediate attention. Training is under way to create a general level of knowledge among all staff on these teams about the unique nature and needs of materials selected for special collections. The intention is not to reassign all staff to work with these materials full time, but rather to have specialists who focus on these materials and generalists who can work with rare and unique materials as part of a larger portfolio of work.

Approaches to Team Integration, Effective Communication, and Achieving Results

Bringing groups of individuals together, particularly those who have not worked together before and who also have varying levels of length of service at the institution, is a challenge that has revealed the need for sensitivity concerning issues of trust, communication style, and past practice. We have been able to move forward with integrating technical services units and creating a dual focus on stewardship and discovery by acknowledging this context of organizational change and departmental integration through intentionally and incrementally creating diverse working groups to accomplish shared goals. Developing these new work teams has allowed us to acknowledge and capitalize on a wide range of individual skills, experiences, and communication styles, all while committing to respecting individual preferences expressed as part of the library reorganization.

We have pursued gradual changes in staffing and communication mechanisms, including expanding lines of communication by e-mail, and also by integrating in a manner such that special collections and non–special collections staff share physical space in new ways. Because consideration for the security of collections is of crucial importance, we have approached the blending of technical services staff in such a way as to introduce new staff into the physical processing area gradually and over time in order to build trust among staff and ensure the integrity of the approach to security for collections. Consequently, we have integrated three metadata staffers including the department head, the experienced cataloging manager, and the metadata librarian into the special collections space over a period of approximately 18 months. These three staff members, along with the senior lead for collections, share an office in the special collections materials processing area to be a visible demonstration of our commitment to unit integration as well as to be an available resource for all special collections staff when issues about collections or metadata arise. Overall, this approach has been successful and is reflective of our commitment to meeting individuals' expectations for in-person communications and respect for individuals' commitment to collection stewardship.

Another substantial change in our work processes has emerged from our decision to develop project and communication plans based around the skills required to complete discretely defined projects. As previously mentioned, a cataloging manager worked with the rare book cataloger in order to define a training plan for MARC-trained staff to be able to work on special collections projects that do not require rare materials expertise. We have approached other projects in a similar manner, including pairing the metadata librarian's expertise in developing project workflows with the processing archivists' knowledge of collections and collection guides in order to evaluate legacy finding aids and develop a plan for mass conversion of this significant body of metadata. Additionally, a group comprising special collections and non–special collections cataloging and processing staff, metadata staff, a grant-funded cataloger, and volunteers meets regularly to discuss shared issues and approaches to metadata creation and management. The importance of these intentional groupings, the cataloging manager with the rare book cataloger and the metadata librarian with the processing archivists, cannot be overstated; alone, none of these halves would be able to adequately plan for or execute the work proposed. It has been essential to our early success in these projects that staff with different backgrounds, skills, and goals can exercise openness to new approaches and be paired in ways that are new for this organization and are fundamental for fostering a climate of trust among staff.

Perhaps most significantly, our approach in forming diverse teams has bolstered our goal of integrating technical services units in order to inform processes, improve communication, and achieve concrete and demonstrable results. Along with the group of integrated technical services staff, we have assembled a pan-university team of experts, including archivists and programming staff, to increase understanding and support for digitization processes, participate in software development, and promote more holistic approaches to metadata creation and management among the newly integrated technical services.

Digitization processes have also improved by virtue of increased overlap between the scanning services unit, metadata experts, and rare materials cataloging staff; similarly, collaboration among archival experts from the University Library and other colleagues across the university have promoted innovation in software development such as implementing ArchivesSpace as a shared tool across the university and in developing a new tool to support conversion of legacy finding aids from Microsoft Word format to valid EAD for migration to ArchivesSpace. In short, by taking a broad view of the skills and experience necessary to provide excellent service both to our researchers and to our own colleagues, we have been able to make decisions with a more meaningful understanding of metadata and collections issues across systems and with a commitment to cultivating deliberate and informed communication.

Strategies for Managing Organizational Change

Integration of staffing for special collections into the Library as a whole has not been without challenges. In examining the status quo of separate staffing for special collections as an operation, many underlying assumptions were challenged, sometimes inadvertently. Individuals have varying reactions to change, as well as responses to how others are responding to change. There have also been varying levels of agreement and acceptance that reorganization was needed or that special collections materials will benefit from an integrated staffing approach. We have found that two approaches to managing and facilitating organizational change have proven fruitful; first, we have engaged in meaningful conversation with staff members to focus on identifying motivations and desires, and second, we have identified specific training needs and developed a plan of action to equip all staff members with skills and knowledge necessary to work in special collections.

Throughout the Library's reorganization, staff members have had the opportunity to engage with library leadership and with their colleagues about what motivates them individually, what they hope to achieve in their new roles, and areas in need of improvement. These conversations have been particularly productive as related to the integration of special collections and non–special collections technical services staff. Broadly speaking, special collections staff have consistently conveyed strong motivation to provide excellent care and stewardship for collections and have continuously identified security for collections as a top priority and motivation in their work. At the same time, those in the metadata units have energetically communicated their desires to create metadata, to analyze past metadata practices and imagine new metadata methods and solutions, and to expose and disseminate metadata as widely as possible. Though different, the motivations and desires of special collections and non–special collections staff are not mutually exclusive and the challenge for managers in the reorganization has been to pair these interests intentionally to leverage passions for institutional benefit.

There have also been near-universal desires on the part of staff that have featured prominently in the Library's reorganization. Most significantly, staff have communicated desire for consistent supervisory and personnel management experience on the part of managers *and* direct reports. To support this need, the Library's human resources unit has devised a four-part supervisory training series to ensure consistent communication in the areas of developing position descriptions, personnel onboarding and off-boarding, and annual evaluation. The supervisory training series was successful in its support of the reorganization not only in that it helped accomplish the shared goal of ensuring consistent experiences for both supervisors and direct reports but also in that it enabled supervisors to be aware of areas of personnel management inconsistency in the previous organization.

As part of our ongoing conversations between and among the newly integrated staff, the need for other types of training has emerged as a critical issue to address. While colleagues previously uninvolved with special collections certainly bring expertise, they may or may not have experience with or understand rare and unique materials, and as noted, retirements and other departures had already depleted the available institutional knowledge. It can be a balancing act to determine when current staff in other units can be tapped for participation and when new hires are needed. Consequently, library management has committed to identifying training needs and investigating and identifying solutions and resources.

Training needs have ranged from practical to conceptual, with many people learning how to physically handle the materials in addition to how these resources may be used by researchers. In a particularly significant example of meeting education needs in the organization, the Library pursued formal training through the Society of American Archivists (SAA) and, in July 2015, hosted SAA trainers to lead a two-day workshop on the theory and practice of archival arrangement and description. The training was extremely successful, with nearly 30 individuals from across the Library and the university participating. Having a large number of staff equipped with a basic understanding of archival material arrangement and description has been critically important to ensuring shared common understanding of metadata creation and management practices and providing a basis for conversations about past practice and ideas for future approaches to metadata management.

In addition to staffing and training, security is an issue for consideration. Determining permissions for building access and stacks access across a broader group of people necessitates more complex decision making and increased communication among stakeholders. Newly integrated staff will need building and collections access and appropriate training and understanding of policy in those areas; and it is possible that we will need to reconfigure access for staff who have been working with these materials for years. Building and collection security policy is not trivial and any change to policy and practice in these areas requires open and sustained conversation with library leaders and managers.

Managing change in a librarywide reorganization and in the integration of special collections and non–special collections technical services units has been a rigorous yet rewarding experience. We know that managing change will continuously require resources both in the form of people willing to engage in new ways of approaching our practices and in the form of monetary resources to provide training necessary to equip all staff with necessary knowledge and skills. Our investment has had excellent returns as we are now able to leverage shared conversation and shared training and learning experiences to make informed, sound, and holistic decisions in ways that were impossible in the previous organizational design.

Outcomes to Date

Though nascent, our efforts to integrate special collections and non–special collections staff into a cohesive unit have resulted in incremental cultural change, two significant and tangible software development accomplishments, and a renewed emphasis on discovery of collections and materials. We acknowledge that not all of the changes will prove successful, however; the organizational structure and impending hires are too new to allow for thoughtful assessment and modification at the time of this writing.

Notably, the MCO and MAD units, at this writing, most directly represent our commitment to technical services integration. Processing archivists have begun to work alongside their cataloging colleagues in the MCO unit to arrange collections and create metadata; similarly, the person selected for the archivist position, a position for which a search is in process, will work with his or her colleagues in MAD to develop metadata policy for archival materials while keeping in mind the broader metadata environment. Furthermore, all staff in the MAD unit (comprising four metadata experts from various departments in the Library's previous structure) have united to deepen their understanding of issues related to archival metadata while awaiting a hire into the archivist position, thus temporarily shoring up the organization while we hire for this vital role.

We also expect that the MCO and MAD units will work in a progressively integrated way as we move forward to accomplish our core goals of appropriate stewardship of collections and increased and enhanced discovery and access of materials. Already the MCO and MAD units have teamed up with the newly formed Library Experience team representing reference and other public service functions to analyze problems that involve metadata and functions such as materials circulation; the combined teams have come together to assess the problems and will reconvene after a period of data analysis to identify possible solutions to various metadata issues such as legacy location codes and integration of researcher-enhanced description. This early example of collaboration among the MCO and MAD units has validated the missions of both teams and will enable us to more adeptly analyze and solve metadata problems in the future.

In addition to the outcomes related to organizational change, we have also had substantial success related to two software projects designed to support manuscript processing activity in the future as well as address digital conversion of legacy finding aids. The first project involves commitment of significant institutional resources in support of bringing ArchivesSpace on-line at the university, and the other involves development of a finding aid converter tool designed for use in transforming finding aids from Microsoft Word format to valid EAD for upload into ArchivesSpace.

Beginning in October 2014, a team began the process of evaluating and implementing ArchivesSpace as the university's choice of software for managing manuscript collections and the collections' attendant metadata. The group included those involved with special collections at all three libraries, as well as metadata expertise from each library. Other team experts included the library IT and programming staff responsible for maintaining the tool, tracking and fixing bugs, and implementing new versions of the software.

The group's charge has been to:

- evaluate ArchivesSpace as software available to the university for management of manuscript collections and metadata;

- develop a styleguide in alignment with *Describing Archives: A Content Standard* (DACS) principles to ensure consistent metadata creation across the three libraries; and

- develop and implement a testing protocol for the tool to ensure that software bugs are identified and reported in such a way as to minimize disruption in collection processing and metadata creation.

We are proud to report that this large group of stakeholders from across the university has well met these goals within one calendar year of the group's formation. Creating this pan-university team representing collections, metadata, and programming skills and experiences has represented for us a considerable advancement forward with regard to convening teams in new ways to achieve shared goals and has reaffirmed our belief that special collections and the Library function more effectively in this new and blended model.

We have also had success in developing software that we hope to use in order to manage even more content with ArchivesSpace in support of our goal to address backlogs of legacy finding aid materials, especially those which are in Microsoft Word format and are only available in paper form at the reference desk in the special collections library. The metadata librarian's initial research revealed that Word finding aid backlogs are a very common problem without easy or quick solutions; in fact, many institutions rely on paying students to copy and paste finding aids into EAD or other archival data management software systems. The metadata librarian mentioned this conundrum to a software engineer who offered to assess the Word documents for viability in developing a tool in support of mass conversion.

Happily, what began as a side research question for a single engineer has turned into a viable project that looks to produce software we've nick-named Transmog, a nod to the transmogrifying effect of converting data from Word to valid EAD. The engineer, the metadata librarian, and the archivist from the health sciences library have met regularly to refine and adapt the tool, and the group is planning to test the tool in summer 2015 to begin to assess the utility of this tool and to also chip away at the finding aid backlog. In a noteworthy act of cooperation across units, the digitization unit in CAD made available to the MAD metadata unit funding in order to hire an intern for the summer to test both the Transmog tool and ArchivesSpace in support of accelerating the pace at which we can make new and legacy collections more widely available. As a result of this cooperation, we hired an intern to use the software to convert over 50 finding aids from Microsoft Word into valid EAD XML for ingest into ArchivesSpace in a fraction of the time it would have taken to copy and paste manually. This level of cooperation, once difficult and infrequent in the prior organizational design, has proven tremendously successful and more easily achieved in the new staffing configuration.

A final outcome of our work to integrate technical services units and form teams of diverse skill alongside successes we've had with bringing new organizational units together and developing significant software tools has been a renewed emphasis on the importance of discovery of collections and materials. As mentioned at the outset of this chapter, we are learning how to support and integrate our staff's sincere passion for care and stewardship of materials (felt most strongly by those who work to acquire and arrange the collections) with the excitement and possibility that other staff feel with regard to making collections discoverable and accessible (felt particularly by the metadata specialists). Developing policies for ArchivesSpace generally and around creating DACS-compliant metadata especially has allowed us to engage with what is rich about our collections and to also emphasize metadata creation and management in alignment with national standards and with an understanding of how metadata for archival collections can interact with other types of metadata at this institution. We are increasingly operating such that those closest to the collections can see the fruit of their arrangement and description labors while those charged with providing leadership for many types of metadata can derive satisfaction and accomplishment through consistent metadata creation and the discovery and access possibilities that result.

Areas for Future Development

We have been pleased with the results of our early ventures with organizing staff around skills and function, regardless of physical location or collections served, in support of our efforts to align with library and university strategic directions. We are excited about these initial successes in the areas of collection processing, metadata creation, and ArchivesSpace implementation; the positive progress we've made in these areas enables us to be hopeful that we will be able to a similar approach in at least four areas.

An area of activity that is an obvious candidate for additional integration between special collections and non–special collections technical services staff involves acquisitions functions. As previously noted, the most significant area of integration of unit mission to date involves the MCO and MAD units; we expect in time to be able to consider RAD, the acquisitions unit, as equally integrated as the other metadata units, and we will surely draw on the same approaches with RAD as we have with the MCO and MAD units with regard to communication strategies and ensuring appropriate skill pairings in functional groups.

A second area of focus in the near future will be the need for the Library to deepen its in-house archival expertise. In addition to hiring for the critical position of archivist, we will also work diligently to equip existing staff with the training and education necessary to be successful as we continue to work together in new ways. Just as we have pursued opportunities for training and education in metadata, we also anticipate the need to expand our expertise with regard to the care and handling of rare and unique materials; fortunately, we have a strong institutional history of such careful collection stewardship, so we will be able to rely on in-house experts to ensure that our teams are equipped with the skills to continue in that tradition of excellence. We expect that training for these two units will be a robust and ongoing endeavor that will be necessary to ensure that staff in our metadata units have a similar understanding of metadata principles and practices as we create and manage metadata over time.

Long a dilemma for the non–special collections technical services, a third realm of activity that will continue our advancement with integrating units within the Library is the increasing challenge of providing description in non-English languages. The centralization of description services into one unit will enable us to confront this challenge in a more holistic way, and will necessitate combining cataloging statistics for non-English resources across the Library, rather than from individual units, in order to analyze the state of cataloging for these materials and investigate and prescribe solutions for all library materials.

The fourth area to which we look forward investing energy and resources is an expanded capacity to share collections and metadata in an increasingly interconnected environment. The University Library participates in resource sharing and aggregation hubs, including Virginia Heritage, the consolidated database of finding aids for archival collections throughout Virginia, as well as the Digital Public Library of America, to which the Library has shared over 30,000 digital objects. We will be poised to contribute to these and other efforts more quickly, reliably, and robustly in the future, having adopted ArchivesSpace as an archival data management tool and by emphasizing sound metadata practice consistent with national standards.

A Model for Change

Beginning in 2013, the University Library has investigated, planned, and implemented a full reorganization for more than two years. The availability of trust, patience, and flexibility is required to make change ebbs and flows among staff individually and as a whole. Despite the challenges that we have described in this chapter in reorganizing staff according to function and in integrating the special collections and non–special collections technical services units, we have found more successes than shortcomings and recommend the arrangement as a viable and worthy model of organizational design.

The Library's reorganization has allowed us to create significant change in at least three ways that position us to align with and carry out library and university directives in ways that were once more difficult. First, and most importantly, we have moved from a decentralized organization in which libraries, departments, and units functioned as microcosms of the whole to a centralized one in which staff and services are aligned around function; this has enabled us to greatly reduce inefficiency while simultaneously promoting consistency in all services. Although this is particularly true for public services, it is also true for metadata creation and management services. As a result of centralization of services, users can expect to receive consistently excellent service and experience with the library, no matter a library's physical location. The centralization of metadata services has meant more satisfying interaction with the library's discovery systems as a result of more holistic metadata management.

Our realignment around function has also had the effect of creating a much more agile organization. By virtue of centralizing staffing and funding, we have been able to deploy resources more effectively. For instance, paying all student employees with a single fund as opposed to the decentralized library model has meant that students are effectively employed by all libraries rather than a single library and can be moved among service points in the organization. Such flexibility was beyond our imagination in years past. Changes in technology systems and paring project management software options from many to a few have had a similar transformative effect in conducting library business and internal communications.

The third type of change that some staff have pursued to ensure alignment with library and university directives has been to use the university's personnel evaluation software called "Lead@" in new ways. Every employee creates, in communication with his or her supervisor, goals and a development plan in the Lead@ system that will provide the basis for the employee's annual performance review. Lead@ allows an employee to connect an individual performance plan to specific organizational and university strategic objectives. Some supervisors and individual employees have begun to experiment with aligning individual performance plans to the university's Cornerstone Plan. We are excited at the potential of this new way of conducting performance review in that an individual connects his or her work to the university's mission and also in that supervisors can ensure that the work of the Library advances the university's mission, values, and goals.

The future of libraries and higher education is such that no unit will survive in a silo. We know this is true for the Library's relationship to the university and is particularly true of the special collections library's relationship to the university library system. Our organizational strategic plans, in the form of the university's Cornerstone Plan and in the form of the Library's new organizational design, necessitate that we integrate and collaborate like never before. At the University Library, our embrace of these new principles has allowed us to achieve goals with such frequency that some staff has wondered why we didn't always operate this way before. Put simply, while there may be varying levels of acceptance of the new organizational model and concerns about the time and training needed to bring about understanding and consistency between previously unconnected work, managers and administrators are able to tangibly see how the new organizational design has made us better at what we do.

Chapter 18
Open Access and Copyright in Archives and Special Collections

Heather Briston

Archivists and special collections librarians often have a complicated relationship with intellectual property law and the impact it has upon our materials, highlighted by avoidance and reluctance. Neither desire makes the underlying issues disappear. We are a profession that endeavors to uphold the law, while at the same time support our researchers, and these ends can conflict. Due to the nature of the materials in our repositories, we cannot act responsibly without understanding how to navigate the primary issues of copyright and how they affect virtual access and use of our materials. Understanding how to make educated choices, leading to decisions and actions within the legal framework, is our greatest tool. The most important thing for archivists and special collections librarians to remember is that we bring a very important understanding and perspective to the table: the mission of our institutions and the knowledge of our materials. This domain-specific knowledge should be coupled with a knowledge and respect for the law, since at times we can approach the boundaries of the law too conservatively.

Many of our repositories have as a mission contributing to learning and scholarship; those that are public institutions also have missions that include the contribution to the public good, and public access to materials. These underline the fact that making materials in our repositories widely available is not only a personal or a professional desire, but often the underlying mission of our repositories. It is important that we increase our understanding of the law and its parameters so that we do not end up abandoning our mission for the sake of expediency. In this chapter, we will put the legal issues of intellectual property in the context of special collections and archives, looking at the effect on open access to our materials, learn about tools to assist in navigating them with an eye toward access and use, and look at the choices repositories have regarding open access and use.

Open Access

"Open access" is a term in the academic library environment increasingly finding its way into the common lexicon. The most typical use of the word is in libraries discussing journal articles and monographs available digitally outside of subscriptions and paywalls. The Scholarly Publishing and Academic Resources Coalition (SPARC), a prominent advocate for open access, uses this definition, "Open access is the free, immediate, online availability of research articles, coupled with the rights to use these articles fully in the digital environment."[1] Since the early 2000s, this discussion of open access has grown exponentially. It has grown to address the larger ethos that scholarly output and research materials of all types (including research data sets, for example) should be freely open and available for all to make use of in their own inquiries. Open access includes many other topics that will not be covered here: the use of institutional repositories in academic settings, issues of evaluating and alternative business models for open access journals, and the topics of open access research data, open textbooks, and open learning objects.[2] While this is predominantly of interest within academia, increasingly governmental entities, funding agencies, and other educational settings are being encouraged to make their materials open access, or encouraging others to do the same.[3]

In this chapter "open access" refers to special collections and archival materials that are open and widely accessible on the Internet; the barriers to access, particularly the requirement of onsite consultation, are gone. We will be looking at it not purely from an academic or scholarly perspective, but from the fundamental prospect of users' access to material and the influence of copyright law and contract law. Why does open access matter to archivists and special collections librarians? First and foremost, our repositories' mission assumes some level of access and use from the general public to within an organization depending on the type of repository. We recognize the fundamental role that the Internet has in making collection materials globally visible to old and new communities of researchers, through openly available online catalogs and the advent of Encoded Archival Description (EAD). This has led to the growing assumption by our users that everything is online. Even our most devoted users are weighing heavily the costs of their actions if the material they need is not readily available online.

Many major grants for preserving or processing collections include access requirements for successful funding. Historically, that was a published finding aid or microfilmed collection. Today, access is an EAD finding aid and/or at least some portion of the digitized materials available online. Some microfilmed collections are receiving digitization grants. Public and private funders understand the need and demand for open access to our "hidden" collections. While general library collections are increasingly more homogenous, special collections set our institutions and repositories apart. Ultimately, open access is important to archivists and special collections librarians because of our mission, our ethics, and our passion. We understand it is key for our collections to become the basis of new research, access, and use.

The Law and Our Collections

Any archivist or special collections librarian, whether in technical, public, or curatorial services experiences the impact of the law on the management of our materials. References to law can include intellectual property, privacy and confidentiality, publicity, and contract law. All of these laws affect whether or not we can make materials available to researchers, under what conditions, and to whom, and then govern the subsequent actions of our users. They touch upon every aspect of access and use that we hold to be an essential part of our mission. Copyright is considered intellectual property. Copyright law has its foundations in Article 1, Section 8 of the U.S. Constitution. This section relates to the creation of works that are the embodiment of creative, useful, scientific expression and an exchange of a limited monopoly for future unfettered public use.[4] Copyright law governs the duplication, display, and other uses of materials that fall within its purview.[5] There are two other areas of intellectual property present in our collections: trademark protects the use of words, phrase, design, illustration, colorways, or other documentable distinctions in commerce, and patent law protects novel or innovative useful objects and processes or additions to objects or processes for a limited period of time.[6] In this chapter we focus specifically on copyright law and contract law, and the affect that these two areas of law can have upon how, where, and under what conditions we provide access to our collections, particularly online.

Copyright

For many archivists and special collections librarians, the relationship with copyright can be frustrating. It is an area where we have little, if any training, although it fundamentally impacts how or whether we can fulfill the mission and values of our profession and our repositories. The application of the law very rarely provides us with bright line rules.

For readers who are new to these questions and for a more in-depth discussion of the law and its application, see Heather Briston, "Understanding Copyright Law" in *Rights in the Digital Era* and other introductory texts listed in the bibliography. At its core the U.S. Copyright Act governs how creative works including books, images, music, computer programs, among others, are used and reused by our repositories and our researchers. The focus of our relationship with copyright revolves around the answers to three questions:

1. Is the work in copyright?

2. If so who owns the copyright?

3. How do sections of the copyright law specify the manner in which the repository can reproduce the work and make it available?[7]

It is particularly important that archivists and special collections librarians not overlook the first question, whether or not the work is in copyright. While it may seem to be the case, not everything is in copyright, for several different reasons: due to date of publication, the formalities of publication at the time, the time elapsed since the death of the creator, federal government publications, and works that are not copyrightable in the first place.[8] Both we and our researchers are freely able to use or repurpose materials not in copyright in our collections and repositories.

If we have determined that targeted materials are within copyright, our next step is to discover who owns the copyright? Identifying the owner, who may or may not be the creator, is important. Determining the copyright of unpublished or recently published materials include factors such as whether the copyright is held by an individual or a corporate entity. If it is an individual, it is his or her life span; for a corporate entity, it is 120 years from the date of creation. For materials published prior to 1989, the prior regime of copyright formalities before the 1976 Act determined whether a work was currently in copyright.[9] In some cases, copyright ownership has been transferred and is no longer owned by the original creator. In these cases, it is important to remember that ownership can only be legally transferred in writing, or by will from an entity that currently legally owns it. It should also be clear that merely owning the item in question does not convey any copyright ownership.[10]

Our materials are meant to be used, and therefore the interplay of exclusive rights and exceptions goes to the heart of managing access and use. The third question is one of copyright's effect on use. It is informed by Section 106 of the Copyright Act, defining activities whose control is exclusively reserved to the copyright holder[11] and in part by the exceptions to those exclusive rights as codified in sections like 107, the fair use exception as it applies to use.

Access and Use

What sets special collections librarians and archivists apart from our information professional colleagues is the extent to which the materials that we manage are composed of a mixture of published and unpublished materials. In many cases, the bulk of the materials that we manage are unpublished. Legislation or the outcomes of litigation are sometimes only tenuously related to the bulk of our collections as solutions and practices tend to be developed for published materials created for commercial purposes.[12] Until 1978, unpublished materials were not covered by federal copyright law, but instead existed in a world of perpetual common law copyright. The trigger for copyright was in publication. This changed with the 1976 Act, when from the point of fixing a work in a tangible medium of expression, the work is copyrighted. It moved the point of copyright from publication, back in time to creation.[13] Thus, with the change in the act, unpublished materials that were in a common law copyright limbo were deemed to be within federal copyright overnight. It was not until 1991 that fair use of unpublished materials was codified in the law. What often sets our unpublished materials apart is the lack of copyright information we have about them. This issue is most prevalent when working with unpublished materials and comes up when discussing orphan works (which will be addressed later). It can have an impact on our professional risk and comfort levels when providing access to our collections online.

Public Domain

For those of us who work with archival, manuscript, or other special collections, the most pressing legal topics are public domain, library and archives exception, fair use exception, and orphan works. The public domain is a trove for archivists and special collections librarians and the users of our collections. These are materials that because of their date of publication, a federal government agency as the creator, the absences of completed formalities, the life span of the creator, or the lack of copyrightable expression, U.S. copyright law does not apply. Therefore, they can be reproduced, and used in whatever way we see fit. There are many tools available to archivists and special collections librarians to assist in determining whether a work is in the public domain.[14] Public domain includes both those materials published before January 1, 1923, and those materials published during periods when specific formalities were required in order to obtain or maintain copyright, or unpublished materials whose creator has been dead for over 70 years.[15]

A robust public domain is vital to the work of archivists and special collections librarians. With the growth of digital projects, these materials have been the target for those who are concerned with the risks of making materials available online.[16] Supporting a robust public domain is part of our mission. We can do this by understanding and ensuring that we have identified as much as we can from the public domain, and do not seek to place additional restrictions on them via contract. The challenge with relying solely on the public domain is that for modern collections, and those who want to engage with the materials of contemporary figures or recent events, public domain is of little assistance when contemplating what can be made widely available online because copyright law does apply.

Library and Archives Exception (Section 108)

For contemporary materials, as well as some surprisingly old materials, we need to explore the fair use and the library and archives exceptions to the exclusive rights of the copyright holder provided for in the U.S. Copyright Act. Many of us are familiar with the Library and Archives exception, Section 108.[17] This exception allows for carefully defined and circumscribed duplication or loan that normally would infringe upon the rights of the copyright holder to be done by librarians and archivists in the name of preservation and access. The details of the section and how it operates are treated more fulsomely in Briston or Hirtle's *Copyright and Cultural Institutions*. For this discussion, it is important to remember that while it provides an outlet for many important preservation and access functions, it doesn't for all. In the realm of open access, Section 108(b)(2) provides little help for making the contents of our collections open and widely available on the web. This is because the section only applies to unpublished text and broadcast news recordings but not to photographs, audio recordings, or other audio visual materials. Also, the exception does not cover digital access to materials outside of the confines of the repository that owns them.[18] Section 108(h) does allow for preservation and access to works in their final 20 years of copyright. This provides a glimmer of hope for access, but also assumes we can determine the copyright duration for our holdings.[19] While Section 108 provides some leeway, with these caveats we need to explore other options, chiefly Section 107, Fair Use.

Fair Use

While Section 108 is of limited help when discussing open access to the materials found in repositories, it is Section 107, Fair Use, which is most frequently referenced when making materials that may be still under copyright available widely. Our relationship with fair use is complicated. As a profession that generally gravitates toward firm, intuitive rules that we can follow, the flexibility of fair use often leaves us stymied, and just a bit unsatisfied; even if it is this part of its nature that provides the greatest opportunity for us to fulfill our missions of open access under copyright law. The courts had referenced fair use for some time, but it was only formally written into the law in 1976.

Fair use is recognition of the fact that there are some uses of copyrighted material that are of such a social and public good that the use should be upheld, regardless of the permission from the copyright holder. It comprises four factors balanced by a court in its analysis of whether or not the use is fair.[20] Section 107 was amended in 1991, to explicitly state that the unpublished nature of a work is not, in and of itself, a bar to a finding of fair use. This is of huge importance to archivists and special collections librarians, not only because of cases prior to the change in the law, where, to our detriment, courts focused on the fact that material was unpublished, but also because of the importance the courts placed in the right of first publication.[21] Despite uncertainty, we evoke fair use to make materials widely available. It is important for us to understand clearly its parameters, and to exercise it purposefully, rather than unknowingly by default.

Orphan Works

The final topic that archivists and special collections librarians address when providing open access to materials is the issue of orphan works. Orphan works are not formally defined or addressed by the Copyright Act. They are understood to be works for which the current copyright holder is no longer identifiable.[22] They are found in both published and unpublished materials, but the scope of the problem is considered to be much larger for unpublished materials. The growth of orphaned works has come as a result of changes in the 1976 copyright law, cemented through subsequent treaties and international agreements. The two main changes are abolishing formalities as a precursor to copyright protection, and the subsistence of copyright from the creation of a work, resulting in bringing scores of unpublished material under federal copyright law, coupled with a copyright term that can last for multiple generations. We know from experience that the copyright holders of much of the material in our collections are difficult if not impossible to ascertain. This uncertainty hampers our ability to provide open access to materials in our collections. It is the risk of the unidentified copyright holder out there waiting to bring suit that presents a barrier for some repositories.[23] While orphan works present a conundrum to archivists and special collections librarians regarding wide virtual access to materials, there is a growing group of tools and workflows developed by our community for managing access issues in copyrighted materials.

Tools and Workflows for Managing Copyright Issues in Access to Digital Collections

When discussing issues related to copyright and making digitized materials online, one of the most common requests is for examples of how others have faced these decisions. We want to know that another repository, just like ours, has done this already and will share their experience. Recently there are more examples being discussed at sessions at conferences, and more examples in the literature. The two most well-known articles are the articles by Dickson and Akmon that discuss two digitization projects where the costs of rights clearance were quantified.[24] These articles do not serve as a template for action, but instead are examples of how the prescribed process as presented by the U.S. Copyright Office for identifying copyright holders and getting permission really does not scale for archival materials. Each proposes a middle way that takes into consideration a certain amount of risk management based on sound analysis.

Examples of repositories that are a part of a digital project and share documentation on their policy and procedures for considering rights, and in some cases also privacy and confidentiality issues, are the University of North Carolina at Chapel Hill (UNC-CH) and the Wellcome Library. UNC-CH had two projects: one a Mellon-funded project digitizing the long Civil Rights Movement and the other funded by the Watson-Brown Foundation to analyze the costs of rights determination. The projects included symposia and reports not only on historians' use and research needs for digital access to unique materials, but also on the intellectual property and privacy issues involved in providing online access to that material.[25] Another recent project is the case study of a Wellcome Library digitization project in the United Kingdom, where staff developed a risk analysis matrix for putting a large amount of material online. While it does deal with archivists working under UK law, it provides a thought-provoking description of a process for dealing with issues of orphaned works, and unlocatable or unresponsive copyright owners.[26]

Recently, the University of California, Los Angeles (UCLA) Library Special Collections released its Digital Project Toolkit, based on one created and released by the Archives of American Art.[27] The toolkit was created as a part of the Los Angeles Aqueduct Digital Platform project, used and refined over several digitization projects at UCLA.[28] It includes documentation for each part of the digital project workflow and extensive documentation, process, and forms for a risk analysis workflow for digital projects.

Various best practices documents for managing copyright-related issues are available for repositories including some that are integrated into and referenced by the UCLA toolkit, depending on the materials in question and the use. The most well-known are the Association of Research Libraries best practices and the Society of American Archivists Orphan Works Best practices.[29] A new set recently released of potential interest to archivists and special collections librarians is the "Statement of Best Practices in Fair Use of Collections Containing Orphan Works for Libraries, Archives, and Other Memory Institutions."[30] The suite of best practices include examples of potential actions that might be taken by repositories in recognizing and reducing risks, providing a framework and lens for decision making.[31] When archivists and special collections librarians think of open access, they focus on materials. However the other side of this relationship is with our users and how the copyright in the materials that we hold and our relationship to it affects our relationship with them.

Managing Rights

We do not often discuss the management of rights that we hold in our collections, since we are focused on the rights that we do not have, or are difficult to uncover. As archivists and special collections librarians, managing copyright in our collections includes performing a copyright audit and making choices about the rights that we hold as a repository. Copyright audits may sound overwhelming, but they can be conducted at any level of granularity, by any size repository. While it is true that the more steps you are able to complete, the more you know, every repository can benefit from an audit, no matter its extent. The end result is a more systematic understanding of current practices in regard to copyright, reviewing deeds and user forms. Depending on the extent of the audit, you will learn specifically what you do and do not know about the copyright in your collections. All of this is useful, and no effort is wasted in this respect.[32]

Most repositories hold some materials for which they own the copyright and can therefore dictate the uses that can be made of that material for a period of time. The most common way that repositories own copyright is via a clause in a deed of gift that explicitly donates those rights to the repository along with the physical collection. The donor can only transfer those copyrights that he or she owns; so commonly in a collection of personal papers, the donor can transfer the copyright in anything that he or she created. This includes such things as outgoing correspondence or personal journals, but not the incoming correspondence of others, or anything that they might have created, but transferred the copyrights to others via licensing or copyright transfer such as for publication. It is very important for archivists and special collections librarians to have a good understanding of copyright transfer with a collection so that they can have an informed conversation with the donor. When donors are unwilling to donate copyrights, it is important to uncover whatever issues might be preventing them from moving forward in this area. Sometimes it is related to concerns that have very little to do with true exploitation of the copyrights that they hold. In these cases it is important to discuss topics of privacy and access, as it may be a situation where the donor is trying to use one area of law to address concerns that they have under a completely separate area of law. (For more discussion of managing rights as part of the acquisition process of digital resources, see Sarah Barsness and Anjanette Schussler, "Digital Acquisitions and Appraisal," Chapter 8 in this volume.) Donors must understand the process of licensing and permission, if they are not currently managing their copyrights, and ensuring that their contact information is up to date, if they take on the responsibility of managing their copyrights directly.[33]

Another way that archival repositories can hold copyrights in their collections is via their parent organization as the institution's archives. The institution is recognized as owning the copyrights, normally as a corporate body. Ideally the repository should have an agreement from its counsel or other administrative body that affirmatively grants permission to the repository to administer the copyright in the materials that it holds. Remember that not everything held by an institution is copyrighted to the institution. The default assumption of the law is that the individual who created the work is the copyright holder. However, there is a specific class of creators for whom this is not the case.

In these cases it is a question of whether or not it is a "work for hire," where as an employee or via a contractual relationship with the organization, the copyright belongs to the organization rather than the individual.[34] For example, most photographers or videographers for hire have clauses in their contracts that reserve the rights in their work to themselves, and if the contract is not closely reviewed, the organization can lose the rights to these materials, outside of the use described in the contract. Whether owned through transfer or via the parent organization, repositories that own copyrights have a pool of material that can be identified for more open access and wider use by researchers. Understanding the breadth and depth of this pool can make planning open access digital projects much easier.

Staff in many repositories find this a challenge, because the records about our collections are not always complete, and resolving the ownership of copyright, even when it seems explicit, can be difficult because of donor understanding and external contractual agreements. With all the work of a repository, the copyright audit can seem like a desirable but unrealistic project, but they can be scaled to the amount of time and resources available and whatever the results of a project, it will lead to improved access and use of the holdings.

Choices in Managing Rights

The second part of managing the copyrights in our collections is the choices staff in our repositories make. We looked at the two primary ways that staff at a repository could get rights in materials in their collections: by deed or via their parent institution. Next it is important for us to look how we as a profession generally, or more specifically as our repositories, choose to exercise those rights.

When a repository holds copyright in a collection, staff members can decide to what extent they will exercise these rights and under what conditions. The decisions can include requiring permission, licensing particular uses, charging fees for those licensed uses, restricting duplication, or restricting access. For repositories that own copyright, these are the choices. However, there are also some repositories that exert similar controls over materials for which they do not hold copyright, but are asserting it as it relates to ownership of the item.

Legal Considerations

When repository staff decide whether to continue or institute permissions, licenses or fees, the first question is: Does the repository have a legal right to do so? If you own the copyright to the item, the simple answer is "yes." Users can still make their own fair use determination and proceed accordingly as with any other copyrighted work. If the ownership is not of copyright, but the physical item, what legal rights accrue? In this case, the repository has the right to control the access to the material. As with any materials where copyright is not held, an argument is made under Sections 107 or 108 if it is still under copyright, whether or not they chose to duplicate. However, once the work is accessed or duplicated, if the repository does not own the copyright, control is limited to the contractual use agreement in the duplication form or other license created. Contract law is different from copyright law in that the only parties bound by the agreement are the parties that signed it. Under copyright law, there can be a cause for infringement not only against the licensee, but also against any subsequent parties that make a use without permission.

If repository staff members are making a contract based on physical ownership, it is very important that they are clear that they are placing requirements on use such as permissions or fees based on ownership of the item *not* on ownership of any copyrights, and there is no copyright permission being granted, and that particularly in the case of public domain materials they are free to obtain copies elsewhere.[35] Once a repository provides access to and duplication of a public domain item, it can only control the subsequent use of that item via the contractual duplication agreement concerning the specific duplication it has made with the researcher for whom the copy was made. Use of other copies not covered by the agreement or by other users not a party to the agreement are beyond the control of the repository. It is important to note here the potential for risk in those cases where use fees are charged for materials where the copyright owner is unknown or the repository does not own the copyright. While it should be noted that this issue has never been litigated so the guidance of a court is not available, there is a risk that the fees could be considered "profits" under the accounting for damages stemming from a cause of infringement.[36] This is often why those repositories with a practice of charging use fees do not do so in those cases of copyrighted material where the repository cannot demonstrate that it is the copyright holder. In a separate but related issue, it is a criminal offense to place a copyright notice on an item when you are doing so with fraudulent intent and know that this is a false assertion; innocent mistakes would not rise to this level.[37]

Ethical Considerations

As with many of our repositories' policies and procedures, there is both a legal and an ethical component to the decision. One ethical question is the contractual relationships that repositories develop over the use of public domain materials. When works are in the public domain, they are not subject to the constraints of copyright law regarding duplication and use. Therefore if a user has access to them, they are free to use them as they wish. The ethical discussions in the profession surrounding permissions and use fees have increased over the past 15 years. An early proponent of discontinuing use fees and permissions was Peter Hirtle, in his presidential address for the Society of American Archivists in 2003. He put forward that because of both legal and ethical concerns, repositories should move from a fees and permissions model to focus on reproduction fees, and charging what our services are worth.[38] Recently, Michelle Light, in her keynote address at the 2014 Rare Books and Manuscripts Section of the Association for College & Research Libraries annual meeting, gave an impassioned call for repositories to get out of the use fees and permissions arena, with examples from around the profession of repositories taking up that decision.[39] In each of these speeches, there was an important focus on the ethical issues surrounding fees and permissions, not just can we, but *should* we as a profession participate in this portion of the market? Ironically, in our arguments about why our repositories should be able to widely use and make accessible our holdings of orphan works or other materials, we look to and argue that our organizational mission makes it an imperative. We cannot ignore that same organizational mission when we then seek to constrict and constrain the use of our collections. We must ensure that all of our policies are in line with our mission.

Enforcement

Along with the legal and ethical choices made when considering charging use fees and licensing their holdings, the costs of enforcing those agreements must be factored into the decision. As a repository, is this something that we really want to embrace? When a repository is only willing to assert its copyright or ownership rights but not willing to enforce them, what does that say about its assertion of rights? Were the institutional costs of negotiating the permissions and collecting the fees worth it? If we want to make sure that our collections are open, available, and used, do we then want to turn around and meter and monitor that use? In her keynote, Michelle Light stated, "I would argue that we improve our society by increasing the distribution of our heritage, by making it more visible and available for inclusion in public discourse."[40] Yes, we want the world to know of the riches of our collections, and we never have enough resources to fulfill our missions, but are use fees and permissions really the way to fulfill those goals? What does this say about our open access desires, remembering that the definition of open access includes both access and use?

Managing Rights—Support for Collections and Services

Most repositories argue that any use fees are collected are returned to support the collection and that this revenue stream is vital for support. While there is no argument that more support is necessary, is this truly a viable option? First, is the use fee revenue channeled into accounts ensuring that the money is always allocated and controlled by special collections? Second, analyze the costs of use fee collection: rights research time, license preparation, and negotiation time. In addition to the staff costs involved in licensing and fee collection, opportunity costs are associated with what that staff person is not doing when focused on this work. In a small staff, this cost may outweigh any revenue. Finally, as Hirtle discussed in his 2003 article, another step is to review the fees for services.[41] Some public repositories are required by policy to ensure that any self-supported services charge fees that fully account for the costs of the service. When we factor in the costs of the person creating the duplication, supervision of the process, and supplies, it is quite clear that many are choosing to subsidize for their users the costs of their services. What would happen if we consistently started to charge what our services were worth?

A growing number of repositories are concluding that extensive use fees and licensing obligations drain, rather than contribute to, their revenue. In the last few years, repositories such as Cornell University, the J. Paul Getty Museum, and the Victoria & Albert Museum have changed their policies.[42] Even more repositories have let go of permission and use fees for public domain or materials that they do not own the copyright with most limiting licensing to commercial uses of copyrights that they hold.[43]

Conclusion

Copyright has always been an issue within collections in our repositories, but with the increasing pressure and desire to make our collections widely available on the Internet, it has become imperative that archivists and special collections librarians thoroughly understand the copyright issues involved in the collections that they manage. Not only will this allow them to professionally and ethically manage their collections, but become advocates for their missions and the needs of their users when legislative bodies look to make changes detrimental to the use of unique and distinctive collections. Finally, this understanding will also help them to approach what it means to be good stewards of our collections.

Notes

1. "Open Access," Scholarly Publishing and Academic Resources Coalition, 2015, http://sparc.arl.org/issues/open-access.

2. "Issues," Scholarly Publishing and Academic Resources Coalition (SPARC), 2015, http://sparc.arl.org/issues.

3. Office of Science and Technology Policy, Executive Office of the President, "Increasing Access to the Results of Federally Funded Scientific Research," February 22, 2013, https://www.whitehouse.gov/sites/default/files/microsites/ostp/ostp_public_access_memo_2013.pdf.

4. U.S. Constitution, Article I, §8.

5. All references to the U.S. Code, Title 17, can be located at http://www.copyright.gov/title17/, to ensure the most recent version of the act. 17 U.S.C. §106.

6. World Intellectual Property Organization, "What Is Intellectual Property?" 2015, http://www.wipo.int/about-ip/en/.

7. Heather Briston, "Understanding Copyright Law," in *Rights in the Digital Era*, ed. Menzi L. Behrnd-Klodt and Christopher J. Prom (Chicago, IL: Society of American Archivists, 2015), 14.

8. 17 U.S.C. §§102(b), 105.

9. 17 U.S.C. §§302, 305. See also Peter B. Hirtle, *Copyright Term and the Public Domain in the United States*, 2015, http://copyright.cornell.edu/resources/publicdomain.cfm.

10. 17 U.S.C. §202.

11. 17 U.S.C. §106.

12. A more expansive discussion of unpublished materials can be found in Heather Briston, "Understanding Copyright Law"; Menzi L. Behrnd-Klodt, *Navigating Legal Issues in Archives* (Chicago: Society of American Archivists, 2008); Peter Hirtle, Emily Hudson, and Andrew T. Kenyon, *Copyright and Cultural Institutions: Guidelines for Digitization for U.S. Libraries, Archives, & Museums* (Ithaca, NY: Cornell University Library, 2009).

13. 17 U.S.C. §102(a).

14. For a list of duration tools, see Stanford University Libraries, "Copyright and Fair Use: Charts and Tools," 2015, http://fairuse.stanford.edu/charts-and-tools/.

15. Note that there are some particular exceptions with foreign works that should be attended to, but they are documented in most good duration estimators.

16. Jean Dryden, "The Role of Copyright in Selection for Digitization," *American Archivist* 77 (April 2014): 64–95.

17. 17 U.S.C. §108.

18. 17 U.S.C. §108(b)(2).

19. 17 U.S.C. §108(h).

20. For a more in-depth discussion regarding fair use and the four factors, see Briston, "Understanding Copyright Law"; Behrnd-Klodt, *Navigating Legal Issues in Archives*; or Hirtle et al., *Copyright and Cultural Institutions*.

21. Harper & Row Publishers, Inc. v. Nation Enterprises, 471 U.S. 539 (1985); Salinger v. Random House, 811 F.2d 90 (1986).

22. Society of American Archivists, "Orphan Works Statement of Best Practices," 1, http://www.archivists.org/standards/OWBP-V4.pdf.

23. For a more in-depth discussion regarding orphan works, see Briston, "Understanding Copyright Law"; Behrnd-Klodt, *Navigating Legal Issues in Archives*; or Hirtle et al., *Copyright and Cultural Institutions*.

24. Maggie Dickson, "Due Diligence, Futile Effort: Copyright and the Digitization of the Thomas E. Watson Papers," *American Archivist* 73 (Fall/Winter 2010): 626–636; Dharma Akmon, "Only with Your Permission: How Rights Holders Respond (or Don't Respond) to Requests to Display Archival Material Online," *Archival Science* 10, no. 1 (2010): 45–64.

25. University of North Carolina University Libraries, *From Investigation to Implementation: Building a Program for the Large-Scale Digitization of Manuscripts,*

"Publications and Presentations," 2009, http://www2.lib.unc.edu/dc/watson/archivalmassdigitization/index.html?section=publications.

26. Victoria Stobo, Ronan Deazley, and Ian G. Anderson, "Copyright & Risk: Scoping the Wellcome Digital Library Project" (CREATe Working Paper No. 10, University of Glasgow, December 2013), http://www.create.ac.uk/wp-content/uploads/2013/12/CREATe-Working-Paper-No.10.pdf.

27. Archives of American Art, "Technical Documentation," 2015, http://www.aaa.si.edu/collections/documentation.

28. UCLA Library Special Collections, "Digital Project Toolkit," 2015, http://www.library.ucla.edu/special-collections/programs-projects/digital-projects-special-collections.

29. Association of Research Libraries, "Code of Best Practices in Fair Use for Academic and Research Libraries," January 2012, http://www.arl.org/focus-areas/copyright-ip/fair-use/code-of-best-practices and Society of American Archivists, "Orphan Works Statement of Best Practices," http://www.archivists.org/standards/OWBP-V4.pdf.

30. American University Washington College of Law and University of California, Berkeley, School of Law, "Statement of Best Practices in Fair Use of Collections Containing Orphan Works for Libraries, Archives, and Other Memory Institutions," February 2015, http://www.cmsimpact.org/fair-use/best-practices/statement-best-practices-fair-use-orphan-works-libraries-archives.

31. For an expanded discussion of risk analysis and best practices, see Briston, "Understanding Copyright Law," 35–41, 45–47.

32. For more details on copyright audits and a checklist, see: Briston, "Understanding Copyright Law," 54–55, 65.

33. For more detail on deeds of gift and working with donors regarding rights managements, see Aprille C. McKay, "Managing Rights and Permissions," in *Trends in Archives Practice: Rights in the Digital Era* (Chicago: Society of American Archivists, 2015), 178–184.

34. 17 U.S.C. §101. A "work made for hire" is a work by an employee in the scope of his or her employment, or as a part of a specially commissioned piece "if the parties expressly agree in a written instrument signed by them that the work shall be considered a work made for hire."

35. McKay, "Managing Rights and Permissions," 199–205.

36. Peter B. Hirtle, "Archives or Assets?" Presidential Address, August 21, 2003, *American Archivist* 66 (Fall/Winter 2003): 238.

37. 17 U.S.C. §506 (c).

38. Hirtle, "Archives or Assets?" 235–247.

39. Michelle Light, "Controlling Goods or Promoting the Public Good: Choices for Special Collections in the Marketplace," June 26, 2014, Presentation at Rare Books and Manuscripts Preconference, Las Vegas, Nevada, http://digitalscholarship.unlv.edu/libfacpresentation/121/.

40. Ibid.

41. Hirtle, "Archives or Assets?" 245–247.

42. J. Paul Getty Museum, "Ordering and Reproducing Images from the J. Paul Getty Museum's Collection," http://www.getty.edu/legal/image_request/; Cornell University Library, "Guidelines for Using Public Domain Text, Images, Audio and Video Reproduced from Cornell University Library Collections," http://cdl.library.cornell.edu/guidelines.html; Victoria and Albert Museum, "Terms and Conditions," http://www.vam.ac.uk/content/articles/t/terms-and-conditions/.

43. Yale University Library, Beinecke Rare Book & Manuscript Library, "Permissions and Copyright," http://beinecke.library.yale.edu/research/permissions-copyright; University of Virginia, Albert and Shirley Small Special Collections

Library, "Publishing," https://small.library.virginia.edu/services/reproduction/ publishing/; University of Wisconsin, Madison Libraries, Special Collections, "Requests to Quote or Publish," http://specialcollections.library.wisc.edu/about/ #permission; University of Wyoming, American Heritage Center, "Copyright Information," http://www.uwyo.edu/ahc/copyright.html; UCLA, Library Special Collections, "Requesting Copies | Service Fees," http://www.library.ucla.edu/use/ access-privileges/print-copy-scan/special-collections-reproductions; UNLV University Libraries, Special Collections, "Reproductions and Use," https://www.library.unlv .edu/speccol/research_and_services/reproductions; University of Texas at Austin, Harry Ransom Center, "Project REVEAL," hrc.contentdm.oclc.org/cdm/reveal.

Bibliography

American University Washington College of Law and University of California, Berkeley, School of Law. *Statement of Best Practices in Fair Use of Collections Containing Orphan Works for Libraries, Archives, and Other Memory Institutions*. February 2015. http://www.cmsimpact .org/fair-use/best-practices/statement-best-practices-fair-use-orphan -works-libraries-archives. (Washington, D.C. : American University, 2015)

Association of Research Libraries. "Code of Best Practices in Fair Use for Academic and Research Libraries," January 2012. http://www.arl.org/ storage/documents/publications/code-of-best-practices-fair-use.pdf.

Behrnd-Klodt, Menzi L. *Navigating Legal Issues in Archives*. Chicago: Society of American Archivists, 2008.

Behrnd-Klodt, Menzi L. and Christopher J. Prom, eds., *Trends in Archives Practice: Rights in the Digital Era*. Chicago: Society of American Archivists, 2015.

Brewer, Michael, and ALA Office for Information Technology Policy. Digital Copyright Slider. 2012. http://librarycopyright.net/resources/ digitalslider/.

Copyright Law of the United States and Related Laws Contained in Title 17 of the United States Code. http://www.copyright.gov/title17/.

Hirtle, Peter, Emily Hudson, and Andrew T. Kenyon. *Copyright and Cultural Institutions: Guidelines for Digitization for U.S. Libraries, Archives, & Museums*. Ithaca, NY: Cornell University Library, 2009.

Hirtle, Peter B. "Archives or Assets?" Presidential Address, August 21, 2003. *American Archivist* 66 (Fall/Winter 2003): 235–247.

Hirtle, Peter B., *Copyright Term and the Public Domain in the United States*. 2015. http://copyright.cornell.edu/resources/publicdomain.cfm.

Society of American Archivists. *Orphan Works: Statement of Best Practices*. January 12, 2009. Revised June 17, 2009. http://www.archivists .org/standards/OWBP-V4.pdf.

Stanford University Libraries. "Copyright and Fair Use: Charts and Tools." 2015. http://fairuse.stanford.edu/charts-and-tools/.

Wagner, Gretchen, and Allan T. Kohl. "Visual Resources Association: Statement on the Fair Use of Images for Teaching, Research, and Study." *VRA Bulletin* 38, no. 1 (2011). http://online.vraweb.org/vrab/ vol38/iss1/5/.

Chapter 19
Leaving Privacy in the Past? Exploring a Curatorial Conundrum

Judith A. Wiener

Judging by the wide and far-reaching literature on the topic, privacy is per-haps one of the most challenging and ever-present curatorial conundrums of archival and manuscript collection work. In many cases, archival and manu-script collections in a wide array of settings exist to preserve the past to inform the future but much of what we preserve and make accessible today was not intended for this purpose originally. For example, personal letters and diaries were written to exchange thoughts and information with limited individuals, doctor's log books were kept to retain specific information related to the treatment of patients, and even interviews were recorded with a spe-cific audience in mind. In many cases, the materials highly sought after by researchers were intended for a far different and less far-reaching public consumption.

As the head curator of a health sciences library special collection depart-ment, I am acutely aware of the challenge of providing greater access to valu-able historical information while respecting the rights of those who have their personal lives reflected in those records. This is especially true in cases where records were created as part of an explicit or understood expectation of privacy. These conundrums are not only present in the health sciences, as archival and library professionals in various areas have been challenged in a similar manner by other circumstances, such as digitizing private citizen letters to their congressional representatives or posting recorded conversa-tions intended for a select audience on institution websites.

Shifting contemporary trends and the modern range of privacy expec-tations often confuse the situation. Patients are openly sharing their medical charts on social media networks and professional historian and archival groups have rallied for legal exceptions to laws protecting the individual's right to privacy. At the same time, international political constituencies have fought for the "right to be forgotten" as a basic human right, and medical institutions are being sued for allowing de-identified patient accounts to appear on reality television shows. Certainly, appropriately curating privacy issues within collections at this time in history is perplexing, especially as greater access to collections through technological means is possible and encouraged. One may wonder if privacy decisions ever become an issue of the past if they rely so heavily on the norms of today.

In this chapter, the unique challenges privacy-sensitive historical records pose within today's shifting access and privacy expectations are examined. The chapter explores how archival and manuscript professionals can provide access to sensitive materials in a responsible and ethical manner. This includes an assessment of points to consider when increasing access to such materials and how to determine which records may legally and ethically demand greater privacy. Areas to be explored include assessing the responsibility of the special collections professional to protect records that were developed with the expectation of privacy and determining how one might balance this against the right to access and maintain such materials to document and understand the past.

Definitions, Laws, and Policy

Much in the same way that public expectations of what is private shift over time, terms concerning the issue of privacy also change. Throughout time, the language used to describe what is private is somewhat ambiguous and can be used interchangeably. In an effort to standardize the terms used when discussing privacy, Menzi L. Behrnd-Klodt and Peter J. Wosh suggest that,

> No single intellectual foundation for privacy exists, although most academics agree that it refers to people and to the purposes for which information is gathered, used, and/or disclosed. Privacy protection generally implies that personal information will not be revealed to others and that individuals will have the right to make private decisions and choices without governmental interference. Privacy also describes the exclusiveness of personal physical and psychological 'space.' Confidentiality, in contrast, refers to the sensitive nature of certain information and to the circumstances surrounding its disclosure or protection.

They further point out that, "none of these concepts exists in a social or historical vacuum. The confluence of history, law, ethics, social sciences, public opinion, and technology all shape the changing definitions concerning privacy."[1]

The law has also tried to define the expectation and rule of privacy as it relates to individuals. This recognition of a personal right to privacy was first articulated in an 1890 *Harvard Law Review* article, "The Right to Privacy," by Samuel D. Warren and Louis D. Brandeis. Their article stated their concern that individuals should have an explicit right to determine if their lives should be made available to the world at large, independent of the commercial or artistic value of their thoughts, emotions, or sentiments. This was a drastic change to previous legal beliefs that privacy breaches could only be realized as damage to property but not to a person explicitly. Based on their article, states began to recognize that individuals had the right to recover damages in court over breaches of their personal privacy, as well as other types of invasions.[2] Since this time, the court system has worked to balance the expectation of privacy against the right to free speech and other societal interests, such as governmental investigations and public safety. Thus, the legal expectation of privacy norms is also consistently in flux and weighed against the demands of changing society.

Additional laws of note in terms of record-keeping have been established to protect the privacy of individuals reflected in specific classes of records. The Family Educational Rights and Privacy Act of 1974 (FERPA), which protects student records from unauthorized third-party review, consistently perplexes organizations holding such records. Similarly, the Health Insurance Portability and Accountability Act of 1996 (HIPAA) posed challenges to a wide array of institutions holding materials that related in some way to patient care, specifically if their institutions were responsible for transmitting information to insurers through electronic means. Both laws were met with controversy from archival and special collections professionals, who felt challenged to understand how the laws governing the administration of modern records related to materials kept for historical purposes and usually accessed for far different reasons than they were created. Given the ambiguity of the reach of these laws on historical records, archivists and manuscript curators have struggled to develop best and standard practices when keeping records under the law, and this has resulted in an uneven and sometimes destructive response to such legislation.[3]

Professional Ethics and Local Policy

Professional expectations, local policies, and legal counsel interpretations may also dictate how privacy expectations are understood and managed at an individual institution level. Despite any sort of overall legislative policy change, archivists and manuscript curators can also be subject to local policy and organizational legal restrictions. Such local interpretation of any privacy legislation can also determine the lengths to which privacy must be protected at any institution. This has meant that many institutions have been asked to follow restrictions based on laws that do not technically apply to them, such as non-HIPAA or FERPA-covered entities being required to restrict patient or student information. These voluntary restrictions can fluctuate, based on the risk aversion levels of the administration and legal offices of one's institution.[4]

The protection of privacy as a professional altruistic quality has long been understood as part of the professional ethical code. The major professional associations, such as the Society of American Archivists, the Association of Canadian Archivists, and the International Council of Archives, have all solidified this expectation into their standards of professional ethics and expectations.[5] But, despite the overall understanding of privacy protection as a standard, the level to which this understanding of privacy is measured against the seemingly contradictory obligation to provide access is something that is highly debated.

Donor requests for privacy may also affect how records are treated in terms of privacy expectations. Archivists and manuscript curators are advised to avoid overly restrictive requests for collection access and to manage any such restrictions in an equal manner in order to meet with ethical professional standards. These donor-specified restrictions are often easier to work with than the concern of protecting the privacy of those whose lives are reflected in collections without their consent or knowledge. For those challenging instances, archives and manuscript professionals are often called upon to make their own best professional judgment and decide whether or not to impose curator-imposed restrictions.[6] These restrictions are subject to the passage of time, however, as the once-taboo topics of today seem less shocking to subsequent generations of researchers. Generally, it is understood that the passage of time lessens the chance of the revelation of once-private matters causing harm or embarrassment. As Tamar Chute and Ellen Swain further explain, "Archivists acknowledge that privacy laws are important; however if privacy is extended broadly after the death of the individual, much archival work is undermined."[7]

Shifting Cultural Norms of Privacy

We live in a time where the line between what is private and what is not is more ambiguous than ever. The rise of the popularity of the Internet and social media outlets, in particular, has contributed to this social conundrum. Outlets such as Facebook, Instagram, and PatientsLikeMe allow people to connect online to intimately share the details of their daily lives and personal experiences as never before. Popular reality television shows, such as *Keeping Up with the Kardashians*, *Wife Swap*, *Real Life*, and *Trauma: Life in the E.R.*, offer a voyeuristic glimpse of the intimate and private lives of celebrities and the general public in a way that may not have been seen as entertainment-worthy in previous eras.

In addition to general public sensibilities, the balance between what is largely of interest for access and worthy for privacy protection has changed among archives and manuscript professionals. For example, records revealing once culturally taboo topics such as homosexuality or mental illness were commonly hidden within collections in the past as a strategy to protect privacy and guard against donor embarrassment or harm. However, today there are professional-led movements to identify and promote such collections as a way to document the "hidden history" of the past and to uncover and celebrate unsung heroes within such movements.[8]

Yet, within these shifting cultural norms, which seem to celebrate openness and technology that provides venues to share unlike never before, there are growing privacy advocates that champion the cause of remaining private or requesting to be forgotten. The European right to be forgotten movement addresses the unique privacy challenges brought forth by the digital era— that it is hard to escape your past when documented so heavily in a variety of digital outlets and archived in the cloud.[9] Although there are variations on the understanding of this right, a simple approach describes it as a right to not be indefinitely linked to the information from one's past. Most notably the right to be forgotten is the right of erasure or the ability to have personal information deleted under certain circumstances.[10] The 1995 European Data Protection Directive solidified the right to be forgotten as a personal right, and this was further upheld in a May 13, 2014, EU ruling that confirmed that even non-European search engines, such as Google, must uphold the right to be forgotten and offer a mechanism of data removal upon request and under specific circumstances.[11] Although the impact of this movement on archival and manuscript collections, especially for records that are born and accessed digitally, is not yet well-defined, the right to force removal of information could conceivably have an impact on the existence of records and how they are kept and managed.

In addition to the right to be forgotten movement, there have been other instances where one's right to privacy seems to be commonly upheld and fought for in the era of social media openness and reality TV. Such is the case when the reality television show *NY Med* featured a de-identified but recognizable dying man onscreen at the New York–Presbyterian Hospital/Weill Cornell Medical Center without his consent or the knowledge or permission of his family and was sued by them for invasion of privacy. Although the case was ultimately dismissed, medical ethicists and organizations such as the American Medical Association have expressed concern that such shows offer patient's pain for mass entertainment consumption. This has led archivists and manuscript curators to question the paradox of not being able to provide access to records of the long-deceased, while such episodes are allowed by their parent institution to air on TV.[12]

Suggested Best Practices

Given these paradoxes and confusion about where we stand in modern times in relation to the shifting cultural, legal, and ethical nature of privacy, a professional may wonder what an archivist or manuscript curator is to do. Perhaps it might make one feel comforted to know that archivists and curators are uniquely positioned to deal with such record challenges. The Society of American Archivists reaffirmed this professional qualifier in its 1986 newsletter response to the debate over access to presidential papers that, "The Society believes that archivists are uniquely qualified to balance competing demands for open access and for protection of confidential information."[13] Luckily, given the pervasiveness of the topic of privacy within archival and manuscript work, much advice and resources exist on managing access while protecting privacy of those whose lives are reflected within the records.

It is important to note that not all materials, even if they contain private or personal information, are subject to privacy or confidentiality concerns to the same extent. Widely published and distributed materials, such as directories, year books, or photo directories, found within libraries and archives are not generally considered to have privacy concerns from a legal or ethical point of view. This is because the records or publications were intended for wide distribution and for public consumption. Materials such as letters, doctor's case books, and registrar data are considered to be much more of a concern because they were created for individual or limited-distribution purposes and often with the expectation of privacy, and they include private data, such as social security numbers, individual grades, or personal health information. Materials available in a digital format also may have greater concern because of the enhanced accessibility to the records via technological means.

For materials with privacy concerns, much can be learned about collections and their privacy disclosure risks at the beginning stages of records or collections processing. Careful assessment at the preliminary stage of collection intake and accession can troubleshoot possible privacy issues in the future. One of the first steps to take is to talk to the donor of the collection, if possible. Whether the creator of the records or the records custodian, the donor often has the best knowledge of the contents of the collection in many cases and can serve to ward off any potential privacy issues in the future. From this predonation interview, the archivist can learn much about the type of information contained within the records and guide the process of what is donated and what is suitable for retention.[14] A discussion with the donor can also provide the archivist with knowledge of anything within the collection that should be flagged for potential access issues. This can include materials copyrighted or owned by another individual and privacy-sensitive materials, such as patient or financial records. The acquisition stage is also an opportune time to discuss any restrictions and have a candid discussion with the donor about the unknown possibilities of future access. Depending on the archives or library, donors should be aware that access is the ultimate goal of the organization and that technology is often used by archival and special collections professionals to increase access to materials. The goal should be to gain and be able to provide as least restrictive and broad of access as possible for the future of the collection.[15]

Often, however, a pre-accession interview is not possible. Donors or records custodians may have little knowledge of the collection materials, or "orphaned" collections may be "discovered" within your institution. In this case, an assessment of archival and manuscript materials for privacy concerns should be made. This is similar to the preliminary assessment already completed for preservation and processing concerns. Records that hold privacy concerns and can be flagged and planned for at the initial stage of processing.[16] This may help a curator decide what processing techniques can and should be utilized. For example, a large part of a collection may be suitable for minimal processing, while sensitive materials may require more time-consuming measures.[17]

If privacy sensitive materials are accepted into a collection, it is possible to deal with them both effectively and ethically to maintain a balance between privacy stewardship and access. The process of providing access should be discussed and advice given at a higher level of your organization, preferably with input from institutional administration and legal counsel. Discussions at this level and even the creation of a policy or general understanding of institutional risk assessment can help frame acceptable access policies. As Sara Hodson explains:

> Both institutions and archivists must determine acceptable risk levels for the possible legal fallout of violating someone's privacy rights. Based on such practical considerations as the time that can be spent on processing collections and the level of detail that the archivist and other staff members can devote to examining individual items, archivists must arrive at policies and procedures that reflect an awareness of both the legal and ethical aspects of individual privacy, without being held hostage by the difficulties of administering the personal papers of modern figures.[18]

The process of restricting any private information and when that information may be open to the public should be addressed within the policy as well. Any solutions should be made with the future possibility of access. Strategies such as hiding records within collections, making them absent from the finding aid, or redacting them to the point of uselessness do not provide an open door for future research access and do not provide opportunities for adherence to future changes in the law or public opinion.[19]

Once privacy-sensitive materials are accepted into an institution, minimal procedures and processes can be put into place to deal with them effectively. Processing decisions can be made to facilitate the processing of the collection while protecting private or closed records. For example, minimal processing strategies can be incorporated for some series, while private records can be carefully excluded or marked for more extensive processing needs.[20]

Information about the existence and access possibilities of private information should be made widely available. Access policies may depend on laws, donor restrictions, or local policies. The process for accessing such records should be detailed. The date restrictions are lifted should be disclosed to the public and the organization should make it part of its internal procedures to regularly review such restricted collections for privacy date expiration in order to make such records more accessible at that time.

Restricted records should also be listed in inventories and within finding aids with as much information provided as possible. For example, mention of the significant patient research files and information contained within the papers of world-renown surgeon Robert M. Zollinger at the OSU Medical Heritage Center (MHC) is included in the collection's finding aid. The information contains a very brief but descriptive title and details about how to access the materials.[21] A more detailed and private finding aid is available to MHC staff-only on a secure and private server. The boxes containing private information are physically marked to provide further on-site access control.

Private information held by technological means, such as digitized documents or born-digital materials, should also receive scrutiny. Redacted copies that still hold valuable information can be included within digital repositories, and files containing private information should receive special attention by the organization's IT professionals to ensure they are held in a secure and encrypted environment.[22]

The possibility for the unintended disclosure of private information should also be planned for by an institution. Accidents of privacy breaches are common within modern records. For example, social security numbers were often used in older modern records and may pose a security risk for identity theft and other violations if disclosed openly. Institutions have dealt with such unintentional breaches by instituting take-down policies that provide a process for having private information redacted or removed from websites.[23] Materials uncovered within the reading room can also be dealt with in a similar manner by instituting a policy by which records can be flagged and reviewed.

Conclusion

The issue of privacy concerns in archives and manuscript collections and how to balance these concerns against access is a constant curatorial concern and one that is unlikely to disappear. Confounding this problem is the fact that laws, technology, and shifting cultural norms and expectations are constantly in flux. Decisions made for such records are unlikely to remain stagnant and the careful curation of such records is demanded in order to meet ethical and legal expectations and standards. However, with a clear understanding of the challenges such records present, planning with the future expectation of access, and policies and practices established with an awareness of organizational risk sensitivities, the management of such records is not only possible but also is an essential role that perhaps only the archival or manuscript professional is qualified to hold.

Notes

1. Menzi Behrnd-Klodt and Peter J. Wosh, *Privacy and Confidentiality Perspectives* (Chicago: Society of Ohio Archivists, 2005), 2.

2. Heather MacNeil, *Without Consent: The Ethics of Disclosing Personal Information in Public Archives* (Metuchen, NJ: Society of American Archivists, 1992), 22–23.

3. Tamar G. Chute and Ellen D. Swain, "Navigating Ambiguous Waters: Providing Access to Student Records in the University Archives," *American Archivist*, 67, no. 2 (2004): 212.

4. Judith A. Wiener and Anne T. Gilliland, "Balancing between Two Goods: Health Insurance Portability and Accountability Act and Ethical Compliancy Considerations for Privacy-Sensitive Materials in Health Sciences Archival and Historical Special Collections," *Journal of the Medical Library Association* 99, no. 1 (2011): 15–22, doi: 10.3163%2F1536-5050.99.1.005.

5. Society of American Archivists, "SAA Core Values Statement and Code of Ethics," approved May 2011, http://www2.archivists.org/statements/saa-core-values -statement-and-code-of-ethics; Association of Canadian Archivists, "Code of Ethics," revised June 1999, http://archivists.ca/content/code-ethics; and International Council on Archives, "ICA Code of Ethics," adopted September 1996, http://www.ica.org/ 5555/reference-documents/ica-code-of-ethics.html.

6. Sara S. Hodson, "In Secret Kept, in Silence Sealed: Privacy in the Papers of Authors and Celebrities," *American Archivist*, 67, no. 2 (2004): 197–200.

7. Chute and Swain, "Navigating Ambiguous Waters," 230.

8. Lorraine Dong, "Taking the Long View of Medical Records Preservation and Archives," *Journal of Documentation*, 71, no. 2 (2015): 394–396; Judith Schwartz, "The Archivist's Balancing Act: Helping Researchers while Protecting Individual Privacy," *Journal of American History*, 79, no. 1 (1992): 180, 188–189.

9. Jeffery Rosen, "The Right to Be Forgotten," *Stanford Law Review Online*, 88 (2012), http://www.stanfordlawreview.org/online/privacy-paradox/right-to-be -forgotten?em_x=22.

10. Anna Bunn, "The Curious Case of the Right to Be Forgotten," *Computer Law and Security Review*, 31 (2015): 338–339.

11. European Commission, "Fact Sheet on the 'Right to Be Forgotten' Ruling (C-131/12)," accessed June 10, 2015, http://ec.europa.eu/justice/data-protection/files/ factsheets/factsheet_data_protection_en.pdf.

12. Stephen Novak, e-mail message to ALHHS-Listserv, January 6, 2015; Charles Ornstein, "Dying in the E.R., and on TV without His Family's Consent," *New York Times*, January 2, 2015, http://www.nytimes.com/2015/01/04/nyregion/dying-in-the -er-and-on-tv-without-his-familys-consent.html?_r=1.

13. Elena S. Danielson, "Privacy Rights and the Rights of Political Victims: Implications of the German Experience," *American Archivist*, 67, no. 2 (2004): 59.

14. Anne T. Gilliland and Judith A. Wiener, "A Hidden Obligation: Stewarding Privacy Concerns in Archival Collections Using a Privacy Audit," *Journal of the Society of North Carolina Archivists*, 11, no. 1 (2014): 26–28.

15. Anne T. Gilliland and Judith A. Wiener, "Digitizing and Providing Access to Privacy-Sensitive Historical Medical Resources: A Legal and Ethical Overview," *Journal of Electronic Resources in Medical Libraries*, 8, no. 4 (2011): 383.

16. Gilliland and Wiener, "A Hidden Obligation," 29.

17. Mark A. Greene, "MPLP: It's Not Just for Processing Anymore," *American Archivist*, 73, no. 1 (2010): 176, accessed June 10, 2015, http://www.columbia.edu/cu/ libraries/inside/units/bibcontrol/osmc/mplp.pdf.

18. Hodson, "In Secret Kept, in Silence Sealed," 211.

19. Schwartz, "The Archivist's Balancing Act," 182–189.

20. Greene, "MPLP," 176–179.

21. For Robert M. Zollinger, MD, finding aid at the Medical Heritage Center, visit https://hsl.osu.edu/sites/default/files/Spec199301Zollinger%20-%20Public%20View_0.pdf.

22. Gilliland and Wiener, "Digitizing and Providing Access," 395–396.

23. Ibid., 399–400.

Chapter 20
Succession Planning for 21st-Century Special Collections Leadership: Initial Steps

Athena Jackson

It is evident from academic programs, conference proceedings, and continuing educational opportunities related to special collections librarianship in the past few decades that we are collectively addressing and considering the special collections library's role in current academic library service models. We are constantly examining our approaches to collection development, reader services, digital partnerships, programming and engagement, participation in the publishing arena, and so on. The ways we are assessing our practical roles in the academic library setting continues beyond the desired focus of this chapter, but suffice it to say, we are not a wait-and-see community when it comes to approaching this hybrid digital and analog research environment. Moreover, given the large number of recent openings in our field from entry-level (and sometimes new) positions to management and leadership roles, we are poised to reflect on what it will require to lead special collections units dedicated to the materiality and context of the historical record in the coming decades. Succession planning for the future is essential to advancing the field and sustaining our value to the academy.

After working in various roles in support of a special collections library, many of us strive to end up in a directorship position—driving the mission of our work, writing provocative annual reports for stakeholders and donors, capturing the requisite statistics to reinforce our successes and challenges that inform our individual decisions and collective vision, managing talented staff as they expand our role in the academic enterprise, and advancing the mission of the broader library in unique and consensus-building ways. That direct avenue, however, is not always one taken by our colleagues as they enter our field. Many thrive as leaders in their respective roles in a special collections unit; underscoring that leadership in any position in a special collections setting can advance the mission of our field into the 21st century. This awareness becomes particularly relevant when considering smaller units where one or two people have many responsibilities that in larger units would be widely distributed among staff. Many of us are called to leadership whether or not we envisioned administrative positions as a career goal. When that happens, we must ensure that those who find themselves in leadership (regardless of intentionality) are prepared and have an awareness of the challenges they may face as well as outlets for guidance and advice.

Therefore this chapter offers useful suggestions for current managers and/or department heads seeking tangible actions they can take to cultivate our next leaders of cultural heritage and historical primary resource collections. Interspersed in the narrative are the echoes and provocations from frank and open conversations (synchronously and asynchronously) I have had in the past several months with close colleagues who also are invested as I am in the next generation of leaders in special collections libraries. It is with their informal and candid responses, coupled with some thoughts on the current trends in educational programs preparing tomorrow's potential leaders, that this chapter describes some first steps for succession planning in special collections settings.

Thoughts on Library and Information Schools' Roles in Leadership Training

In most cases, the path to leadership begins in the classroom—in the academic programs that are available to students who are training to become professional librarians. Thus, it is imperative that we ask ourselves a fundamental question: Are our library schools equipping the next generation of managers and administrators with the skills they will need to address real-world challenges of in the future? Without trying to force a simple affirmative or negative response on this question, it is fair to say that there is room for improvement. As Lester and Van Fleet summarized in their 2008 study:

> [a]s evident to anyone who pays even the slightest attention to such matters, there is ongoing tension between LIS schools and those engaged in the daily practice of being a library and information science professional. While there are many, diverse reasons for this tension, a constant issue revolves around what the schools should be producing as entrants to the field and how the education of those entrants should be shaped.[1]

Two professional organizations closely tied to the special collections field, the Society of American Archivists and the Rare Books and Manuscripts Section (RBMS) of ACRL-ALA[2] provide core competencies[3] and similar documentation[4] that describe the desirable skills and background needed for success in the profession. However, the role library and information schools play in cultivating practical leadership skills is not always evident in their pedagogical approaches. Moreover, the findings from a 2008 study of an analysis of 55 library schools programs revealed that "not all schools mention competency statements or use of a statement from professional associations in their program presentations."[5] Having discovered such a sobering fact, the study's authors do note however that

> [o]f the specific competency statements included in the study, the one most frequently observed ... was the Special Library Association (SLA) document, referenced by 19 schools. The second most prominent was the Medical Library Association (MLA) statement (14 schools), followed closely by the American Association of School Librarians (AASL) document (13 schools), the *Society of American Archivists (SAA) statement (12 schools)*, and the American Association of Law Libraries (AALL) statement (11 schools). [emphasis added][6]

It is refreshing to learn that a dozen programs, and maybe more since 2008, have been emphasizing SAA's role in shaping future professionals, but it is still unclear based on the scope of this study how many of these programs extend their curricula toward addressing the specific challenges and demands of leadership roles.

Another study, exploring a 2008 informal blog survey of LIS courses and their importance ranked by students, noted that "the topic of management is covered to some extent in most of the courses examined, but there does not appear to be significant focus on the development of supervisory or management skills."[7] With this in mind, I reviewed recent course descriptions listed from 16 ALA-accredited programs with "Academic Libraries," "Management and Administration," and "Special Collections" focuses identified in their descriptions.[8] I examined fall and spring course listings (that were available) with the hope that they might reveal courses related to management of archives and/or special collections units. Table 20.1 illustrates the list of courses found while reviewing websites from each institution. There are certainly some encouraging signs to be taken from this cursory evaluation (that is, just in the most recent semester programs). For example, I found several courses relevant to leadership training with titles such as Ethics, Leadership, Management in Museums and Administration and Management of Libraries. Unfortunately, I also found very few courses that focus specifically on leading special collections. Nevertheless, it is assumed that many of these classes would offer tips and techniques that are translatable to our realm of academic librarianship, particularly courses related to museum and historical agency administration.

What advocates of strong leadership training face, in short, is a challenge on two fronts. First, we need to reckon with library school programs' seemingly slow adoption of professional guidelines for practitioners; and second, we have to acknowledge the difficulty in discovering special collections–specific leadership courses in these same programs. Given the complexity of this challenge, it is no surprise that Aaron Purcell in his 2012 comprehensive book *Academic Archives: Managing the Next Generation of College and University Archives, Records, and Special Collections* identifies what he calls a "crisis of leadership and direction in academic libraries." Crucially, though, Purcell does not despair. Instead, he sees an opportunity for thoughtful collaboration that can meet the crisis directly. He writes:

> [t]here is a strong possibility that graduate library programs will work with professional organizations such as the Association

Table 20.1 Courses Identified from Recent Listings Offered by ALA-Accredited Programs Focusing on Academic Libraries, Management and Administration, and Special Collections

State	Program	Sample of Courses Found Relating to Management
AL	University of Alabama	Management Theory & Practice; Introduction to Philanthropy and Institutional Advancement; Advanced Topics in Library Management
NY	University at Albany, SUNY	Administration of Information Agencies
AZ	University of Arizona	Leadership and the Information Organization
CA	UCLA	Management Theory and Practice for Information Professionals; UCLA Summer Course: Cross-Cultural Communication and Management in a Global Workplace
PA	Clarion University of Pennsylvania	Administration of Libraries; Administration & Management of Libraries
IL	Dominican University	Leadership and Strategic Communication; Management of Libraries and Information Centers; Advanced Seminar: Management and Organizational Theory; Administration & Management of Libraries
HI	University of Hawaii	Library Leadership Seminar; Management of Libraries & Information Centers
IL	University of Illinois at Urbana-Champaign	Change Management; Higher Education and Information Professionals; Contemporary Academic Librarianship
IN	Indiana University	Academic Library Management
NC	University of North Carolina at Chapel Hill	Management for Information Professionals
CA	San Jose State University	Seminar in Library Management ["Examples of topics studied include: Advocacy, Conflict Management, Digital Assets Management, Financial Management, Human Resources Management, Leadership, Managing Information Technology, Grant Writing."]
MA	Simmons College	Principles of Management
SC	University of South Carolina	Master of Management in Library and Information Science
TN	University of Tennessee	Management of Information Organizations
ON	University of Toronto	Management of Information Organizations; Ethics, Leadership, Management in Museums
MI	Wayne State University	Library Administration and Management; Administration of Historical Agencies

Note: This is not a comprehensive list of all management courses taught in library and information school programs. This list is generated when all three descriptors ("Academic Libraries," "Management and Administration," and "Special Collections") were identified by the ALA-accredited institution listed and whose courses were easily found by searching their program and course description websites, fall 2015.

of Research Libraries (ARL), the American Library Association
(ALA), and Association of College and Research Libraries (ACRL)
to create specialized programs in academic librarianship.[9]

Collaboration with professional organizations around this issue of leadership training is one concrete measure we can take to ensure that library
schools are effectively preparing students for the issues that managers and
administrators deal with every day. Our library and information school programs have to cover a wide array of topics and to cultivate expertise during
a finite amount of time with their students and our future colleagues.
This is not an easy task. However, in a time of rapid change when the need
for strong leaderships increases, we should evaluate the curricula for our
field to identify any gaps that might hinder us from addressing that need.
Moreover, this is not a burden that practicing special collections professionals should leave entirely to our academic partners. Rather, we need to
be active participants in the conversation. We should share in shouldering
the responsibility for cultivating tomorrow's leaders today.

Before Entering Special Collections

No one path taken to special collections librarianship naturally segues
into a leadership position. By a quick mental cataloging of my colleagues serving in leadership roles, I realize my professional history is one among many.
Some rose to management from curatorial appointments, some from technical
services, many from archives and manuscripts, others from specialized humanities backgrounds, some from other parts of the academic library or institution,
and others like me, with a completely different agenda in mind before entering
the field. Having started my career in management in the electronic publishing
industry with a fantastic (and supportive) boss who had an MLS, I envisioned
myself in her position someday: as a production or editorial executive at a publishing firm with a foundation in librarianship. I applied to library school with
this goal in mind. Like many of my colleagues, one professor's lecture in a
graduate class on special collections encompassing our community's common
trait of insatiable curiosity, intellectual fervor, and scholarly engagement led
me to realize that I finally found the vocation that met all of my professional
interests. I quickly switched gears toward special collections librarianship and
targeted my study in that direction as much as possible.

When I started my position as associate director of the Special
Collections Library at the University of Michigan, I began to think about
what it would mean to accept a more administrative role, which would
require me to end the daily instructional, curatorial, and outreach aspects
of my earlier positions. My concerns were alleviated as I realized quickly
the impact my leadership could make on the unit's mission and the overall
work of our field. The energy used to develop interesting pedagogically
focused instruction sessions or to manage a grant-funded historical newspaper digitization project transferred nicely to overseeing the operations of
a special collections library and participating in vision-setting with other
library administrators. Retaining secondary curatorial responsibilities in
this role allowed me to continue to hone my collecting skills and stay connected to the collections, the reason I was I drawn to this field in the first
place. Concomitantly, the scope of my service to my professional community
also grew. After serving on various committees spearheading diversity

initiatives and mentoring new professionals in our field, I was elected to serve on the Executive Committee of RBMS and appointed to cochair planning an annual conference for this community. In each role and professional service I performed, I endeavored to fill discovered gaps in my skillsets so that my next step would be better informed and strategically placed.

Passing the Baton: Actions Today's Leaders Can Take to Ensure Success for Tomorrow's Leaders

Managing the work of a busy special collections library requires an established skillset that should include at least one vital component of the diverse work that is special collections librarianship (collection development, bibliography, cataloging, public services, community outreach, archival processing, and primary source instruction, to name a few), as well as accepting the reality that administrative duties will require one to expand his or her focus on tasks and projects to include wider initiatives of the entire academic library and institution. While many of us specialized in one or two skills as we entered the special collections milieu, the quotidian experiences we quickly faced as managers surfaced new skills we needed to succeed, such as managing personnel and budgets and advocating for resources.

Special collections leaders have to balance focus in many directions: our administration, our donors, our staff, our faculty, our students, our colleagues, and the general public. Our roles adjust to meet the needs of our institutions and also the realities of our budgets and spaces (online and physically). We often have to shift our communication approaches to the wide audiences with which we engage. One may have dust off a curatorial hat when chatting with donors, refer to a rusty cataloging prowess when collaborating with library digitization units, or cultivate new skills when translating efforts to a metric-minded academic leadership. Passing the baton to future leaders is a daunting task. Where should we focus? What is most important to share, to train, to anticipate?

Diversity

As we think about the future of our field, I would be remiss not to first comment on recruitment. The collections in our settings illustrate the range of humanistic creation from the collections of men and women of letters to archives representing voices from marginalized cultural and social communities. Rare books, early manuscripts, and papers of established leaders in various disciplines will always be of importance to understanding the humanistic record, but voices heretofore unheard are also integral to shaping a comprehensive historical landscape. Concurrently, our national demographics are changing toward a more culturally diverse population; students and researchers will continue to represent this shift.

Having diversity in perspectives, backgrounds, and racial and ethnic representation must be a priority for our field. Diversity initiatives extend beyond hiring for entry-level positions toward cultivating leaders in our profession from these backgrounds. We must have representation at the decision-making table with respect to resource and budget allocation and collecting initiatives. Without diverse perspectives, we risk maintaining a status quo of priorities that may not mirror those of our constituencies or contemporary histories. My goals have always been buttressed by a deep personal interest in history and culture as a first-generation Mexican-American. My background is an asset to my institution and my field, directly connected to a sense of responsibility to surface and document the *whole* of the cultural record in the academy where all voices are given agency and are present because they are of value to scholarly inquiry. The future of recruiting and developing leaders should always start with finding the best fit for the job, but we should also be proactively seeking professionals from underrepresented groups that may not typically pursue careers in our field.

Increasing scholarships to our professional conferences and continuing educational programs have demonstrated positive results, embracing a thriving community of burgeoning professionals from diverse backgrounds.[10] But, recruitment can and should be more creative. Consider reaching out to local or nearby high schools that have a population of students from underrepresented backgrounds. Prepare and support public programming that highlights collections with which these students could identify. Reach out to your international students and first-generation undergraduate students to promote the profession and the importance of their considering this as a possible career goal. A useful resource for starting this type of endeavors in your region is the RBMS Diversity Toolkit.[11] This guide offers professionals the resources, sample outreach tools, and suggested discussion topics for presenting to groups from underrepresented communities. The guide can be modified to consider a specific audience's expertise and possible talking points to engage all levels of interest and backgrounds.

To be culturally sensitive, one must be culturally literate. Welcoming colleagues from diverse backgrounds exposes our field to customs and community practices that we need to somehow address in our work. Diversity in our profession will make us all more culturally literate and able to better preserve and describe materials with community investment from groups who may have been reticent in the past to provide their materials to our collections, thereby making our collections richer with their inclusion.

Mentorship

As we prepare and plan for our successors, retaining and mentoring aspiring leaders in the workplace seems the logical place to start. First, we must instill in our colleagues the importance of having a strong understanding of the rich history of our field. We must align cultivating technological skills with nurturing an understanding of how our collections were developed and described, and how their material composition impacts learning and study. A strong understanding of the impetus of our field make the next crop of leaders better suited to tell our story and advocate for our profession. Our roles as scholar-librarians should not be discounted given the depth of support we provide our patrons, but this aspect should not (and cannot) be the only facet of our work in the future.

Preparing tomorrow's leaders also requires humility on our parts. Our field is brimming with innovative, passionate, and creative early career professionals accustomed to sharing widely and learning through collaborative networks. Open-mindedness is required when hearing suggestions for streamlining, and sometimes jettisoning, that which has always been done for alternatives more innovative and efficient that serve the same and perhaps additional purposes. Our colleagues' energy and cross-technological approaches will open doors for us to new users and may surface an aptitude for leadership ripe for development in their current positions.

First Steps

So, how do we consciously start now to plan for the future? Some examples of tangible ways the above could be incorporated into daily activities are listed below. Not all of these can be a part of a busy work environment, but perhaps they will serve to engender an atmosphere during the workday where knowledge-sharing and apprenticeship are integral to shaping professionals with leadership ambitions, and nurturing those who have not considered administrative roles but demonstrate the desirable skills. Of course, these activities should be performed with proper oversight and training, but we should also remain cognizant that creativity and fresh ideas come from empowered colleagues who have a sense of ownership of their efforts. This list is a starting point upon which we can all build.

- Allow aspiring leaders to chair meetings not only internally in the department but also on behalf of the unit with external audiences, even when the stakes are high. Learning how to communicate our work and efforts with different audiences bolsters confidence and inspires collaboration with colleagues across the library. Aspiring leaders learn quickly that our unit missions must align with those of other units in the library and the institution. Understanding the symbiotic relationships we share across the academy ensures that our work is on target with the stakeholders who provide resources and funding.

- Encourage improving interpersonal, diplomatic, and consensus-building skills in the same way we encourage technical or skills training. Bring new employees to donor events with an assignment to discuss one communication goal that you wanted to share with your audience. Prep them well for the delicate conversations they may face with audiences with different levels of expertise and types of investment. When they start to demonstrate confidence in this arena, encourage them to seek opportunities for nurturing relationships with new and potential donors.

- Hold brainstorming meetings regarding new collecting avenues or budget allocation where new colleagues are asked to provide suggestions and justification for any new activities or collections they would like to pursue. This exercise may segue nicely to grant-writing opportunities or cross-institutional collaboration common to the administrative activities suite.

- Provide space for risk, mistakes, and experimentation. Many of us learned on the job. Affording opportunities to try new things in a "sand box" provides something that many of us did not have: a safe space to learn from mistakes, receive practical guidance, and develop new skills.

- Encourage periodic and frank discussions about career goals. Identify ways for motivated colleagues to channel ambitions for tomorrow to applicable hands-on experience today. Foster professional development opportunities by supporting their taking management classes. Consider nominating potential leaders to established leadership institutes in our field such as the ARL Leadership Fellows Program,[12] Harvard's Leadership Institute for Academic Librarians,[13] and many more that can be found listed at ALA's website.[14]

- Refrain from romanticizing a past from which we are now at a temporal and cultural distance. Our past is still relevant to the work we currently do, but it need not be presented as a long-lost possibly never-to-be recreated expertise rather than a useful activity worthy of mastering today given the proper exposure and training.

- Talk about the future of the field, regularly. Be open to suggestions and carving new paths for the unit to explore.

Complement all of these tasks with frank and constructive advice. Define benchmarks so that your colleague can measure success tangibly and will feel empowered to perform his or her new skill when the opportunity next presents itself. While many topics regarding personnel issues or librarywide planning that is not quite established warrant discretion, many more topics are and should be ripe for discussion. Encourage transparency in documenting policy and information sharing through questions and answers. Ultimately, sharing with our intrepid early career colleagues our successes and failures will provide a true picture of what they will be facing when taking over the helm.

Conclusion

The enterprising and collaborative spirit of many of my colleagues generated a cohort of current and rising leaders invested in acknowledging our profession's past accomplishments while not seeking to rest on our and our predecessors' laurels. The past decade or so has seen a spike in outreach and engagement online and in our libraries. The work we do is vital not only to our local institutions but also to promoting the intrinsic value of preserved cultural and historical memory. The collections we build today demonstrate a strong awareness of capturing contemporary, multicultural, diasporic, and marginalized voices, essential to supporting the scholarship taking place in the academy. Indeed, our current leadership community is setting a solid foundation for the 21st century collecting and service, but more can and will be done.

Future special collections leaders will have a strong mandate to encourage and make avenues for connections across our collections, both in our physical spaces and also in the digital sphere. They will need to foster agile settings for cross-training and collaboration; carefully design redistribution and reallocation of funding and support for collections as needed. I see a future in which successful leaders manage and guide their staff to talk to and work with all of their library colleagues in creative endeavors, with less emphasis on territory and more emphasis on common ground. Combining proactive recruitment efforts to professionals from underrepresented backgrounds with measurable and tangible opportunities for our early career colleagues in the workplace, we will be better suited to transition leadership in ways that will continue celebrate our past while also embracing the future.

As I conclude this chapter, it is serendipitous that at present I am leaving my associate director post and soon to be in a director's role of a special collections library. Reflecting on this narrative and my initial intent for writing it, I am in a unique position to enact all that I recommend—to pay it forward. It is a task that I take seriously and am enthusiastic about its outcome.

Notes

1. J. Lester and C. Van Fleet, "Use of Professional Competencies and Standards Documents for Curriculum Planning in Schools of Library and Information Studies Education," *Journal of Education for Library and Information Science* 49, no. 1 (2008): 60.

2. Association of College and Research Libraries of the American Library Association.

3. Guidelines: Competencies for Special Collections Professionals, http://www.ala .org/acrl/standards/comp4specollect.

4. So You Want to Be an Archivist: An Overview of the Archives Profession, http:// www2.archivists.org/profession

5. Lester and Van Fleet, "Use of Professional Competencies," 43–69; Web, 49.

6. Ibid., 50.

7. Edgar C. Bailey, Jr., "Educating Future Academic Librarians: An Analysis of Courses in Academic Librarianship," *Journal of Education for Library and Information Science* 51, no. 1 (2010): 30–42. Web, 40.

8. Searchable DB of ALA accredited programs, http://www.ala.org/CFApps/lisdir/ index.cfm.

9. Aaron D. Purcell, *Academic Archives: Managing the Next Generation of College and University Archives, Records, and Special Collections* (Chicago: American Library Association, 2012), 286.

10. http://rbms.info/committees/scholarships/.

11. RBMS Diversity, http://rbms.info/files/committees/diversity/RBMS_Diversity Toolkit-2014-10-03.pdf.

12. http://www.arl.org/leadership-recruitment/leadership-development/arl -leadership-fellows-program#.Vo0EGVJh3EY.

13. https://www.gse.harvard.edu/ppe/program/leadership-institute-academic -librarians.

14. http://www.ala.org/offices/hrdr/abouthrdr/hrdrliaisoncomm/otld/leadership training.

Chapter 21
Toward a Culture of Social Media in Special Collections

Colleen Theisen

The call for a shift to user-focused philosophies to guide our work in special collections has been resounding for more than 25 years, even before the introduction of the World Wide Web.[1] A majority of special collections librarians and archivists believe in user-focused philosophies, and special collections literature and conferences continually reflect the belief in the importance of outreach work as a core function.[2] In the beginning of the 21st century, this translates into a culture of social media. However, in the day-to-day work in overstretched and underfunded systems, belief does not always equate with action.

Social media sites are increasingly important and even beloved spaces for expressing identity, connecting with communities, finding entertainment, and keeping informed. "Go where your users are" is a common marketing mantra. Americans are increasingly investing in social media but special collections lag behind in connecting with them there. Public library adoption of social media (not including blogs) was 70 percent in 2012.[3] Amid this dramatic increase in information seeking and connecting online through social media, a 2013 survey of social media adoption for special collections found that just 20 percent, or one in five special collections, used either a blog, Facebook, or Twitter.[4]

The choice for a special collection site to invest in social media cannot be limited to a decision to take a few photos and post them to Twitter; it demonstrates a commitment to adopting user-focused philosophies and the cascading changes that come from that commitment. With limited staff, investing in an emerging work function often means making the choice not to invest in another activity or to let something go that has always been done. Therefore, sustainable and effective outreach through social media has to be guided by an investment and vision from the top to set those priorities, or traditional job functions will always win this competition for time in the long run. Most special collections have too few staff, competing priorities, processing backlogs, and mile-long to-do lists. Why on earth would we choose to focus on social media as e-mails go unanswered and the processing backlog grows?

The answer lies in envisioning a broader view of our work and our mission. For many people, "library" equals "books," and special collections or archives—if known at all—call to mind dust and irrelevance. If those limited views of the value of cultural heritage persist in the mind of the public, they also persist in the minds of the entities that determine our funding and our survival. How can a special collection survive if housed in a college that closes its doors? Times of fiscal austerity require more focus on outreach, not less. Things that are invisible are easy to make disappear. If we want a world where cultural heritage institutions are understood, valued, and embedded in the day-to-day life of vital communities, we have to participate in building that world and make our value and purpose visible to a broader public. No one else is going to tell our story.

Special collections researchers, supporters, or online fans are not born; they are made. "Research in primary sources is a habit that must be cultivated, all the more so in an era of convenient alternatives."[5] Participating in social media makes it possible to connect with a new group of potential patrons and generate excitement to inspire a new generation of users and supporters. Connecting with local donors and local communities is already vital to our work in individual institutions. Inspiring a broader audience of new supporters must also be done, extending beyond the borders of any particular special collections, archive, historical society, or museum.

This work unites us together in advocacy. The Society of American Archivists called upon the archival profession in 2015 to dare to "live dangerously" by "taking some concerted actions to increase awareness of and advocate for archives." President Kathleen Roe noted that "[Advocacy] is not something that most of us have been trained to do, and it is something that for many of us is a bit beyond our comfort zone (hence the element of "danger").[6] Creating an internet presence primed with opportunities for anyone anywhere to discover, connect, be inspired, and learn about special collections is a different model for outreach than special collections have traditionally embraced. It allows anyone, anywhere, to be transformed into a potential user.

Working together, across institutions, in online communities that have no geographic boundaries is the best solution for answering the questions that face cultural heritage institutions: Why do we as a society pay all of this money to keep collections at all? What is a special collection for? What is the value of a public good? Why does history matter?

The possible audiences in online spaces are as varied as our collections. Public library lovers, education advocates, railroad enthusiasts, Trekkies, performance art lovers, dancers, crafters, or anyone filled with a bit of awe and wonder when presented with a medieval manuscript can be inspired to new interest and connection. Increasing awareness and cultivating new interest are particularly well-suited goals for social media outreach. Social networks of connected individuals have overlapping areas of interest that match our collecting areas. When a user is inspired to share a post from a special collection, that work can spread quickly through networks of like-minded interconnected individuals more likely to also be inspired and learn from that content. Network effects make it possible to have far-reaching impact.

Special collections–centric social media work can create spaces where the spark of an interest in history begins, and where people envision themselves as connected to the long arm of history for the first time. For an individual to decide to become a new user of our collections, they must first value that we exist and understand what we do, whether or not they take advantage of our services at this time. Before a person envisions him- or herself as a user of special collections or archives and decide to take an action, he or she must first:

1. care about history, books, or research in some way;
2. know that special collections and archives categorically exist;
3. know what a special collections or archives does;
4. know what types of collections a special collections might have;
5. know what "use" of a collection looks like;
6. have a need;
7. know what to do to access;
8. overcome any anxiety;
9. have time.

Knowing what a particular special collections or archives does, what it holds, and anticipating their reception as welcoming if they ever might have a need creates the optimum environment for the day when they turn into a user. These criteria can guide social media outreach. We can and should build an internet culture where the past is embedded in the present to grow our potential user pool.

What then, does social media look like if the goal is to inspire, delight, and educate? A cultural heritage institution that is reaching out to those who know nothing about what a library or archives actually does should try to:

1. build awareness that special collections and archives exist;
2. inspire, delight, and build wonder;
3. educate what a special collections or archives does and the collections one might have;
4. demonstrate what "use" looks like;
5. increase understanding and appreciation of the past;[7]
6. be visible as a model.

Providing content that fulfills these six goals arms new users with what they need to grow into a supporter: the necessary knowledge, a reduction of anxiety, and a changed perspective.

The future conflict that cultural heritage institutions face in taking on this advocacy work is that the reach of a social media network is not limited by geography. People's interests, passions, and research are driven by topic and do not stop at the doors of a particular building or collecting institution. Yet the money that pays for most outreach work does come from one geographic area and one institution. While it is possible to tailor social media use to the platforms and methods that reach an audience that is geographically nearby, shared advocacy cultivates the largest possible pool of supporters. Reaching out by topic and spreading through supporters' networks defy geographic boundaries. Successfully inspiring people to value cultural heritage enough to take an action might send them clicking through digital collections or walking through the doors of an institution anywhere in the world. Advocacy on behalf of one is advocacy on behalf of all.

Taking on this work is fraught with repercussions. For an increasing number of Americans, life is spent living with intertwined physical and virtual spaces, but that adoption has been unequal. Asking our staff to suddenly take on work in virtual spaces that they do not use can be time-consuming, as each site can have a huge technical and cultural learning curve. Participating in social media spaces can require facing exhausting or emotionally taxing challenges. It is necessary to determine whether you create separate work, home, and community profiles and carefully manage and separate distinct audiences, or present an identity that mixes together previously separate contexts (e.g., day job versus family or pet photos). Posting to social media opens us or our work environments up to a new transparency. Fear of critique, fear of harassment, and fear of public embarrassment are all rational fears in social media spaces and are not faced equally by all librarians because race, ethnicity, gender, appearance, or any myriad of intersectional factors can make participation online a safer choice for some than others.

And what if we succeed? Cultivating new fans and supporters may mean more reference questions to answer, more donations, more processing, and more classes, and yet may not ever yield more staff to help manage that increased work. Overwork, stress, and damage to the collections through increased use could be the only result.

Whether we change our work to reflect it or not, the Internet has already changed everything.

We can answer a reference question through e-mail, connect with colleagues via Skype, and digitize our collections and provide online access. We can collaborate to bring together collections by a single author from institutions all over the world into one virtual collection.

Sharing an image of a small piece of manuscript waste from a binding can inspire scholars from three countries to transcribe and argue over dating the fragment in the comments. Putting up an image of an unusual book can yield a call within an hour from a follower in France who wants to let us know that it is one of a pair, shares the story of how it came to their family, and what it means to them, and believes donating it to a library halfway across the world is the fitting next step so as to unite the two. It is even possible to have a new freshman walk into special collections on his or her first day on campus and say, "I'm finally here; where are the miniature books?"

The expertise and services that our librarians provide move with the librarian wherever they go, physically or virtually. Online life is real life and online relationships are real relationships. Deciding to live and work as an advocate for special collections in social media spaces requires adapting to potentially overwhelming and cascading changes. It is also an opportunity to translate our love and enthusiasm for history and historic collections into spaces that matter to people.

Defining Ourselves through Content Choices

As a person watches each photo, link, or text update, each piece of content that scrolls by contributes to expectations and associations that are developed through time. What does this special collections choose to post? Is it funny, poignant, political, bizarre, or awe-inspiring? Does the person posting sound like someone I would want to be friends with? Do they sound honest, authentic, and trustworthy? Are they always there consistently as a comfortable part of my daily life, reminding me again and again of all those posts that I found valuable in the past? Or do they disappear for six weeks just as I started to look forward to their content?

A post on social media is about a subject or content but it is also contributing to the intangible emotions and impressions which form the start of a relationship. With limited time and attention to go around, every post on social media inspires an evaluation: Is this post worth my time? Even if the content is quickly forgotten, some lingering feelings and impressions remain and build through time, post by post. The most basic choice on social media is the decision present with every post: Do I keep this page in my feed for another day, or has it become annoying or turned into noise so that I should unfollow?

When people find a particular piece of library or archives' content inspiring or valuable enough that they share it, they are associating it with their identity and sending the message to their own followers that it is worth paying attention to. Their followers make the same assessment: Was this valuable? Annoying? Sharing is a reputation exchange between a person and his or her network. There is always a risk that their friends and followers would view the choice to share our content as adding annoyance or noise. Are we entertaining, informative, useful, or inspiring enough to be worth the risk?

A special collections can tell the world that history matters 100,000 times, and tell people who are unaware of us that they should listen or care. A few will hear us. But if we provide an inspiring story of value and someone hears it from a friend who chose to share it, that is more meaningful. By sharing through a trusting relationship, established through time, each person who makes the choice to share our content lays the groundwork for others to become our potential followers, even though the collections or archive has had no direct contact with them. We ask for time, attention, risk, and love from our followers. Are we invested enough in our social media to be worth it? Do we consistently tell stories that are relevant to their interests?

Advocacy is a form of teaching. How do we build, inspire, educate, or demonstrate anything in a noisy multipurpose social media feed full of cat videos, family members' updates, advertising, news, photos, and more? Even without preexisting personal interest, if someone has grown to care for a guide, a topic can be framed by the relationship with that person so that they see the topic in a new way. A beloved or respected teacher, infectious enthusiasm, and a good story can inspire new interest and appreciation for a topic, even one that might have seemed dull in the past. John Overholt described the mix of inspiration and education required to find and convert a nonuser into a user or supporter:

> [Undergraduates] must be reached early and often with a message that mixes the genuine pleasure and wonder of our collections with a much more practical one: our library and the people who work there can make your research easier and its products better. Only the most motivated students will cross our thresholds on their own.[8]

The biggest change in online outreach in social media spaces is a move toward idiosyncratic individuals working visibly and being known by name. It is difficult to take an anonymous active role in a community, and it is more difficult to be perceived as trustworthy and authentic when speaking in the voice of "The Institution."

Eric Stoller also advocates that higher education professionals model how to be an authentic individual in professional roles online by "practicing vulnerability."

> Life is messy. Professionals learn much from observing other professionals. Performing an online brand pushes us further away from our authentic selves. Social media conversations matter when they are honest. What happens when professionals start playing a part?[9]

A personal relationship with a real-life librarian or archivist counters the pervasive stereotypes of dusty irrelevance. Cultural heritage professionals on social media can meaningfully demonstrate their love for their work and rare materials. A known individual who is able to express his or her occasionally idiosyncratic opinions is perceived as more trustworthy than an anonymous institutional voice. This association between "authenticity" and trust is even more pronounced the younger a person is.[10]

Learning, research, and, eventually, using a special collections or archives for research requires openly asking a question, even though it may point out ignorance. Curiosity and learning require being willing to voice your ideas, though you may be proven wrong or ridiculed for them. All of these culturally contentious skills are required for education, critical inquiry, and historic research, and ultimately to ensure the survival of libraries. To ask a question is an act of courage. Modeling how to ask questions and demonstrating that vulnerability, especially as a professional, is modeling the vulnerability and courage it takes to learn.

Serving as Role Models

Our institutions and professionals connected with them are often tasked with preparing students with information literacy and modeling for them how to exist as an intellectual, a scholar, or a responsible adult. Our presence, through what we choose to present and share, and the rhetoric we use to do so model that emerging cultural norms and understanding about how to participate in online spaces as a responsible citizen.

Information literacy, ethics, and codes of conduct guide us and our institutions to participate in a manner sometimes at odds with the culture of a social media site. We must balance that culture with institutional policy when deciding how to proceed. For example, how do you participate in Twitter as a professional under your own name when social media audiences can be a mix of family, community connections, work colleagues, acquaintances, celebrities, and strangers? Do you have to make separate accounts and separate your life into professional and private categories? If you mix them together, how do you do that rhetorically in a space of "collapsed context" where it is impossible to separate divergent audiences?[11]

Serving as a model may also mean modeling use of the collections. If a librarian participates in a community that uses the animated GIF as a rhetorical device (such as Tumblr) for communicating, and creates a short animation using an item from the collection, that GIF speaks in the language of the site while modeling a use of the collections in a way that is relevant to that community. When that content is shared and brings joy to a person's followers, it is received as a gift and inspires creations in return, strengthening relationships and building trust with the library and the librarian at the center. Serving as an online advocate, guide, teacher, or model may require a librarian to be an active creator and participant, not speaking to the community but as part of a community. Creating scholarship to guide new scholars, crafting to guide the crafters, and modeling data to guide the budding digital humanists may be a more active role than traditionally thought of as part of librarianship.

Participating in these spaces creates a teaching opportunity not only through our content, but also through our methods, including the much discussed issue of how to contribute to and develop the norms and standards regarding responsible and ethical use and reuse of images and how to cite them.[12] Library and information science is a home for all of these ethical and practical concerns about the online use and sharing of information and images. Librarians can lead the discussion and provide a model of what an optimal but fun, ethical, and effective use of social media looks like that can influence how others use the Internet as well.

Practical Implementation

If an institution does not have an established social media presence, the process of choosing where to invest your time is a daunting challenge. Starting a channel with high energy and expectations that goes silent after three to six months as day-to-day concerns grow to take precedence and the novelty wears off is a common tale. Consistency of content production is important when establishing trust on social media. Will you continue to be there? Can you be relied upon? Where will you find an audience that is interested in the content you want to make? Goals can help determine where to place your efforts. The next step is asking what is sustainable.

Contributing to one or more social media channels is not an all-or-nothing choice. Choosing where to put your time and effort on social media is extremely complex because of the proliferation of channels. The more library, museum, archives, historical society, and higher education channels there are, the more they divide the attention of the audience we want to reach, an audience for whom the distinctions between channels are fairly moot. Where can you find the best fit between the content and the audience?

Reflecting on the goals you have for contributing in online spaces, the best answer to reach those goals is not always to launch a new channel on a new site. Analyzing identity and the intersecting identities of related channels may bring to light other solutions to collaborate and join an existing community instead of starting from scratch. Every channel out there has the same need for an endless supply of good content.

Particularly if an organization has limited staff, establishing relationships with existing channels where an audience would want to see your content is a great way to invest your limited time to have an impact. A stand-alone channel is easier for branding, but depending on goals, a collaborative partnership with a local museum, library, or government institution may push the content out to more potential users. Establishing collaborative relationships makes it possible down the road to launch a stand-alone channel for particularly successful content series, with a built-in audience who already follow it from the collaborative channel.

Assembling a team is crucial for sustainability. Sometimes the decision can come from the top and social media participation can be encouraged or assigned to a team. Sometimes you have to recruit willing individuals from within the department or the organization, or even reach outside the institution and let the content guide the choice when finding participants.

Coordinating the contributions of a team of collaborators is key to long-term sustainability, and yet collaborations are complicated and often fail. There are several methods then for coordinating the efforts of a team to both allow for a contributor to have a sense of ownership that is motivating and allow for maintaining a consistent voice. Social media contributions can be divided by platform, assigning different staff members to their most comfortable venues. Feeling like a social media site, "belongs" to them can give a feeling of responsibility to the community there, allows for a person to know one community very well, and makes it easy to maintain a consistent voice. However, platform-based divisions make it difficult to coordinate cross-posting that content to other sites if you have several social media sites. Different contributors can choose a topic area that will be theirs to curate and be responsible for creating content and reformatting it in order to tell the world all about that topic across social media sites on an agreed-upon frequency.

This new collaboration space is messy. Crisis is often the biggest motivator for collaboration, spurring action, but what happens when the crisis abates? What happens when your channel grows, when you are seen, when you're no longer invisible? Motivation has to shift from the excitement of building something to the responsibility to the community that is following what you built.

Therefore, creating collaborative social media projects that have short predetermined time frames gives a chance to harness and renew the excitement of working on something new, and set it aside before it becomes rote and enthusiasm tapers away, resulting in a silent social media channel. Set date ranges and make a short series. For example: A month of [xxx], Three months of [xxx]. The collaboration can then be evaluated at the end of the series, and can always be renewed if there are more stories to tell.

Hevelin Collection Tumblr[13]

The Hevelin Collection Tumblr from the University of Iowa posts images from pulp magazines from the 1920s, 1930s, and 1940s. With bright colors and lurid illustrations, pulp magazine covers were already popular and circulating widely when the University of Iowa joined that space. Tumblr does not have a culture of attribution. However, Curator of Science Fiction and Popular Culture Peter Balestrieri, the page's manager, would include a full citation and was careful to find the artist's name who was responsible for the artwork on each cover and include that name post. Over time, another of the main Tumblr pages in the pulp image community *also* began to include the artist's name with each of their posts. Modeling the use of citations began to influence the community to include further citation. The library can and does contribute to community norms and rhetoric, modeling practices with wide-ranging effects on our communities.

Throwback Thursdays (#tbt)

Archives are a rich source of stories that matter to an existing academic institution's students, faculty, and alumni around the world. The University of Iowa has only one archivist with many demands on his time. With this in mind, special collections staff established a relationship with the social media manager for the University of Iowa's main channels. A partnership was reached to deliver a single piece of content relating to the history of the University of Iowa each week, not on special collections channels, but onto the main University of Iowa channels for Throwback Thursdays. Growing out of the Instagram community, the Throwback Thursday hashtag (#tbt) is an established weekly event across social media channels, featuring images from the past. The university archives weekly #tbt post is the piece of content from across the University of Iowa special collections that has the most views, interaction, comments, and shares of any piece of content each week, though it is the one piece of content that is not shared on our own channels. It is the perfect match between time investment, channel, and audience.

Iowa Women's Archives Tumblr[14]

The University of Iowa special collections already had an established identity on Tumblr in 2013, when it partnered with staff from the Iowa Digital Library to create a weekly post featuring digitized content specifically from the Iowa Women's Archives. This promoted both the Iowa Digital Library and the Iowa Women's Archives simultaneously, and with two full-time staff members, the Iowa Women's Archives had found it difficult to fit in creating content on its own. "Women's History Wednesdays" proved to be a slightly unusual fit on the main Tumblr channel, which was primarily book history–related content but spread like wildfire among the feminist community on Tumblr, and so the team decided with all of the newly established interest that it could sustain itself as a Tumblr on its own. When this decision is made, the next steps are easy. Make a new page. Announce to the audience that have been following that they can follow the new site. Continue to reblog the new channel content onto the original channel. On its own, the Iowa Women's Archives Tumblr now has over 12,000 followers.

Iowa City Past[15]

When the Iowa City Public Library digitized its local history collection and put it online as a digital collection, librarians from the University of Iowa Libraries and the Iowa City Public Library formed a Tumblr together to collaboratively share images from Iowa City's past. The collections share the same topic, and collaborating makes it possible to share the workload, making it possible to sustain the project.

John Martin Rare Book Room

The John Martin Rare Book Room houses medical rare books in the Hardin Library for the Health Sciences at the University of Iowa. For a short time there was a graduate student who was available for project work who created a series of guest posts from the John Martin Rare Book Room to appear as a short-term weekly series on the Special Collections Tumblr, giving collection access to an interested audience without having to build one, and without the burden of worrying about long-term sustainability. For special collections that meant more great content for its page, easing the burden and freeing up time to invest in planning for what will come next after the collaboration runs its course.

Conclusion

Collaborating across a library, institution, campus, city, or connected collections across the country means first abandoning ideas of competition. The prevalent notion that with mass digitization the answer to the future of academic libraries is to brand ourselves based upon our unique items—our special collections—is at its heart a competitive idea. It ignores that there are similar budgetary and philosophical forces that are acting against all cultural heritage institutions, and it ignores the fact that following the trail in pursuit of answers to a research question is a pursuit without boundaries. Each special collection, library, historical society, museum, or archive online is part of an ecosystem with other similar local, national, and international institutions with complementary goals. We are stronger together than on our own. Choosing a noncompetitive philosophy is important in online spaces when the goal is to reach and teach nonusers—to whom the distinctions between us matter little. You do not help your collection by proving that your stuff is better than other stuff out there.

Once you decide on the parameters of what topics fit your channel, reblog others who are having the same conversation, to introduce those creators or institutions to your community. The community norm is that others will also reblog *your* posts. Thus, all of us can have an impact and spread through different but related communities. Reblogging increases the amount of good content on your page, making it more enjoyable for your followers; they will pay more attention to you as a provider of the best, most valuable content. And finally, when a new library comes online, tell everyone in your feed to follow it so it does not have to start from zero.

Given the large audience out there with an interest in history and books who do not know about special collections, imagine the impact if special collections, archives, historical societies, and even art museums team up to collaborate on group social media channels. Maybe in the future we will develop social media consortia where high-quality contributions could be weekly, monthly, or even just a few times a year, but bringing together enough contributing institutions that it can be a sustainable, vibrant, and beloved part of online life. From Whitman Collections to medieval manuscripts, scholars, crafters, or even just fans could follow their interests across the boundaries of our institutions.

When the goal is to cultivate a large community of supporters who may grow into users, the possibility of danger, discomfort, identity realignment, and time-consuming change are all real and possible outcomes of investing in outreach work in online communities. Each change may require another change. Priorities for aligning our time and therefore support for outreach have to be guided from the highest levels of the institution in order to succeed. If our institutional leaders instill a focus on outreach and inspiring the next generation of users, allow for the time to develop and change, and place a priority upon that work, special collections can be beloved: embedded in an online community of supporters that will be there to answer if we ever need to call for help. We will be actively creating the networks, communities, and society that are informed by and values the past, whether online or off.

Notes

1. Timothy Ericson, " 'Preoccupied with Our Own Gardens': Outreach and Archivists," *Archivaria* 31 (1990): 114–112.

2. See, for example: Kate Theimer, "The Future of Archives Is Participatory: Archives as Platform, or A New Mission for Archives," *Archives Next*, April 3, 2014, http://www.archivesnext.com/?p=3700; Sidney E. Berger, *Rare Books and Special Collections* (Chicago: Neal-Schuman, 2014); John Overholt, "Five Theses on the Future of Special Collections," *RBM: A Journal of Rare Books, Manuscripts, and Cultural Heritage* 14, no. 1 (2013): 15–20.

3. Megan Wanucha and Linda Hofschire, *U.S. Public Libraries and the Use of Web Technologies, 2012 (Closer Look Report)* (Denver: Colorado State Library, Library Research Service, 2013).

4. Sean Heyliger, Juli McLoone, and Nikki Thomas, "Making Connections: A Survey of Special Collections' Social Media Outreach," *American Archivist* 76 no. 2 (2013): 374–414.

5. Overholt, "Five Theses," 19.

6. Kathleen Roe, "The Year of Living Dangerously for Archives," *Off the Record*. September 3, 2014, http://offtherecord.archivists.org/2014/09/03/the-year-of-living-dangerously-for-archives/.

7. Theimer, "The Future of Archives Is Participatory."

8. Overholt, "Five Theses," 19.

9. Eric Stoller, "Our Shared Future: Social Media, Leadership, Vulnerability, and Digital Identity," *Journal of College and Character* 14, no. 1 (2013): 7.

10. Dan Schawbel, "10 New Findings about the Millennial Consumer," *Forbes*, http://www.forbes.com/sites/danschawbel/2015/01/20/10-new-findings-about-the-millennial-consumer/#1bc310b728a8.

11. Michael Wesch, "YouTube and You: Experiences of Self-Awareness in the Context Collapse of the Recording Webcam," *Explorations in Media Ecology* 8, no. 2 (2009): 19–34.

12. Sarah Werner, "How to Destroy Special Collections with Social Media," http://sarahwerner.net/blog/2015/07/how-to-destroy-special-collections-with-social-media/.

13. Hevelin Collection, hevelincollection.tumblr.com.

14. Iowa Women's Archives, iowawomensarchives.tumblr.com.

15. Iowa City Past, iowacitypast.tumblr.com.

Afterword

Lynne M. Thomas and Beth M. Whittaker

At the beginning of this volume, we stated our intention to provide a snapshot of special collections and archives as a field at the beginning of the 21st century. That is, of course, easier said than done, requiring dozens of people and a tremendous amount of coordination. All of our contributors juggled the writing and editing process with demanding day jobs, for which we are duly grateful.

Life in special collections libraries and archives encompasses a diverse group of materials and activities and individuals and institutions that steward them. We all, no matter how specialized, wear a lot of hats. We are absolutely certain that there are topics we missed, or did not cover as thoroughly as we would have liked. Our profession changes far too quickly to be comprehensive, and books are, by their nature, static works. This project began in mid-2014; by the time you read this, it will be at least three years since we set out to publish. The irony of this constant change in a field that is assumed to be particularly focused on "dusty old books" is not lost on us.

We will refrain from rehashing the points made by contributors to this volume. The authors in this volume know what they are talking about, working in these environments daily and thoughtfully engaging with the broader community and profession. If, after reading even just a few chapters, readers miss that it is important to carefully consider the impact of your programming or to build relationships with other cultural heritage organizations or to begin to tackle the challenges of digital preservation, no summary we can provide here will be useful.

Therefore, we thought a more fruitful approach would be to highlight some of what *we* learned over the course of this book. Although we are both firmly mid-career special collections librarians, with decades of experience under our belt (and hopefully decades yet to come) we were struck by some important points that were either new to us, or might be new to our readers.

- Most practitioners are doing the best they can, yet rarely feel as though they are doing enough—or doing it well enough. At the initial proposal stage, authors were sometimes unsure whether their work was "important enough" or "special enough" or "well-known enough." We are a modest bunch, and we tend to sell ourselves, and the work we heroically do every day, short.

- One of the biggest challenges we face is having the time and space to look around at what others are doing, and to then reconsider or adjust our own practices. Many institutions, both state-supported and private, are facing ever reduced levels of support; calls for accountability and efficiency get louder with fewer staff to complete the work and demonstrate the efficiencies. We are loath to stop doing things we believe are important, so we continually feel like we must fit something "new" into an already full day. We will need to choose carefully which activities to continue.

- Despite the existence of standards and competencies, there is a wide variation in special collections practice. That variation is directly impacted by (and impacts in turn) our access to basic special collections knowledge (e.g., acquisitions, collation, metadata, and digitization), best practices, and emerging technologies.

- As a field, special collections librarians and archivists often find ourselves explaining exactly what we do, and why, to our colleagues, our administrators, and the public. The number of venues for doing so has expanded and shifted, and web discovery and online spaces make this even more complex.

- We've seen an increased emphasis on making special collections and archives (and cultural heritage work in general) more "open," ranging from individual universities adopting open access mandates to national funding agencies requiring that project results coming from their funding be made as open as possible, as quickly as possible.

- There are still great opportunities for professional growth in special collections; our field remains full of dynamic individuals ready and willing to take on new challenges. Several of our chapter authors left positions for new ones as this book moved forward.

Our hope is that the sheer breadth of projects, experiences, and viewpoints laid out in this volume inspires you to take a moment to look around, and consider how to steward the changes that the rest of the 21st century will invariably bring to our profession. We turn this volume over to you, even more excited about the possibilities of the future of special collections than we were when we began. We hope this book helped kindle (or rekindle) a similar sense of optimism in you, dear readers and colleagues.

Index

About the Editors and Contributors

PRISCILLA ANDERSON is Senior Preservation Librarian at Harvard University, providing preservation consultation and services to over 70 libraries and archives that make up one of the world's largest academic library systems. Anderson practiced rare book conservation in museums, libraries, and private practice prior to moving into preservation, and holds master's degrees in both Art Conservation and Library Science.

ANNE BAHDE is coeditor of *Using Primary Sources: Hands-on Instructional Exercises*. A special collections librarian in the Special Collections and Archives Research Center at Oregon State University, her research interests include undergraduate use of primary sources and methods for enhancing access to archival and manuscript materials with digital humanities tools.

WHITNEY BAKER is Head of Conservation Services at the University of Kansas Libraries. She also teaches preventive conservation in the graduate program in Museum Studies at the University of Kansas. She holds a master's degree and Advanced Certificate in Library and Archives Conservation.

SARAH BARSNESS is the Digital Collections Assistant at the Minnesota Historical Society. She collaborates with curators and other staff to move digital collections from acquisition to long-term preservation. Sarah got her MA in Library and Information Studies (2011) from the University of Wisconsin–Madison.

HEATHER BRISTON is the University Archivist for UCLA. She was also an archivist at the University of Oregon and the University of California, Berkeley. She received an MS in Information (Archives and Records Management) from the University of Michigan, and a JD from Syracuse University, with a focus on intellectual property law.

AMY CHEN is the Special Collections Instruction Librarian at the University of Iowa's Special Collections and University Archives. Previously, she was a 2013–2015 Council on Library and Information Resources Postdoctoral Fellow in the Division of Special Collections at the University of Alabama, where she oversaw instruction, exhibitions, and social media. In 2013, she received her PhD in English from Emory University with a dissertation on the acquisition of literary collections.

AUDREY MCKANNA COLEMAN, CA, is the Senior Archivist of the Robert J. Dole Archive & Special Collections and Assistant Director of the Dole Institute of Politics. She has 15 years of professional experience in museum, archives, library, and visual resources fields, and is a lecturer in the University of Kansas Undergraduate Honors Program. Audrey has served on the Kansas Historical Records Advisory Board since 2013 and is a current member of the Kansas Humanities Council Speakers Bureau and Rotary International. She has a BA in Spanish and MA in Museum Studies, both from the University of Kansas.

LISA L. CRANE (MLIS, San Jose State University, 2006) began working at the Claremont Colleges Library in 2007, and since 2010, she is the Western Americana Manuscripts Librarian in Special Collections. She has volunteered at the Museum of History and Art, Ontario, in a myriad of capacities since 2004 including secretary and treasurer of the board for the Museum Associates. She was a member of the original docent class of 2005.

SHANNON DAVIS has worked in the Scholarly Publishing unit of Washington University Libraries since 2007, where she has held several positions. Ms. Davis is currently Digital Library Services Manager and oversees numerous projects. Her work focuses on digital project development, project management, and collaborative initiatives with on and off campus partners. Ms. Davis received her BFA in Visual Communications from Washington University and earned a Master of Arts in Information Science & Learning Technologies from the University of Missouri.

CHRISTINE DEZELAR-TIEDMAN is Metadata and Emerging Technologies Librarian at the University of Minnesota Libraries, and has worked as a cataloger in academic libraries since 1995. She received her MLIS from the University of Iowa and is active in the Rare Books and Manuscripts Section of the Association of College & Research Libraries.

MEREDITH R. EVANS is the Director of the Jimmy Carter Presidential Library & Museum. Among other positions she served as an Associate University Librarian at Washington University in St. Louis and the University of North Carolina at Charlotte. Her experience includes archives and special collections, fund-raising, staff and collection development, and the formation and integration of digital programs and data curation. Evans earned degrees from Clark Atlanta University, North Carolina State University, and University of North Carolina at Chapel Hill.

IVEY GLENDON is the Manager for Metadata Analysis & Design at the University of Virginia Library in Charlottesville, Virginia. She received her MLIS from Florida State University and focuses on metadata schema, controlled vocabularies, and project management.

MELANIE GRIFFIN is Special Collections Librarian at the University of South Florida, where she serves as curator of the science fiction and children's literature collections and as coordinator of special collections cataloging. Melanie holds an MLIS with a concentration in Rare Books Librarianship and an MA in British Literature, and she is currently pursuing a PhD in Children's Literature.

ATHENA JACKSON is Dorothy Foehr Huck Chair and Head of Special Collections at Penn State University Libraries. She was previously the Associate Director of the Special Collections Library at the University of Michigan. She has served on various committees of the Rare Books and Manuscripts Section, such as Member-at-Large of the Executive Committee and the Diversity Committee. She has spoken nationally on diversity in the special collections profession and on digital access to rare and unique materials.

JENNIFER KIRMER received her B.A. in Anthropology from the University of Kansas and her M.A. in Library Studies at the University of Wisconsin-Madison. Kirmer has worked in multiple archival institutions including the Dole Institute of Politics and the Art Institute of Chicago. Upon completion of her graduate work, she took the role of Digital Archivist at Washington University in St. Louis, working on projects in digital preservation and curation. Kirmer received her Digital Archives Specialist (DAS) certification from the Society of American Archivists (SAA) in February 2015. Jennifer recently left WashU to take a position at MasterCard International.

MAUREEN E. MARYANSKI is a Reference Librarian for Printed Collections at the New-York Historical Society. Trained at Indiana University's Lilly Library, she specializes in rare books and manuscripts. She also focuses on women's history and writes dance history essays for the Dance Heritage Coalition.

MELANIE MEYERS is the Senior Reference Services Librarian, Special Collections at the Center for Jewish History, New York City, where she oversees all aspects of unified special collections reference for five partner organizations. She has worked with special collections in a variety of settings, including private, nonprofit, and academic institutions.

DANA M. MILLER is the Head of Metadata and Cataloging at University of Nevada, Reno Libraries. As a graduate student in the Simmons College Archives Management program, she benefited from student positions and internships, and as a professional archivist and librarian, she has enlisted students and volunteers in multiple settings in successful large-scale projects.

ALLISON JAI O'DELL is Metadata Librarian at the University of Florida Libraries, where she is experimenting with Linked Data applications to expose special collections to new discovery and purpose. She comes from a background of special collections cataloging, book arts, book history, and database management.

JOHN OVERHOLT is Curator of the Donald and Mary Hyde Collection of Dr. Samuel Johnson and Early Modern Books & Manuscripts at Harvard University's Houghton Library. In 2015 he was elected Vice Chair/Chair Elect of the Rare Book and Manuscript Section of the Association of College and Research Libraries.

CHARLOTTE PRIDDLE is Librarian for Printed Books at the Fales Library & Special Collections, New York University. This role includes responsibility for acquisitions across all collections, instruction at various levels, digital projects, outreach and donor relations, and exhibition planning. She also coteaches an undergraduate seminar in the History of the Book at NYU.

MARILYN RACKLEY was most recently the Aeon Solutions Manager at Atlas Systems, where she helped libraries and archives around the United States implement and use the Aeon system to improve access to their collections. Prior to joining Atlas, she worked with special collections libraries and archives at Harvard University.

SONYA ROONEY has been University Archivist at Washington University in St. Louis since 2005 and has worked in archives for sixteen years. She received her MA in History with a concentration in Museum Studies from University of Missouri-St. Louis in 2002 and is also a Certified Archivist.

JENNIFER O'BRIEN ROPER is the Director, Acquisitions & Discovery at the University of Virginia Library in Charlottesville, Virginia. She received her MSLS from the University of North Carolina at Chapel Hill and has spent 20 years working in academic libraries to connect scholars to resources.

ABBY SAUNDERS is Curator of the Cassady Lewis Carroll Collection at the University of Southern California Special Collections. She has previously worked at Roger Williams University and Brown University. She holds a BA in English from Rhode Island College and a MLIS from Simmons, with a concentration in preservation.

JAIME L. SCHUMACHER is the Scholarly Communications Librarian at Northern Illinois University Libraries and coleader of Digital POWRR, a group of professionals dedicated to discovering reasonable, yet robust, digital preservation solutions and providing pragmatic training to archivists and librarians. Jaime has taught POWRR workshops across the country and is passionate about the long-term preservation and accessibility of cultural heritage materials. She received her MS in Library and Information Science from the University of Illinois Urbana–Champaign and holds a BS in Computer Technology from Purdue University.

ANJANETTE SCHUSSLER is a Government Records Assistant with the State Archives at the Minnesota Historical Society, where she processes government records and works with records retention schedules. She has a degree in Library and Information Technology from Minneapolis Community and Technical College and has been involved in libraries and archives since 2010.

MATTIE TAORMINA is the Head of Public Services and is a Processing Manuscripts Librarian for Stanford University Special Collections and University Archives. She is the coeditor of book *Using Primary Sources: Hands-On Instructional Exercises* and the Vice President/President Elect for the Society of California Archivists.

COLLEEN THEISEN is the Outreach & Engagement Librarian for the University of Iowa Special Collections where she coordinates social media including the UISpecColl Tumblr (uispeccoll.tumblr.com), named *New and Notable* by Tumblr in 2013, and directs and hosts the YouTube channel *Staxpeditions* (youtube.com/uispeccoll). Theisen holds an MS in Information from the University of Michigan, where she specialized in Archives and Records Management, a BA in Art History & Archaeology from the University of Missouri–Columbia, and a certificate for 6–12th grade art education from Clarke University. In 2015 *Library Journal* named her a "Mover & Shaker," for her work as an educator in both online and offline spaces.

LYNNE M. THOMAS is the Head of Distinctive Collections, Curator of Rare Books and Special Collections, and Associate Professor at Northern Illinois University in DeKalb, Illinois, where she is responsible for popular culture special collections that include the literary papers of 70 contemporary science fiction and fantasy authors, dime novels, children's literature, comics, and much more. She is the coauthor of *Special Collections 2.0*, with Beth Whittaker (Libraries Unlimited, 2009), as well as academic articles about cross-dressing in dime novels, using libraries to survive the zombie apocalypse, and embedded curatorship for documenting particular communities. She periodically teaches a special collections course for San Jose State University's iSchool. In her spare time, she is a three-time Hugo-award winning podcaster and editor, and a big geek.

JUDITH A. WIENER, MA, MLIS, is an Associate Professor and the Assistant Director for Collections and Outreach at The Ohio State University Health Sciences Library. She is the head curator of the OSU Medical Heritage Center. Her research interests include special collections administrative issues, particularly in relation to privacy and health sciences collections.

BETH M. WHITTAKER is Assistant Dean of Distinctive Collections and Director of the Kenneth Spencer Research Library at the University of Kansas, where she leads special collections, archives, conservation, and international collections initiatives. She served as the editor of *RBM: A Journal of Rare Books, Manuscripts, and Cultural Heritage*, an ACRL journal, from 2008 to 2014. She is the coauthor, with Lynne M. Thomas, of *Special Collections 2.0: New Technologies for Rare Books, Manuscripts, and Archival Collections* (2009) and has published dozens of articles in numerous journals on a variety of topics related to special collections, cataloging, and cultural heritage.

SHERYL WILLIAMS is Curator of Collections at Kenneth Spencer Research Library, University of Kansas. She also serves as Curator of the Kansas Collection, a position she has held since 1979. Her degrees include a MA in Library Science from the University of Oklahoma, and a BA in History from Kalamazoo College. She is an active member of the Society of American Archivists.

SUPRIYA WRONKIEWICZ has worked with dance-related collections since 2010 while working with the Dance Heritage Coalition and the Museum of Performance + Design as the archivist for the San Francisco Ballet. Supriya is a member of the Society of American Archivists and the Society of California Archivists. She is a Certified Archivist and holds an MLIS from San Jose State University.